GENDER AND GENERATION
ON THE FAR WESTERN FRONTIER

Gender and Generation on the Far Western Frontier

CYNTHIA CULVER PRESCOTT

The University of Arizona Press   Tucson

The University of Arizona Press
www.uapress.arizona.edu

Printed in the United States of America
21 , 20   19   18   17   16   7   6   5   4   3   2

ISBN-13: 978-0-8165-2543-0 (cloth)
ISBN-13: 978-0-8165-3413-5 (paper)

Cover photos: *front*, Sarah and W.A. Finley as bride and groom, 1866
(courtesy Oregon State University Archives, Harriet's Collection);
back, Backenstos' Ranch, Marion County, Oregon, circa 1889 (courtesy
Oregon Historical Society)

Library of Congress Cataloguing-in-Publication Data
Prescott, Cynthia Culver, 1975–
  Gender and generation on the far western frontier / Cynthia Culver
Prescott.
     p. cm. — (Women's western voices)
  Includes bibliographical references and index.
  ISBN-13: 978-0-8165-2453-0 (hardcover : alk. paper)
  1. Women pioneers—Oregon—Willamette River Valley—
History—19th century. 2. Pioneers—Oregon—Willamette River
Valley—History—19th century. 3. Rural families—Willamette River
Valley—History—19th century. 4. Frontier and pioneer life—Oregon—
Willamette River Valley. 5. Farm life—Oregon—Willamette River
Valley—History—19th century. 6. Sex role—Oregon—Willamette
River Valley—History—19th century. 7. Intergenerational relations—
Oregon—Willamette River Valley—History—19th century. 8. Middle
class—Oregon—Willamette River Valley—History—19th century.
9. Willamette River Valley (Or.)—History—19th century. 10.
Willamette River Valley (Or.)—Social conditions—19th century.
I. Title.
  F882.W6P74 2007
  306.8709795'309034—dc22
                        2007020512

♾ This paper meets the requirements of ANSI/NISO Z39.48-1992
(Permanence of Paper).

CONTENTS

ILLUSTRATIONS

Figures

Tables

ACKNOWLEDGMENTS

Many people's insights and perspectives are woven into the fabric of this project. Stephen Aron guided and prodded me throughout my graduate career and beyond. Steve, inasmuch as this book has a point, it is thanks to you. The assistance of Ruth Bloch and Judith Seltzer was invaluable in developing the project and improving my writing. The WHEATies (Michael Bottoms, John Bowes, Lawrence Culver, Samantha Holtcamp Gervase, Kelly Lytle Hernandez, Arthur Rolston, Rachel St. John, Lissa Wadewitz, and Allison Varzally) contributed to the project in numerous ways, not least of which was helping me to maintain my sanity through my six years at UCLA. Mary Bywater Cross contributed valuable insights about quilts and textile research. Michael Lansing, Colleen O'Neill, and the anonymous readers for the *Western Historical Quarterly* pushed me to clarify my thinking and strengthen my arguments.

Funding from the University of California Regents and the Center for the Study of Women at the University of California, Los Angeles supported this research. An internship and research fellowship at the Autry National Center supported me while I was writing, introduced me to the world of public history and material culture, and sent my research in new and exciting directions. Thank you to Michael Duchemin, Louise Pubols, Marva Felchlin, Linda Strauss, Rebecca Menendez, and the entire Collections Management staff for providing access to the Autry Museum's diverse holdings and guiding my study of material culture. A grant from Loyola Marymount University's Bellarmine College of Liberal Arts contributed to the costs of publishing this book. Thanks also to Father Michael Engh, John

Popiden, Deena González, Edward Park, and Loyola Marymount University for accommodating my schedule in the final stages of this project.

This project would not have been possible without the collections and staff of the Oregon Historical Society (OHS). Special thanks to Todd Welch and everyone on the OHS research library staff for their guidance and assistance with everything from accessing manuscript collections to photocopying historic photographs. Anne Wheeler and Marsha Takayanagi Matthews enabled me to work with the OHS Museum's textile collection. Marsha and Lucy Berkley assisted me with many of the photographs illustrating this work.

Many other libraries and museums also supported my research. Thank you to Normandy Helmer and the staff of the University of Oregon's Knight Special Collections Library and University Archives. The Oregon State Archives provided access to valuable materials, and its staff hauled scores of boxes for me with good humor. Thanks also to the Clackamas County Historical Society Library, the Marion County Historical Society Library, the Washington County Historical Society Research Library, the Oregon State University Special Collections Library and University Archives, the Los Angeles Regional Family History Center, and the Oakland Museum of California for providing access to valuable resources.

I also wish to thank the University of Arizona Press for believing in this project. Laura Woodworth-Ney pursued and embraced my work enthusiastically. Thank you to my editor, Patti Hartmann, for her support of this project. Thanks also to anonymous readers for their comments and to Jason S. Ninneman for working with me on technological issues.

Finally, I wish to thank my family and friends, who have supported me both emotionally and financially through this journey. Thanks goes to the members of Graduate Christian Fellowship for being a second family to me in L.A. I am indebted to the Yung and Neel families, who so graciously and generously opened their homes to me during my journeys to archives. Special thanks to my parents, whose love and generosity have sustained me throughout my life and helped to make this book possible. Lastly, thanks to my husband Tim, whose unwavering faith in me often exceeds my own.

GENDER AND GENERATION
ON THE FAR WESTERN FRONTIER

INTRODUCTION

While traveling westward with her family on the Overland Trail in 1852, young Mary Ellen Todd secretly taught herself to crack the ox whip. She had envied the men in the wagon train for their ability to crack the great whip, thereby controlling the movement of the entire wagon train, and found "a secret joy in being able to have a power that set things going." Mary Ellen's mother, however, believed that cracking the ox whip wasn't "a very lady-like thing for a girl to do."[1] Although she accepted her daughter's assistance with such traditionally male work as herding cattle, she did not share her daughter's exhilaration regarding the opportunities to step into male roles discovered on the trail. Instead, she worried about the blurring of gender roles and the loosening of feminine constraints found in trail life, and she looked forward to reestablishing distinct gender positions upon reaching Oregon. The concerns of Mary Ellen Todd's mother tempered the girl's excitement with a sense of shame at her overly masculine accomplishment.

Seven-year-old Hamlin Smith, who was born near Salem, Oregon in 1862, helped his family by driving cattle on their donation land claim (DLC). By age fourteen, he worked more independently, plowing, harvesting wheat, and hauling manure. He attended the local school only during the winter months, while his sister, whose labor was less needed on the farm, graduated from Willamette University. Long after he married and began farming his own land, Hamlin continued to exchange labor with his father and extended family. Later in life, he embraced new technologies, becoming a streetcar conductor in the growing city of Salem.[2] While participation in urban life eventually altered the nature of his work, throughout his life Hamlin lived out the gender ideals instilled in him by his settler parents.

Like Mary Ellen Todd, many young people experienced flexible boundaries for gender behavior while traveling on the Overland Trail or growing up on the Oregon frontier in the mid-nineteenth century. As these children's parents became established in the Willamette Valley, however, they sought to reestablish the gender roles they had known "back home"—and to a large degree, they succeeded. Favorable economic conditions permitted first-generation settlers to build boundaries between men's and women's social and work spaces and to teach their sons and daughters to complete gender-specific labor. Yet as members of the second generation grew up, they adapted their parents' gender ideology in ways the early settlers never anticipated. Even while Hamlin Smith and many others labored within their accepted work roles, some of their siblings and peers enjoyed new educational, social, or occupational opportunities. Ultimately, second-generation Oregonians acknowledged their parents' gender division of labor and domestic ideals, but contested the rigidity of women's role by embracing more egalitarian marriages, a new consumer culture, and greater female participation in the public sphere.

In 1979, frontier historians John Mack Faragher and Julie Roy Jeffrey published groundbreaking studies of gender in nineteenth-century westward migration. They found that settlers coming to Oregon from the Midwest ascribed to eastern middle-class gender ideals of separate "spheres" for the sexes, seeking to match their daily lives to those ideals. While Faragher and Jeffrey argued that life on the Overland Trail forced men and women to more frequently cross the boundaries between masculine and feminine behavior than they had in their former home, the far western frontier did not, as these scholars anticipated, liberate women from the restrictions of domestic life. Instead, they found, the challenges of the trail and frontier reinforced the emigrants' desire to create separate spheres for men and women.[3]

Overland Trail and frontier studies completed during the 1980s confirmed Jeffrey's and Faragher's findings that the first settlers retained their traditional ideals. Yet none of these subsequent studies followed western settlers long enough to prove or disprove Jeffrey's suggestion that women on the frontier ultimately matched their social roles to the established domestic ideology. This book revisits these westering men and women, lingering longer on Oregon's Willamette Valley frontier to explore the long-term impact of migration on rural families' gender roles.[4]

Table I.1

Population of the Willamette Valley, 1850–1900

	White	Black	Indian	Chinese	Japanese	Aggregate
1850	11,580	51	N/A	N/A	N/A	11,631
1860	38,860	59	82	N/A	N/A	39,001
1870	60,190	273	109	597	N/A	61,169
1880	95,182	287	617	3,060	2	99,148
1890	176,345	767	397	6,152	25	183,686
1900	221,346	898	961	8,470	1,586	233,261

Source: United States Census.

The lack of first-generation ideological change identified by Faragher and Jeffrey can be partially explained through insights from immigration historians. These historians identify relatively little cultural transformation among the first generation of immigrants to the United States, who came to the country as adults. However, George Sánchez, Judy Yung, and others have identified much greater cultural change among the second generation, who grew up in the United States and mediated between their ancestors' culture and that of their new home. In particular, Yung found that cultural conflicts between first-generation immigrants and their children often centered on gender behavior. This generational model of cultural change makes Jeffrey's finding of consistent ideology among the first generation of Oregon settlers unsurprising. I argue that, while the first generation of settlers spent their lives trying to match the gender ideology described by Jeffrey and Faragher, the second generation—who grew up on the Oregon frontier and were influenced by an increasingly national, rapidly shifting culture—exhibited significant ideological change as they sought to mediate between their parents' teachings and modernizing influences.[5]

Although the American West is now recognized as an area of complex interethnic and intercultural interactions, Oregon's Willamette Valley stands out as a place where Frederick Jackson Turner's conception of an orderly Anglo-American migration westward is not far off the mark.[6] The Willamette Valley was 99.6 percent white in 1850 and 1860 (table I.1),[7] and during the latter decades of the nineteenth century, the valley's white popu-

Table I.2
Population of Oregon, 1850–1900

	White	Black	Indian	Chinese	Japanese	Aggregate
1850	13,087	207	N/A	N/A	N/A	13,294
1860	52,160	128	177	N/A	N/A	52,465
1870	86,929	346	318	3,330	N/A	90,923
1880	163,075	487	1,694	9,510	2	174,768
1890	301,758	1,186	1,258	9,540	25	313,767
1900	394,582	1,105	4,951	10,397	2501	413,536

Source: United States Census.

lation decreased only slightly relative to people of color, becoming 96.0 percent in 1880 and 1890.[8] As late as 1890, only 18.3 percent of the state's aggregate population had been born outside the United States (table I.2).[9]

The majority of Oregon settlers migrated as family units from the Ohio Valley. Nearly a third of Oregon's 1850 population was born in the midwestern states of Indiana, Illinois, Ohio, and Iowa, with an additional 30 percent of Oregon settlers hailing from neighboring Missouri and Kentucky. While the typical Willamette Valley settler migrated to Oregon from the frontier states of Indiana, Illinois, Iowa, or Missouri, many had been born in the older states of Kentucky, Tennessee, or Ohio and had children who were born in Iowa or Missouri.[10]

Although gender imbalance did characterize the early years of settlement in Oregon, the Willamette Valley was more balanced than other frontier regions, particularly California. In 1850, the Oregon Territory's sex ratio was 154.2 males per 100 females, and among adults over the age of twenty, men outnumbered women more than two to one (table I.3).[11] However, in rural Benton and Linn counties, sex ratios were relatively balanced at 126.8 and 126.4 men per 100 women, respectively (table I.4).[12] This is in direct contrast to the population of the state's gold-rich neighbor to the south—in fact, California's residents were as much as 93 percent male in 1850.[13] Thus, comparatively, Oregon was home to quite gender-balanced communities of rural families.[14]

Many scholars have treated California as a historical anomaly because of its Spanish and Mexican past, the predominately male gold rush experi-

Table I.3
Sex ratios in the Oregon population, 1850–1900

	Males	Females	Males per 100 Females	Aggregate
1850	7,202	4,671	154.2	11,873
1860	31,591	20,874	151.3	52,465
1870	53,131	37,792	140.6	90,923
1880	103,381	71,387	144.8	174,768
1890	181,840	131,927	137.8	313,767
1900	232,985	180,551	129.0	413,536

Source: United States Census.

ence it offered, and its ethnically diverse population of settlers lured by gold. The gold rush in fact helped California become a particularly unsettled region in the 1850s and 1860s, a prime example of the mythic "wild West" characterized by a distinctively male culture and few community institutions. In striking contrast to California, Oregon was geographically and culturally very much like the Midwest.[15]

The midwestern farming families who settled in the Willamette Valley during the 1840s and 1850s migrated for fundamentally conservative reasons. They hoped that access to free farmland in an amenable climate would enable them to provide for their descendants and more fully live out their domestic ideology, which historians refer to as the "cult of domesticity." This set of gender ideals led them to expect men to work outside the home while their wives maintained it as a haven from harsh public life, supporting an idealization of the home as a female-dominated refuge that was central to the culture of the antebellum-era middle class. This class set itself apart more through social conduct than through wealth, so that genteel behavior —characterized by emotional restraint, superb manners, and other gender-specific traits—was crucial to establishing and maintaining one's class membership. "True women" were pious, pure, and submissive, remaining within the domestic sphere, while their husbands demonstrated their gentility through discipline and duty. Although most American families—and particularly those living on the frontier—could not truly hope to meet these

Table I.4

Sex ratios in urban and rural
Willamette Valley counties in 1850

	Males per 100 females
Urban counties	
Washington	210.4
Clackamas	154.6
Rural counties	
Benton	126.8
Linn	126.4

Source: William A. Bowen, *The Willamette Valley: Migra-tion and Settlement on the Oregon Frontier* (Seattle: University of Washington Press, 1978).

exacting standards for behavior, many nonetheless identified with the urban middle class and sought to adopt its lifestyle as much as possible. Ultimately, however, favorable farming conditions in the Willamette Valley failed to insulate Oregon settlers and their children from the development of a new middle-class consumer culture that arose in the late nineteenth century.[16]

The Willamette Valley's climate was, as settlers had been led to believe, ideal for American subsistence-surplus farmers. The region's moderate climate attracted farmers accustomed to the harsh, snowy winters and hot, humid summers of Illinois and Iowa. Here, steady, gentle rains fell from September to April, averaging up to sixty inches each year, and melting snow from the Cascades swelled rivers and streams flowing down into the valley as winter rains subsided. Valley weather remained mild year-round, with a mean temperature of forty degrees Fahrenheit in the coldest months (ten degrees warmer than central Illinois) and sixty-seven degrees in summer. Even occasional warm spells seemed tolerable thanks to the summer's relatively low humidity, and midwesterners used to warm, muggy nights required "two quilts and a flannel blanket" to stay comfortable on summer evenings in the valley.[17]

Like its weather, the Willamette Valley's geography was also well suited to farmers (fig. I.1). Stretching one hundred miles south from the Columbia

River and measuring twenty to thirty miles wide, the area was covered in rich grassland with ample rivers and streams that appealed to farmers accustomed to Ohio Valley slash-and-burn land-clearing techniques. The valley floor's rich black loam was primarily covered with thick grasses such as sloughgrass (*Beckmannia syzigachne*), whose growth had been encouraged by annual burnings by local Kalapuya Indians. Gallery forests lined the Willamette River and its tributaries, while forests of fir trees (*Pseudotsuga menziesii* and *Abies grandis*), pine trees (*Pinus ponderosa*), and hardwood trees such as the bigleaf maple (*Acer macrophyllum*) lined the foothills that formed the eastern and western edges of the valley. By building their homes on the edges of these forests, farming families had easy access to ample supplies of wood and water, while their crops and livestock spread across the grasslands of the flat valley floor.[18]

These grasslands had been created and maintained by the indigenous Kalapuyas' seasonal burning techniques. But by the 1840s, the Kalapuya population had been devastated by diseases spread through contact with European and North American explorers and fur traders. In the last quarter of the eighteenth century, scholars believe, the Kalapuya numbered about 13,500, or about fifty people per one hundred square miles.[19] By the time the 1843 Great Migration brought between seven hundred and one thousand Anglo settlers overland from the eastern settlements, this native population had been drastically reduced by smallpox, malaria, dysentery, tuberculosis, and venereal infections, as well as by subsequent starvation as their lessened numbers disrupted seasonal and daily activities. Contrary to the impressions of many early settlers who dwelled on frightening interactions with indigenous people, by 1850 there were probably fewer than five hundred Kalapuya and Chinook remaining in the Willamette Valley.[20] Beginning in 1829, some French Canadian trappers who retired from the Hudson's Bay Company chose to settle with their Indian wives and métis children in what became known as French Prairie. But like the surviving native population, this settlement (numbering some 350 in 1841) was small enough for most Anglo-American settlers to ignore. From their perspective, the valley remained empty, awaiting their "improvements" of cabins, fences, and plowed fields to be set up on large grants of free land.[21]

In fact, the Oregon provisional government's first land law, created in 1843, allowed claimants to take up to 640 acres of free land. This was superseded in 1850 by the federal Donation Land Law, better known as the

I.1   The Willamette Valley, 1875. (Map by Michael W. Pesses)

Donation Land Claim Act (DLCA), which granted land to settlers who established residence in the Oregon Territory prior to December 1, 1851. Under this act, single white men could claim 320 acres, while 640 acres went to married couples to be shared equally between husband and wife.[22] Single men who arrived in Oregon after December 1, 1851 could receive title to 160 acres, and a married couple could receive 320 acres. In all, 7,432 donation claims were made under the DLCA, consisting of some 2,614,000 acres—most of which were within the Willamette Valley (fig. I.2). By 1857, the territorial surveyor general declared the Oregon frontier closed, stating, "The greatest part of the most valuable lands in Oregon has been taken by actual settlers under the donation laws . . . Now there is but little vacant good land west of the Cascade Mountains."[23]

Under the terms of the DLCA, Anglo-American families could claim farms several times larger than those they had worked on in the Midwest. Donation land claims (DLCs) offered more security than did the midwestern custom of squatting, and if families became dissatisfied with their land, they were free to sell out (if only for the value of the improvements they had made) and begin again elsewhere in the Willamette Valley. The land allotments were generous even in comparison to those of the more famous Homestead Act of 1862, which allotted 160 acres per family in less-productive regions. But even a successful frontier farmer typically planted only about forty or fifty acres in crops, holding an additional twenty to forty acres for pasturage, a woodlot, and other needs. To plant more than forty acres would require a significant quantity of hired labor, which was in short supply on the frontier. In the early days of settlement, farmers therefore could scarcely dream of actively tending 640 acres—a full square mile—of Oregon farmland.[24]

Why, then, would men and women brave the hardships of the Oregon Trail in search of land they could not hope to till in their lifetimes? The promise of large land grants lay not so much in immediate wealth as in securing a patrimony for their descendants. Settlers believed that generous land grants would permit them to provide viable farms not for only one but for all of their sons—and perhaps for their daughters as well. The DLCA offered these farmers and farm wives an opportunity to live out their conventional dream of settling their children and their children's children on their lands, prompting them to move thousands of miles and cut kinship

I.2 Habersham's Sectional and County Map of Oregon, by J. K. Gill & Co., 1874. Fertile soil, a mild climate, and large quantities of free land granted through the 1850 Donation Land Claim Act encouraged the rapid settlement of the Willamette Valley. More arid land east of the Cascade Mountains was settled far more slowly. (Courtesy Department of Special Collections, Charles E. Young Research Library, UCLA; Collection 990 [Collection of Pamphlet Maps, 1750–], box 25)

ties in the hope that their offspring would not need to repeat the frontier process in the next generation.[25]

To a large extent, this hope was realized. The Willamette Valley's relatively low mobility rates during the mid-nineteenth century represented a change from a long-standing American pattern of movement and out-migration. In the typical western Oregon farming community of Sublimity, for example, 42 percent of 1857 taxpayers were still living there in 1870, and 38 percent of 1860 household heads remained a decade later.[26] In contrast, about 90 percent of the 1850 population of Grass Valley, California, had left the area by 1856.[27] Even in the typical midwestern farming community of Sugar Creek, Illinois, which was first settled in the 1820s and 1830s, only 30.5 percent of household heads remained from 1830 to 1840, and only 22.2 percent remained between 1850 and 1860.[28] Aided by generous land laws, rich farmland, and a mild climate, families established unusually successful and lasting farms and communities in the Willamette Valley.[29]

I contend that the first-generation settlers' economic success eventually enabled them to live out their gender ideology to an extent that was impossible in the Midwest during their time. However, their dreams of reproducing generations of "true" women and men on their land claims would not be realized. Just as their children came of age in the late nineteenth century, American standards for middle-class membership began to change. Increasingly, participation in a new culture of consumption and refined leisure—rather than good manners—became the marker of the middle class. Shopping in urban department stores, riding bicycles, or vacationing at resorts such as Niagara Falls replaced reading or playing piano in the family parlor as ideal leisure activities. Meanwhile, building on decades of women's charity work, middle-class people with resources to spare sought to help the less fortunate through progressive political and social reform.[30]

As middle-class culture shifted from an emphasis on genteel behavior to genteel consumption, technology increasingly tied rural America to its urban centers. By the 1880s, a vast network of railroads and telegraphs connected the Willamette Valley to the rest of the nation. A newly national print culture arose, and lower printing and shipping rates enabled Oregon residents to participate in new cultural trends through fashion magazines and mail-order catalogs. As urban centers grew, developing stronger trade and communication ties to the surrounding hinterlands,[31] so did opportunities for many Americans—including those on the western frontier—to mimic those living in eastern cities. I argue that this confluence of favorable farming conditions and rapid incorporation into the American nation caused the frontier period to pass more quickly in the Willamette Valley than in midwestern and other western locales. Thus, second-generation Oregonians were forced to grow up negotiating between their parents' old gender ideals and new, all-encompassing middle-class standards. By the time they reached adulthood, the sons and daughters of Oregon settlers were adopting new attitudes toward marriage, work, consumption, and sociability.

Chapter 1 of this book focuses on mid-nineteenth-century farming families' gender ideology and its expression in their separate spheres for men and women. In this section, I show that during the early years of settlement, life on the Willamette Valley frontier required a significant degree of fluidity in the boundary separating men's and women's work, and flexible gender roles were necessary. However, over time, Oregon women were gradually freed from field labor and men were freed from assisting with housework, actually enabling settlers to live out their domestic ideology more fully than had been possible in their former homes. Even as they grew older, when infirmity inclined men and women to abandon many tasks proper for their sex, they found ways to retain their traditional gender roles. Thus throughout their lives, men and women were able to adapt to new work realities without losing their traditional identities.

Chapter 2 focuses on men's gender identity and how it was expressed through their labor. First-generation men demonstrated their masculinity by providing for their families and making decisions on their behalf. But as the second generation reached maturity, tension developed between fathers and sons. Many sons had to choose between an extended period of semi-dependence on their fathers and continuing the frontier migration pattern by striking out on their own outside the Willamette Valley. Ultimately, fathers became farm managers, making decisions for the household and directing their sons' work long after they stopped working in the fields themselves. For the second generation, being "manly" required not only that they provide and make wise decisions for their families but also that they exhibit the self-restraint associated with middle-class status.

In chapter 3, I compare the marital relationships of first- and second-generation Willamette Valley settlers. It is shown that first generation couples married at a young age and largely out of necessity, forming economic partnerships that they hoped would develop into loving relationships. Those who were born and raised on the Oregon frontier waited longer to marry, seeking companionship and more equal power relations, as well as desiring romance more than financial security. But they did not wholly reject their parents' largely practical view of marriage.

Chapters 4 and 5 focus on second-generation women. Whereas the first generation strove for middle-class status through refined behavior and separate spheres of work for the sexes, the second generation sought to meet the new class standards developing in eastern cities. Refined consumption, particularly revealed in women's clothing and the trappings of a formal parlor, replaced refined behavior, and education, paid labor, and other opportunities allowed some second-generation females to become "New Women" who took on a more prominent role in the public sphere. Some even became proto-feminist activists, seeking a career on par with men or fighting for women's suffrage. Still, even those with the most radical political views framed their arguments within the context of domestic ideology. And while increased mechanization and availability of cheap, convenient products reduced the burden of women's productive work, their domestic responsibilities did not change significantly. Whether they pursued higher class status through consumption (chap. 4) or struggled for greater political rights (chap. 5), second-generation women did not *fundamentally* challenge their parents' beliefs in separate social roles for men and women.

Finally, chapter 6 examines first- and second-generation Oregonians' attempts to reconcile the changes in men's and women's ideal roles at the turn of the century. New Women's roles were disturbing to first-generation Oregon settlers that clung to their domestic ideal, hundreds of whom joined organizations memorializing their accomplishments as "Oregon pioneers" and "pioneer mothers." But even within these pioneer groups' realm of inherently conservative goals and perspectives, growing participation by the second generation brought with it ideological change, leading these organizations to accept somewhat more equal roles for women and men. Thus, pioneer children were able to develop expectations for masculinity and femininity and observe a more permeable boundary between men's and women's spheres—without entirely abandoning the first generation's faith in domesticity. In honoring their memories of the Oregon frontier, they balanced their own more liberal gender identities with the respectful acknowledgement of their parents' traditional ideology.

CHAPTER 1

Fashioning Women and Men on the Frontier

Like most rural women, first-generation Oregonian Maria Locey completed a wide variety of domestic tasks each day. Although a committed diarist, she rarely wrote about these chores. Only late in life did Locey enjoy sufficient leisure time to record her daily routine.

> I do not often write down anything about my work but I thought one day last week I would pay attention and it ran some thing like this
>
> > Got up at five and got breakfast.
> > Went into the sitting-room and assisted at family prayers.
> > Prepared the little boy's dinner, washed him and made him ready for school (his mother is away) on their homestead.
> > Skimmed and strained the milk.
> > Went to the henhouse to feed my setting-hens, swept and dusted the sitting-room.
> > Washed the break-fast dishes.
> > Then ironed till eleven.
> > Got dinner, rested for an hour.
> > Made the beds, worked at mending or some other necessary work for an hour or two, then got supper, washed dishes again etc.
>
> This is about a sample, with a change of sometimes instead of ironing I put in the time washing, house-cleaning, gardening etc., with many occasional stoppages and side-tracks. Sometimes in the afternoon I write a letter, and so far this year I have read three chapters in the Bible each day besides the ones we read at family worship.[1]

As can be seen in this passage, the work done by farm wives like Maria Locey—those who had been living in the Willamette Valley for some time—consisted primarily of domestic tasks. But during the time on the trail and early years of settlement, the strains of frontier life made women like Locey responsible for many non-domestic, "masculine" tasks as well, all of which were crucial to their families' survival.[2] It was not until Willamette Valley farms became more established that these women were able to focus solely on domestic work and religious activities, enhancing their status as proper ladies by leaving the field work to their husbands.

Following the work roles of Oregon's settlers throughout their lifetimes reveals that their ability to live out their gender ideology varied over different life stages. In their younger years, as the first settlers were just starting to build their farms, they had to work hard to gradually reestablish a clear gender division of labor. Over time, however, the barnyard became a defined border between women's place in the home and men's place in the fields and in society, effectively creating a distinct sphere of work for each sex. Later, as first-generation settlers aged, infirmity forced them to redefine the boundary between men's and women's work once more. But regardless of how they negotiated their family's division of labor—and regardless of the life stage they were in—first-generation settlers did not abandon their belief in men's and women's fundamental differences.

The Midwestern Frontier

Almost all mid-nineteenth-century Americans believed that men and women should have distinct economic and social roles, but easterners lived out this belief to the fullest—while midwesterners merely strived to do so. The eastern middle class was largely set apart by its separation of men's and women's spheres of work, with men working outside the home and women taking care of the home and children and making only a limited contribution to their household's economic production. Such separation was not possible for farm families, particularly those living on the frontier. For them, all production and child rearing took place right on the farm. Nonetheless, men and women divided their tasks by gender. Men worked in the fields, planting and harvesting crops and tending livestock. They also cleared new fields, cut lumber and firewood, and hunted. Meanwhile, their wives stayed in the home, preparing hearty meals for their families and preserving foodstuffs for winter use. In addition, they made, laundered, and mended the family's clothing. But frontier conditions required men and women to remain flexible about this spatial division of labor. Women sometimes helped in the fields, particularly during planting and harvesting, and men assisted with domestic tasks such as pumping water and chopping firewood.[3]

Both husbands and wives worked in the barnyard—the transition zone between the house and fields. This space represented a kind of borderland of overlapping interests and cross-gender cooperation.[4] Yet what might appear to be a grey area of shared labor was actually a checkerboard of interlocking but distinct tasks. Within this shared space, husbands and wives divided their work based on each task's similarity to their other work. Thus men cared for horses and oxen, while women cared for hogs and poultry. In some cases, men and women subdivided specific tasks within a category of work. For example, men herded and fed the milch cows, but women milked them and churned the milk and cream to make the butter. Similarly, men turned the soil for their wives' household gardens and "truck patches." They also slaughtered livestock and cured the meat, while their wives ground the scraps to make sausage. In all these ways, men and women shared the work of the barnyard while maintaining distinct gender roles.[5]

As can be seen in children's chore assignments, midwestern girls' and boys' respective gender identification became more pronounced with age. For the first few years of life, children of both sexes wore dresses and performed household tasks appropriate to their limited physical strength and dexterity. For instance, girls and boys alike would begin to feed the poultry and gather eggs in the barnyard at the age of four. By the age of six, however, children were primarily working within gender-specific boundaries. Boys wore pants and began to do outdoor chores such as carrying firewood, and by age ten, they were apprenticed to their fathers to learn field work. Their sisters remained in the home, learning to cook, sew, and tend smaller siblings. Although young children were more likely to be called upon to cross gender boundaries than were their parents, by the time they reached puberty, boys and girls were responsible for gender-specific adult labor.[6]

When the combined efforts of the nuclear family were insufficient, midwesterners relied on their neighbors to assist with pressing labor needs. Men gathered outdoors to build houses, split rails, husk corn or shear sheep, spurring one another on through masculine competition. Meanwhile, their wives gathered within the domestic space to prepare meals for the male workers or to complete a quilt. Men assisted men and women assisted women within their respective work and social spaces.[7]

Because hard labor was required to support a family on the midwestern frontier in the mid-nineteenth century, men's and women's distinct work spheres often overlapped through necessity. Despite this forced flexibility of gender roles, they retained and lived out their original ideology as much as possible, raising their children to do so as well. Life on the Oregon Trail, however, challenged the boundaries between male and female work more than ever.

The Oregon Trail

Migrating overland to Oregon in the mid-nineteenth century required four to six months of daily toil, and challenges that settlers encountered along the trail required an even greater degree of gender role flexibility than they had known on the midwestern frontier. But while migrating families' daily lives did change significantly as a consequence, men and women continued to divide their work along gender lines. Even operating within condensed workspaces, westering men and women succeeded in creating at least an illusion of separate roles and spaces for the sexes.[8]

The Scott family is a typical example. Father Tucker Scott, assisted by eldest son Harvey, fourteen, drove the family's wagon. Eldest daughter Mary replaced her invalid mother as cook. Tucker's second daughter, nicknamed "Jenny," kept the family journal each day, and fifteen-year-old Margaret assisted both her older sisters with their tasks.[9] Catherine, age thirteen, tended the two youngest children (ages five and three), who were too small to contribute much labor. Finally, old enough to contribute labor but young enough for flexible gender roles, eleven-year-old Harriet and nine-year-old John helped drive the loose stock. Gender and age thus combined to determine the responsibilities assigned to each member of the household.[10]

Husbands' and wives' roles became less defined through close physical proximity and pressing needs. Most women temporarily took over the driving of the family wagon at some point. Similarly, many men helped their wives in times of hardship. But men and women still found ways to retain distinct workspaces, often assigning labor to young people and hired hands, who demonstrated more flexible gender roles than did married men and women. Both boys and girls in their teens, for example, often drove the loose stock and carried firewood and water. In some cases, families assigned hired hands to drive the wagons, freeing the household heads to do other, higher-status work such as serving as a captain or scout for the company, or letting them pursue pleasurable activities such as hunting. Clearly, tasks that were not categorized precisely as either men's or women's work were often done by people of lesser social status.[11]

The Early Years in the Willamette Valley

When Oregon settlers arrived in the Willamette Valley, they saw the opportunity to more concretely establish the gender division of labor they had known in the Midwest. Men once more worked out in the fields and women stayed within a more permanent domestic sphere. However, as with life on the trail, their great labor needs required frontier families to remain flexible about their work roles during the first years of settlement.

As they had done in the Midwest, first-generation Oregonians divided their responsibilities roughly based on location, more frequently sharing labor within the transition zones of the barnyard and garden than in the more clearly gendered spaces of the fields and the home. It was acceptable, therefore, for some men to work in the family's garden on a regular basis, particularly if it was especially large. In contrast, only bachelors regularly washed and repaired their own clothes, although married men might occasionally help with heavy chores such as laundry. The ways in which men and women negotiated gender boundaries within the barnyard borderland varied based on the labor required on a given farm.[12]

The first few years of farming required intensive labor, necessary for clearing and fencing the land and breaking the soil to a plow. Paid field laborers were scarce, forcing farmers to rely on the work of their wives and daughters. But men continued to do the most physically demanding field labor such as clearing new fields, plowing, and harvesting, while women generally did easier tasks such as threshing or winnowing grain. To protect their distinct gender identities, early settlers considered women's field work to be "helping" their husbands, and a woman's femininity was not questioned so long as she was only assisting with tasks that were clearly not her own.[13]

Settler women's daily responsibilities did not differ dramatically from their work in the Midwest. A great deal of their time was given to feeding and clothing their families. Just as they had done "back home," these women prepared three meals a day, tended extensive kitchen gardens, preserved produce for future use, and raised eggs and chickens. If their family owned cows, women usually milked them and churned the milk into butter. They typically boiled and scrubbed their family's laundry using homemade soft soap. "Everybody has to be their own tailor here," settler Margaret B. Smith wrote to her sister back home. "I have made six pairs of pants, five aprons, five sheets . . . I have a great deal of sewing to do yet."[14] Because cloth was expensive, women often repaired damage to their family's clothing using patches and darning needles and cut down worn adult clothing to create children's clothes.[15]

Women also contributed various forms of paid labor to the household economy during these first years. In the early 1850s, the California gold rush and continuing emigration to Oregon created a ready market for farm produce including fruit, vegetables, eggs, and butter. Many households relied on women's surplus eggs and butter to pay for goods that they could not produce themselves—dry goods, farm equipment, wool and cotton cloth, salt, and luxuries such as coffee and tobacco. For this reason, farm wife Synthia Applegate milked thirty-two cows each day to make about one hundred pounds of butter and cheese per week, which she then sold for twenty-five cents per pound—a significant contribution to the family's income. Likewise, many women did laundry, kept paying boarders, or sold their sewing or baking to more recent emigrants or to men bound for the mines. Some better-educated women taught temporary subscription schools until public schools could be established with male teachers. In later years, these women and their children proudly described the creative ways in which they had utilized their domestic and maternal skills to contribute to their family's welfare.[16]

During the time just after settlement, industrious and hard-working women were particularly esteemed. Any wife seeking a divorce, like settler Harriet Coulton, typically tried to establish her legal reliability by emphasizing that she "managed the household affairs of her said husband with prudence and economy."[17] Similarly, it was good to be presented as productive to the extreme, as was Lucinda Coones by her neighbor, who testified in court: "[I]n the community where she lives, everybody speaks well of her. I know that she has always worked hard to support her family."[18] With so much to be done, it is not surprising that women's domestic labor contributions were greatly valued by their frontier society.

Separating Men's and Women's Roles

It became increasingly possible for Willamette Valley men and women to separate their roles as farms became established and the second generation grew old enough to contribute gender-specific labor. Men's and women's workspaces continued to overlap in the barnyard, but this region developed into a less-porous border separating the home from the outside world. In addition, families began to rely on technology or hired labor to replace direct assistance from the opposite sex, further contributing to the growing gender divide.

Families' early years in Oregon were not unlike frontier life elsewhere in North America. But once they established working farms in the Willamette Valley, the area's political and geographic differences soon enabled many Oregon settlers to economically surpass those living elsewhere. Thanks to the Donation Land Claim Act (DLCA) of 1850, most emigrants who had arrived over the Oregon Trail with little more than the clothing on their backs could quickly gain a large farm of rich land and wood lots. The valley's combination of open grassland, wooded areas, a mild climate, and reliable rainfall was ideal for farming nearly all year. Further, livestock animals grew fat on winter's rich grasses, freeing their owners from raising large quantities of feed. With all of these advantages, many men and women were gradually able to relieve themselves of assisting one another with gender-specific tasks. While mothers continued to tend infants, supervise toddlers, and teach young children to do simple chores, as boys grew older they were able to replace their mothers in the fields. Sons became strong enough both to assist their fathers and to hire their labor out to neighbors, and daughters were able to help their mothers with household jobs.[19]

As they were freed from field labor, Willamette Valley women could fully focus on domestic tasks that they had previously struggled to complete. Besides growing large and varied gardens and increasing their production of butter, cheese, and eggs, they also made finer clothing. Before, clothing had been basic at best—one woman recalled trading for a small piece of cloth "that made a covering. And that was about all; it could hardly be considered dresses."[20] Now, women could replace such simple coverings with more carefully tailored clothing and more varied bedding, continuing to devote a significant portion of their time each week to washing, ironing, and mending. Despite a greater availability of cheap fabrics, women carefully patched, mended, or cut down each article for children's use as they had during the early years, and when clothing became worn beyond repair, it was cut up to make quilts, comforters, and rag rugs that were both functional and attractive. This frugality did not subtract from the fact that settlers' clothing was much improved—on the contrary, it meant that women had more time and resources to devote to such efforts.[21]

Actually, even as women were relieved from field work, many learned with dismay that their domestic tasks expanded to require nearly every waking moment. Mary Coe, for one, lamented that she was unable to keep up her diary, write poetry, or use elegant penmanship as she wished. She asked a woman friend to forgive her hasty letter, for: "[D]oes not a house-keeper have her hands full without writing letters? Certainly if she is a good house-keeper."[22] Mrs. Woodward, another early settler, had looked forward to doing spiritual work alongside her missionary husband, but found that she could barely keep up with the tasks of her household and had no time or energy left for work outside her home.[23] For four decades, Maria Locey found time to teach Sunday school in addition to her wifely responsibilities, yet she rejoiced when she finally had a "quiet, peaceful Sabbath at home."[24] Thus even without doing field labor, these women discovered that endeavoring to be a "good house-keeper" left little time for activities that they truly valued or enjoyed.

During their first years in Oregon, women did allow themselves to set aside pressing household tasks in the cause of helping one another. Many traveled significant distances to assist neighbors in times of childbirth and severe illness, and as the countryside became more densely settled, Oregon settlers continued to turn to neighbor women rather than male doctors for medical care—particularly in the case of childbirth, which remained an explicitly female experience. Older women frequently stayed with their neighbors or grown daughters to assist with birth and remained to help with domestic work until the new mother was strong enough to do it herself. But women offered aid not only during hard times; they also assisted one another with routine, labor-intensive tasks whenever possible. For example, a woman came to help first-generation settler Emma Guthrie cut out dresses for Guthrie and her daughters, then remained to sew the dresses for her.

Similarly, a skilled seamstress helped Mrs. James Knox with her sewing. In return, the Knox family loaned the seamstress a light spinning wheel for flax, on which she taught her daughters to spin. Women also gathered to finish quilts that individuals had pieced beforehand, or to hold other work "bees" to pool labor and enjoy one another's company. This female assistance helped settler women overcome the isolation of frontier life.[25]

Although women gradually reduced their participation in "male tasks," they remained important partners for their husbands in the busiest times of the year, helping in their own ways with projects such as harvest and slaughter. While sons or neighbors assisted their husbands with harvesting the grain, for example, women prepared hearty meals for the large harvesting teams, occasionally also helping to rake or clean the wheat as they had in previous years. In late autumn when men slaughtered hogs, women processed lard and made sausage, and throughout the year, while men were responsible for mucking out stables and hauling manure, women sometimes cleaned manure out of the chicken house. When the Locey family moved into a new home, Cyrus moved the heavy furniture, but his wife Maria and her daughter cleaned and settled their belongings in the new house. In ways like these, women contributed to household labor needs without abandoning their domestic role.[26]

Women also shared responsibility for the family orchard with their husbands. Many families in the Midwest had maintained small orchards for household use, but Oregon's milder climate made it possible to grow a wide variety of fruit trees and berry bushes, encouraging a few settler families to turn their properties into nurseries or vast fruit farms. Subsistence-oriented farmers also emphasized fruit production more heavily in Oregon than they had in the Midwest. In Oregon orchards, men continued to plant the trees but became even more occupied with tending the grown trees and harvesting the fruit; in addition, they were involved in cider making, which required male strength for operating the presses. Men's concern with growing and processing fruit increased with its relative importance to the family's production strategy. But in general, once the fruit had been harvested, most of the responsibility shifted to women, who dried it or made preserves. As with other tasks in the transition zones between men's and women's work, men did the most physically demanding labor, while food processing was primarily the women's job.[27]

The barnyard increasingly formed a clear—if never completely solid—boundary between men's and women's responsibilities, a fact that becomes quite evident in examining the tasks involved in dairy production. Men fenced in pastures where the dairy cattle and other livestock grazed, raised hay for feed, and built and mucked out the barn, while women performed the milk processing. Responsibility for the milking itself remained flexible, depending on the labor available within a given family. Children learned to milk cows by age six; in fact, according to young settler Lucy Robinson, "[I could not] remember the time I didn't milk. . . . My sister and I pailed thirty-five cows night and morning right along."[28] After the initial years of settlement, as cattle herds grew and children learned to do more skilled labor, responsibility for milking the cows sometimes transferred from women or children to male field hands. But processing the fresh milk and the tedious task of churning and working butter generally fell to farm wives.

As the boundary between men's and women's workspaces became more defined, women took over butter and other household production almost exclusively. Many families had relied heavily on women's butter making during initial settlement, when butter prices were high due to the California gold rush and cash was scarce. As butter prices leveled off and men's grain production became more central to the family economy, women's butter and eggs became a small part of a larger household economic strategy, but farm account books indicate that women's butter, cheese, and egg production still often constituted a significant portion of the family's income.

The importance Oregon women placed on butter production is reflected in the diligence with which they clipped butter-making suggestions from local newspapers and saved them in their journals. Men, on the other hand, appear to have had little interest in the job of butter churning, rarely commenting on it except on the few occasions when they were forced to assist their wives with this labor. Maria Locey regularly recorded her domestic accomplishments in her diary, demonstrating particular interest in butter production and occasionally complaining about the labor required to churn butter or accomplish other tasks. When she maintained her husband's journal in his absence, however, Maria adopted his disinterest in such tasks: although one day she spent at least two hours churning fourteen pounds of butter, she wrote simply, "Nothing of importance occurred today."[29] While Maria clearly valued her own daily labor, she apparently assumed that her domestic tasks were unimportant in her husband's eyes. Dairy production's absence from men's otherwise detailed records of farm work indicates that it remained women's separate responsibility.[30]

As long as dairy and eggs constituted women's individual contribution to the household expenses, these products remained virtually invisible to men. An exception to this rule, however, occurred among families that shifted toward large-scale production, when men's interest in dairying increased significantly. By the 1880s, first- and second-generation men in the Willamette Valley and on Oregon's Pacific coast had converted some family farms into commercial dairies, at which point producing milk, cheese, or eggs became not simply women's work, but the family's business, replacing the traditionally male-dominated industry of grain crops. When this happened, farmers took over supervision and control, becoming businessmen as they hired other men to do the milking that had traditionally been done by unpaid wives or children.[31]

Although wives were, of course, unpaid for most of their own domestic chores, Oregon women did have the financial advantage of enjoying more liberal property rights than their counterparts elsewhere in the United States. As has been mentioned, the DLCA of 1850 enabled married women to claim up to 320 acres of Oregon farmland, and two years after the act was passed, the territorial legislature secured this land to their separate use and control. Over the next two decades, state laws extended to married women the right to retain separate ownership of property obtained outside marriage. In addition to having the traditional life interest in one-third of their husbands' estate, widows were permitted to set aside domestic property such as butter churns and poultry prior to estate sales. These liberal property rights provided Oregon women with unique opportunities to enhance their economic standing.[32]

Rather than using their property rights to gain financial and social standing on men's terms, married women took advantage of these laws to expand their own domestic production or to enhance their domestic sphere. More than one-third of the sixty-two Linn County women who declared separate property during the nineteenth century set apart dairy cattle, indicating their desire to profit from selling butter or other household products. Nine Linn County women sold their donation land claims (DLCs) or other land holdings to men, investing the proceeds in personal property such as milch cows that would improve their domestic efficiency, or buying other goods that would not require them to relinquish control of their property to their husbands or to hire male farm workers. For example, Marietta Eddy sold land that she owned prior to her marriage in order to purchase fourteen cows, a milk bucket, a team of horses, and a wagon and harness. Nearly two-thirds of Linn County women likewise set apart horses, and one-third set apart wagons or equipment, which could enable them to trade their dairy products or garden produce with neighbors or at the nearest general store. About one in twelve women declared a sewing machine or other domestic equipment that could ease the burden of their household labor—or that perhaps enabled them to do paid work within their home—and a handful of women invested in equipment and merchandise for a candy, millinery, or jewelry store. Several women similarly chose to establish hotels or boarding houses, as did Henrietta B. Gore, who sold her half of the Gore DLC to purchase twelve beds and bedding, a stair carpet, and an organ, along with furnishings for a bar, a dining room, and a kitchen with two stoves. About one in five Linn County women invested in household furniture or luxuries such as pianos, which enhanced their status as wives. Thus, instead of joining the men in the highly valued world of land and grain crops, these women invested in the domestic sphere and further emphasized the divisions between men's and women's work.[33]

Women's focus on domestic production is also reflected in inheritance patterns. While most Oregon fathers divided their estate among all of their children, many men left money or other household goods to their daughters in place of land. Daughters often invested this cash in dairy cattle or other personal possessions, as reflected in their declarations of married women's separate property. Mothers showed an even stronger interest in providing for their daughters' household production, giving them milch cows or household goods as wedding gifts, or setting these things aside for daughters in their will. For example, Mary C. Cline gave her daughter Nellie Cline a sewing machine. Nellie also brought a piano to her marriage.[34]

Most mid-nineteenth-century Willamette Valley families had few resources available for investing in new equipment of any kind, let alone luxuries such as pianos. Not surprisingly, male household heads prioritized increased grain production ahead of easing their wives' domestic work. As was the case with their counterparts in the Midwest, these men's highest priority was to purchase plows, reapers, and other farm equipment intended to improve crop productivity. Over time, however, men discovered that labor-saving domestic devices not only relieved some of women's drudgery but also freed them from their responsibility to assist with women's work.

During the first years of settlement, only the wealthiest men were able to afford household luxuries for their families, so the acquisition of such things indicated financial success and a step toward the more refined life that had drawn settlers to the Oregon frontier in the first place. This is seen in pioneer reminiscences recorded at the turn of the century, in which several men and women remember with pride their families owning the first sewing machines or large musical instruments in Oregon. For example, Nicholas Lee "was a systematic farmer," whose success enabled his family to acquire "the first piano and first sewing machine in the neighborhood."[35] Sewing machine ownership was considered an indication of progress for the community and forward thinking by the household head. Yet for women, sewing machines represented something far more tangible: a significant help in one of their most time-consuming domestic tasks. Just as women helped one another with their heaviest work, women fortunate enough to own a sewing machine shared this valuable convenience with their neighbors.[36]

Men's primary motivation in providing domestic conveniences may have been to relieve themselves of helping with domestic labor, but they also often wrote of pleasing women by doing so. "Uncle Billy," an old man who lived with Jesse Applegate's family, "was always trying to please the Missus with some article of household use to lighten her labor—washboards, churns, cheese hoop and press—always made unsolicited—and given as a surprise."[37] In similar ways, a number of husbands appear to have used their mechanical skills to craft simple equipment for their wives.

For many men, the first significant step toward easing their wives' burden was to buy a cookstove. Although the initial learning curve for their use was steep, these wood-burning stoves cooked more evenly, were easier to control, and required less constant attention and labor than the open hearth. Later in the century, hand-powered washing machines made wash day less taxing for many women. In addition, a few husbands recognized the value of sewing machines long before they became affordable and widely available. One of these men was Henry Caples, who while at the Idaho gold mines instructed his wife to invest the gold dust he sent home in a sewing machine. While men did continue to value plows and other field equipment over domestic conveniences, those who chose to invest time or money in labor-saving devices for women received in return both their wives' appreciation and greater freedom from domestic labor for themselves.[38]

Not all husbands were as quick as Uncle Billy or Henry Caples to recognize the value of sewing machines and other conveniences, many believing they could not afford such a large investment in women's labor. In fact, sewing machines were so rare well into the 1860s that at least one woman—long after a stove freed her from cooking over the fireplace—remembered with regret, "[I]n those days there were no labor-saving conveniences. Mother . . . did all the sewing by hand."[39] But although men's grain crops often seemed to them more pressing, those men who were willing to consider purchasing a sewing machine soon became convinced of its value. In 1859, Seth Lewelling visited neighbors and experimented with their sewing machine by sewing a pair of pants for his son. He apparently was impressed by the practicality of the investment, for soon after this visit he purchased a sewing machine for his wife at the extravagant price of $140, or nearly twice the price of a horse.[40] Cyrus Locey finally purchased his family's first sewing machine in 1872, hoping it would be "the means of helping out Mollie [his wife, Maria] in her work." Having once invested $85, he apparently became more enthusiastic about the piece of equipment—he purchased a new sewing machine in 1886, and Maria received new sewing and washing machines regularly from that time on (although it remains unclear whether Cyrus purchased them or whether Maria bought them with earnings from her fledgling dairy business).[41] Women, who benefited most directly from domestic technology and valued it much more than did men, were grateful when their husbands bought it for them. In addition, many were quite possessive of it—in cases of divorce or when probating their husbands' estates, women often attempted to set items like sewing machines apart from their husbands' personal property. Some settler women also gave their daughters sewing machines as they prepared to marry and establish households of their own.[42]

Labor-saving devices, especially sewing machines, gradually became standard among Oregon families. In 1875, the Master of the Oregon State Grange reported that he had "made positive arrangements to supply [the] Order with Family Sewing Machines of the best quality, at greatly reduced rates, and fully warranted."[43] The Grange's interest in securing reduced prices for sewing machines reveals the extent to which rural men had become convinced of their value, and the Master's use of the phrase "Family

Sewing Machines" suggests that they were no longer luxury items, but had become an integral part of rural household economic strategies.[44]

Some husbands also sought to ease their wives' burden by hiring domestic workers to assist them, but these workers were rare. Although most men brought their families with them to the Oregon frontier, there was a shortage of Anglo women during the early years of settlement. This shortage was keenly felt by bachelors who needed a domestic worker for financial success, or to claim the land promised to wives through the DLCA. As one recent arrival wrote to his family back east, "women is scarce here, and [there are] a great many batchelers that is well Situated & wants wives."[45] These conditions meant that domestic servants were difficult to find even if families had sufficient resources to pay for them, so most women had to find ways to do their work and help their husbands as needed. They kept their children out of school for varying periods of time to help with pressing domestic tasks, and a select few families managed to hire Indian women or neighbors' daughters to assist them. On the whole, Willamette Valley settlers hired persons of color—and particularly Chinese men—as domestic servants far less frequently than did farming families in California.[46]

But as settlers became more financially secure, and as the state's sex ratio became more balanced, families were better able to hire at least occasional domestic help. Young Anglo women and widows were more available for paid assistance with laundry, cooking, and other repetitive tasks, and the first-generation women who employed them developed close relationships with these hired "girls," treating them almost as surrogate daughters (in contrast to housewives in eastern cities, who enhanced their class status by emphasizing differences between family members and servants). Late in life, settlers like Maria Locey rejoiced at having a domestic "to do the hard work of the kitchen," freeing them for less physically taxing but apparently more rewarding tasks like cleaning the pantry, quilting, and sewing new linens and curtains.[47] Still, while women greatly appreciated assistance, most 1870s men were more interested in hiring male hands to do field labor, commonly paying domestic workers $3 per week while offering male field hands from $1 to $2 per day. Thus, when settlers hired Indian or Chinese men to do domestic tasks, it suggested that these men's ethnicity made them less masculine and more suited to poorly paid feminine work. Anglo-American men did not usually hire out as domestic servants, but found more highly paid field labor.[48]

Very occasionally, men did assign Anglo male hired hands to assist their wives with the housework, but when possible, these employees only temporarily assisted with the most physically challenging tasks (such as laundering or churning butter). Often, they performed masculine jobs that were recorded as merely *supporting* women's domestic tasks—as when Edward E. Parrish's hired hand worked on the wooden quilt frames that his wife and female domestic servant used to complete quilts. Farmers seemed eager to assign these low-skill and low-status jobs to their hired hands, yet by recording their employees' labor as they did, these men maintained for themselves at least part of the credit for helping their wives. Designating the work as "helping" also protected these Anglo hired hands' gender identity. While Indian or Chinese men were considered suited to domestic work and were degraded by their association with it, Anglo employers and employees maintained their masculine status by helping women without considering the work to be their own.[49]

Seeking Domesticity

As desirable farming conditions in Oregon enabled more and more settlers to match their lives to eastern ideals, Willamette Valley farm women were able to at least partially display the refined behavior these ideals called for. In doing so, they effectively set themselves apart as members of a middle class that had grown and become established in mid-nineteenth-century eastern cities.[50]

Once successful farms had been established and women were able to focus their attentions on domestic work, they commonly saw field labor as socially undesirable. German immigrant Catherine Wehnum, for instance, believed that to be accepted as a proper woman in Oregon, she must not toil as a farm worker as she had in Germany and on the Michigan frontier. So intent was Catherine on establishing herself solidly within the domestic sphere that in 1871, she sought a divorce on the basis of cruelty because her husband, Henry, made her do field labor. She complained that Henry "required and compelled pl[ainti]ff to work for def[endan]t as a common farm laborer, in harvesting, grubbing, building fence, planing and hoeing and cultivating the farm, working on the roads, &c, in addition to the ordinary duties of a housewife, and during all that time [the defendant] was in good pecuniary circumstances." Abandoning her earlier willingness to do outdoor work, Catherine adopted her neighbors' belief that women should not work outside the home: "I didnt work out[doors] here the same as I did there because it was not fashionable and I would not do it." In contrast, her husband clung to German cultural standards, rejecting the value of a wife "that he had to make a living for." Both Catherine and Henry recognized that their marriage was an economic partnership, but they disagreed about where and how clearly the boundary between men's and women's work roles should be drawn. Catherine appealed to her neighbors' growing expectation that, when "pecuniary circumstances" permitted, women should be freed from field labor to develop the "fashionable" traits of an ideal housewife.[51]

Nineteenth-century American gender ideology held that it was women's domesticity that set the middle class apart from the laboring classes. Thus Oregon settlers, like their counterparts in the Midwest, accepted women's field labor only when they deemed it necessary for survival, expecting that women's work and social roles would take a conventional form when circumstances permitted. The Wehnums' divorce proceedings reveal the different extents to which husband and wife had adopted this American view of social class. In fact, Catherine had willingly worked in the fields both before and after immigrating to the United States, and her husband asserted that before their marriage and financial success, she had preferred outdoor work to domestic tasks. Apparently, then, although Willamette Valley wives could not remove economic production from their lives and their homes, they sought to use their domesticity to demonstrate their increased class status.

Social expectations for women in the valley changed as farms and communities grew. During the early years of settlement, women were highly valued for their contributions to household labor needs. As Oregonians became more established, however, settlers increasingly expected women to be not only useful but also ladylike, following eastern rules for refined behavior. Beginning in the 1850s, local newspapers frequently reprinted articles from eastern periodicals directing women to be "true ladies" and focus their attention on the family home, and as soon as they were able, women sought to do so.[52] Rural families could not afford for women to be merely ornamental, but they agreed with these eastern authors that wives should be homemakers first and foremost. Beyond cooking and cleaning,

Oregon settlers expected women to create a welcoming and morally upright environment to which their "menfolks" would be anxious to return.

Among the middle class that developed in the mid-nineteenth-century eastern United States, the home was seen as a haven from the world, particularly from the world of business. This message was reinforced by publications such as *Godey's Lady's Book* and the many etiquette books that appeared at the time. But in reality, the division between the home and the outside world was less clearly defined than these publications suggested, even among the urban middle class—and for rural Oregonians, it was even blurrier. Although Oregon women gradually withdrew from field labor, they continued to do productive work both inside and outside, and men, similarly, brought tasks such as mending harness within the home, sometimes remaining to assist their wives with domestic work. Many families continued to live in cramped cabins that bore little resemblance to the domestic paradise described in the prescriptive literature, but they matched their homes to the eastern domestic ideal as closely as possible.[53]

Actually, Oregon men and women found many ways to make their homes more comfortable and upscale. Men replaced small, crude log cabins with larger frame houses or built shelves, furniture, and other conveniences. Besides making curtains, quilts, and rag rugs that provided both beauty and utility, some women found time for "fancy work" such as embroidered samplers with which to decorate their rooms. Wives, valued for their hospitality to friends and strangers alike, also played a key role in creating an emotionally welcoming environment within the family home.[54]

Oregon men greatly valued this domestic romanticism. Although their work on the farm was far more insulated from "the world" than was that of eastern businessmen, they nonetheless desired their homes to be refuges from work and male responsibilities, places to bask in the service and adoration of their wives and children. This becomes clear as settler Justin Chenoweth waxes poetic about the farmer's nightly return home from the fields:

To a lovely wife in good cheer.
There, prepared and offered,
By those whom he truly loves
The plainest food becomes
Ambrosia, equal to Jove's. . . .

Then his clustering children
While amusing, with emulous prate
Heed not the trappings of men
But deem their sire absolutely great.[55]

This poem clearly shows that Chenoweth and his counterparts throughout Oregon desired to replace the struggles of frontier life with the promise of domestic joy.

As good Willamette Valley wives embraced this idea, they trained their daughters to be similarly "lovely wives" to their future husbands. As one mother wrote to her daughter, "[O]f course it is onely right that you should do your share in building up the home + makeing it a pleasant one for your husband."[56] A number of other women collected eastern prescriptive literature that was frequently reprinted in local newspapers, and a few even penned fiction that instructed their daughters in ideal feminine behavior. In these stories, young women learned that a husband's role was to go forth into the wider world and to do dangerous things; a woman should maintain the home as his retreat.[57]

Despite the popularity of this literary genre, Oregon women and men did not always adopt the prescribed behavior. For example, one female author cited advice from men found frequently in contemporary periodicals: " 'If a woman would retain her husband's affections, and make his home attractive, let her always meet him as he returns from labor, with her sweetest smile and in her most attractive dress.' " The author then described her own failed attempt to follow this advice. Rather than pleasing her husband, she irritated him with her frivolity. Furthermore, she soiled her good dress while simultaneously preparing dinner for her husband and tending her young son. Through this experience, the author learned to be more practical, dressing for her domestic work just as men dressed for their own tasks. She thus acknowledged that some aspects of eastern ideology did not apply to real life on an Oregon farm. Yet the moral of the story was that men should limit themselves to advising fellow men rather than instructing women in things about which "they know little and understand less." That is to say, although this author recognized the limits of strict domestic ideology, she nonetheless concluded that even Oregon men's and women's lives ought to be as separate as eastern principles dictated.[58]

The gap between the genders' spheres was great when applied beyond work roles to prescribed behavior, because while men were primarily valued for their achievements and labor, women's work was less valued and less visible to the outside world. Therefore, like their middle-class counterparts in eastern cities, Willamette Valley women were judged primarily on the basis of their behavior and social graces. A proper lady was self-controlled, gracious and gentle to her family and friends, eager to assist anyone in need, and good at exerting a moderating influence over her husband and all with whom she interacted. She presented her most "polished side" to everyone she met. Like settler Martha Ann Maupin, "she faithfully observed her marriage vow, conducted herself with propriety, managed the household affairs with prudence + economy + treated her said husband with kindness and forbearance."[59]

The ideal woman was *necessarily* virtuous. Adultery was not tolerated even during the earliest days of settlement, and it was one of the most readily accepted causes for divorce. Inappropriate public intimacy constituted solid evidence of the crime of adultery. For example, John Harris was granted a divorce after only two months of marriage to his seventeen-year-old wife Anna, who "did allow the said A J Gann to hug, kiss, and fondle her, and do things that a good wife would not have done."[60]

Chastity grew more important as communities became more established, and gossip was a powerful form of social control. Dayton resident Sarah Smith, for instance, by innocently accepting social visits and practical assistance from another man during her husband's absence, became the subject of widespread rumors in the town. An individual's reputation in the neighborhood became even more important when couples found themselves in court, as can be seen when male witnesses placed defendant Elizabeth Stege in a hurdy-gurdy house. One witness explained that he "wouldn't think it was a place for a chaste and virtuous woman to be found even if she had business with the occupants."[61] And as the case turned out, Stege's mere presence in such a rowdy place appears to have been sufficient proof that she was unchaste, supporting her husband's claim of adultery (although the male witnesses' presence there appears not to have endangered their reputation at all). Even slightly suggestive behavior on the part of any woman, such as exposing some of her leg while in her own home, could prove that she was not a lady. It was no longer sufficient for a woman to be a productive housewife who avoided adultery. A lady's behavior must be beyond reproach.[62]

Besides being required to appear as perfect ladies, women were also expected to embrace motherhood, which Oregon settlers considered to be the pinnacle of women's work and identity. "The woman who has never had a baby of her own is only half a woman," declared one local newspaper article, "and only half knows the sweetness of life."[63] It is not surprising, then, that among the forty-six families in this study for which complete family genealogies were available, first-generation settlers had an average of 8.8 children, and only one family had fewer than five children.[64] Women spent a significant portion of their adult lives pregnant or nursing an infant and thus, in addition to their daily tasks in the house and barnyard, they also had to tend to their many children. To relieve wives of some of their work—as well as for educational purposes—older daughters were trained to do all the household tasks that would be required of them when they married and began families of their own.[65]

Motherhood—and the importance of raising virtuous children—brought upon women yet more behavioral requirements. Maternal imagery centered on goodness and love, suggesting that a proper mother was self-sacrificing, always placing the good of her progeny ahead of herself. She created a comfortable home in which to raise her children, and consoled both children and adults in times of sorrow. She taught sons and daughters to be upstanding, moral young men and women and raised her sons to be upright citizens. Fathers provided discipline, but mothers guided by example and gentle correction, providing nurturance and guidance without challenging their reputation as a proper lady.[66]

Old Age Blurs Gender Distinctions

While middle age brought greater financial security and a more clear gender division of labor for most Oregon settlers, as they grew older, both men and women gradually withdrew from the most physically demanding work related to their respective roles. Aging women relied on others to do taxing domestic tasks. At the same time, their aging husbands passed field work to younger men and once again assisted their wives with domestic labor. As the boundary between their workspaces became permeable once more, men and women renegotiated the meanings of the domestic sphere.

Retirement was a gradual and incomplete process that typically began between the ages of sixty and seventy. At this point, women sought less-challenging work that reinforced their status as "queens of the home" or proper ladies. Like Maria Locey, who found time to record her daily schedule late in life while caring for her young grandson, many women increasingly emphasized nurturing their families. Others focused on literary pursuits or decorative crafts like completing complex patchwork quilts or fine needlepoint that expressed their artistic and sewing abilities and made their homes look more like those of eastern middle-class families. Often, women became more active in caring for their neighbors, delivering babies, or attending to the emotional and spiritual needs of others in their community. All of these women shifted their attention from physically challenging daily chores such as churning butter or carrying water to domestic work that carried with it the prestige of acknowledged skill and wisdom attained over a lifetime of domestic labor. As this occurred, many older women turned to unmarried daughters and domestic servants to take on the majority of their chores, or they looked to their husbands or their husbands' field hands to help with their more taxing responsibilities.[67]

As men had sometimes had to do during the early days of settlement, aging husbands again consented to assisting their wives. Those who had carefully avoided "women's work," particularly once their farms became established, grew more willing to help with demanding jobs such as churning butter. But while men gradually took over the churning itself, they deferred to their wives as the experts on butter production, emphasizing that their labor was merely *helping* the women. Thus Cyrus Locey recorded in his journal, "I *helped* Mama churn today. *She thinks* we churned about 6 Lbs. butter churning about one hour."[68] Cyrus provided the labor, but the process remained his wife's responsibility, and she provided her expert opinion on how much butter his labor had produced. Similarly, while an elderly Edward E. Parrish regularly recorded the work done by his wife in his daily journal, Parrish consistently prefaced his remarks with the words "I notice," emphasizing the effort he exerted even to be aware of his wife's labor at a stage when his own daily labor was decreasing.[69] Men still desired to be useful, but they did not want advanced age to take away the gender identity so long defined by their work. Therefore, they carefully maintained their distance from feminine work by framing their participation in terms of helping their wives—just as they had done in earlier years, when they or their hired hands had given similar aid.

Many men appear to have more readily contributed to tasks that were not considered strictly domestic. In particular, although they consistently recorded their butter churning as merely helping, they were often willing to directly identify with garden work. At age eighty-two, in fact, Edward E. Parrish wrote frequently of gardening with his wife, once declaring in his journal: "My work these days is tryig to help the garden to master the weeds, &c."[70] In this way, Parrish claimed command over his labor, "helping" the garden itself rather than assisting his wife. Work in this former transition zone between home and fields appears to have been more easily accepted as men's work than was the clearly feminine task of making butter.

Elderly men's interest in household tasks grew as they tended toward more high-level management positions. As they had done in previous years, men built fences and houses for chickens in the barnyard; now, they also became more involved in selling chickens and eggs and keeping detailed records of the quantities sold. They still rarely recorded contributing to daily tasks such as feeding the chickens and collecting eggs. This may mean that men added these tasks to their usually unspecified list of daily chores, but it is much more likely that their wives or paid laborers remained responsible for them. Thus, just as older women shifted their focus to more esteemed domestic tasks that drew on their expertise, their husbands took on a managerial role that lent prestige to what otherwise would have seemed low-status domestic work.[71]

To men and women who had worked throughout their lives to distinguish their gender's economic and social role, the inability to live out this role in their old age posed a problem. But as both sexes were able to take on higher-status work functions, the aging first generation even now managed to maintain a boundary between the genders. Since they had first come to Oregon, their work roles had in a sense come full circle.

Conclusion

Overall, gender roles were quite similar for families in the Midwest, on the Overland Trail, and during the early years of settlement in Oregon's Willamette Valley. Men worked in the fields and tended livestock, while women did housework, sewed clothing, raised poultry and produce, and made butter. While at first husbands and wives frequently assisted one another with the most pressing or challenging tasks, over time, prosperity provided them with domestic servants, hired hands, and new technologies that allowed the sexes to retreat into their separate spheres of work. Men and women cooperated within the barnyard, each doing gender-appropriate tasks, and when women needed assistance with "women's work" such as churning butter, they turned to their children, to female domestic servants, or occasionally to male hired hands. This clearly defined division of labor created an efficient partnership within the household and, perhaps more importantly, it enabled couples to more fully match their lives to the eastern domestic ideology, permitting women to approximate genteel behavior and create the domestic environment that marked membership in the mid-nineteenth-century middle class. Even men and women who survived past age sixty, when physical impairments forced them to abstain from certain tasks, were able to maintain social distance from gender-inappropriate work. Thus even this renewed crossing of gender boundaries ultimately failed to challenge the old ideals that settlers had brought with them from the Midwest.

CHAPTER 2

Masculine Providers and Manly Men

Throughout his teen years, Oliver Jory helped his father with their family's fruit-growing and -drying business just south of Salem, Oregon. Like many second-generation male settlers, Oliver served an informal apprenticeship to his father, gradually assuming more responsibility for the family farm and business. Beginning in his early twenties, Oliver also traveled around Oregon to events such as the Portland Mechanics Fair to sell fruit-drying machines made according to his father's patents. But despite his growing independence, Oliver felt too economically insecure to marry his fiancée, Ella, who remained with her family 175 miles away in Coos County, and he bemoaned having full responsibility for the drying business whenever his father was away. In 1892, when Oliver was thirty-two and his father was approaching sixty, Oliver built a factory to produce the fruit-drying machines his father had designed. His father then focused his attention on the farm and agreed to exchange labor with his son, who ran the factory portion of the family business. Not until 1901, when Oliver was forty years old, did he feel self-sufficient enough to finally marry Ella. While his eighteen-year engagement bordered on absurd, Oliver Jory's prolonged semi-dependence on his father and his struggle to establish his independence were typical of young men who came of age in the Willamette Valley during the late nineteenth century.[1]

First-generation Oregonians sought to become either masculine providers or feminine homemakers. Toward that end, men strove to relieve their wives of field labor. They trained their sons to do "men's work" in preparation for the day that they, too, would be independent farmers. In the process, fathers sought to instill their own gender ideology in their sons, showing them proper behavior and wise decision making. Yet that very training in autonomy and wisdom, along with the relative abundance of undeveloped land claimed by the first generation, led to intergenerational conflicts as fathers clung to their positions as household heads and their sons sought independence for themselves and their own families.[2] Ultimately, the second generation did become independent providers, but often at a significant cost to their fathers' own masculine identity. As settlers' sons grew up, and as new economic and social trends developed around the country, second-generation men largely redefined standards for manly behavior.

Providing for the Family

As the first Oregon settlers established successful farms and distinct male and female workspaces, the genders' differing economic roles reinforced their differing social roles. Although wives' and children's work remained critical to survival, Oregonians believed that it was men's responsibility to provide their families with food, shelter, and at least a few small comforts. If they failed in their role as providers, first-generation Oregon men faced social and sometimes legal censure. Perhaps even more problematic, their masculinity was called into question.

Because farm work required seasonal peaks of productivity, first-generation men cooperated with their neighbors at times of great labor needs, just as they had done in the Midwest. They maintained records of exchange with their neighbors and local merchants, trading goods and days of labor. Farmers and merchants typically "settled up" approximately once per year, and farmers would pay the balance that they owed in cash, produce, labor, or a "note" (a slip of paper recording the amount owed, interest rate, and terms for repayment, which could also be signed over to a third party in lieu of cash). This informal exchange was particularly important during the 1850s and 1860s, when cash was rare and few could afford to hire workers. Periodic labor exchanges offered not only improved work efficiency but also an opportunity to socialize and reinforce social ties among men in the neighborhood.[3]

Whether the labor need was seasonal, occasional, or acute, men assisted men and women assisted women. The differences between men's and women's work—and the resulting social implications—are reflected in one second-generation woman's recollection of pioneer cooperation:

When I was a girl, if a woman got sick . . . [her female] neighbors came in, did the housework, took her children to their homes to care for till she was well, brought her home-made bread and jellies and other things, and if a man met with an accident or was sick, all the men in the neighborhood would put in his crop for him or reap his grain, making it a day's picnic, just as if they were going to a house-raising. If he was out of wood they would haul wood and cut it up, and in every way the neighbors showed a spirit of helpfulness and service.[4]

As this reminiscence reveals, not only work roles but also styles of assistance varied by gender. Individual women worked within their nurturing role, providing nursing skills, childcare, and emotional comfort. In contrast, men worked as teams to accomplish a major task, turning it into an opportunity for camaraderie and teamwork as well as assistance to their neighbors in need. Women rarely enjoyed such extensive opportunities for teamwork, except when attending and supporting their husbands' work bees through cooking and other domestic labor.

Although men's patriarchal authority declined in the nineteenth century, male heads of household nonetheless held significant power as providers for household members.[5] A man was "the head of his family, & consequently the provider," as Margaret Waddle proclaimed in her 1858 divorce complaint. In the Waddles' case, Margaret argued, her husband was at fault in the collapse of their marriage, for he took all the cash in their house when he departed for the mines and left Margaret to work to support herself.[6] In contrast, in another divorce case nine years later, a young Marion County man testified that his father had treated his mother "as a man should treat his wife . . . provided her a good home, a good house to live in. He worked hard and furnished her with plenty to eat and wear."[7] In addition to providing material comforts, supporting one's family meant freeing one's wife and daughters from field labor; thus, masculinity was also symbolized by a wife who remained in the home. By this reasoning, settler Maria Watson was married to an excellent man, for her spouse "never allowed outside work to fall to her, and . . . the cows on the farm always ran if they saw a woman coming."[8]

The fact that Oregonians were highly critical of men who failed to provide for their families can be seen through witnesses' depositions in divorce trials. In general, witnesses testified on behalf of Oregon men more frequently than they did for women, but they consistently testified against men when they were convinced that the men had failed in their provider roles. For example, a male neighbor who took a position against settler William Taylor reported that he had urged Taylor to return home from the gold mines and accept responsibility for his family. "I told him the conditions of his wife + children and his obligations that he was under to that wife and children . . . and he was acting very bad not to make some provision for [his children's] support." When Taylor still refused to return to his family, this neighbor took over as their provider, helping the family financially as well as by testifying against Taylor at his divorce trial.[9] In a more extreme case, German immigrant Henry Wehnum's son declared in court that Henry "didnt want a damned bitch that he had to make a living for. He wanted one to make a living for him." This testimony revealed Henry to be in direct conflict with Anglo-American gender ideals.[10]

Few husbands seemed as clearly unwilling to support their wives as Henry Wehnum did. Yet many men, including American-born Oregonians, nonetheless failed to adequately provide for their wives. Some simply deserted them and moved away in search of a living somewhere else. In Marion County alone, 388 women sued their husbands for divorce due to desertion between 1848 and 1899, constituting 35 percent of divorce complainants who filed during that period; another 20 percent argued that their husbands had neglected them or failed to support them.[11] In Lane County, seventy-one women sought divorces for non-support between 1853 and 1891, representing nearly one-quarter of all divorce complainants during those years (but less than 5 percent of all women living in the county).[12] Further, because divorce brought with it great social costs to both men and women, it is safe to assume that many more Marion and Lane County women—whose populations more than quadrupled from 1860 to 1900— also suffered desertion or neglect but failed to report it.[13] By society's standards, these women's spouses failed as husbands and fathers. Furthermore, by neglecting their provider role, they failed as men.

Fathers and Sons

Like rural men throughout the United States, first-generation Oregon fathers trained their sons to be good providers and good men, teaching them all the skills necessary to raise crops and run a farm. During their informal apprenticeship to their fathers, sons experienced a stage of semi-dependency similar to that of farmers' sons in colonial New England.[14] As first-generation men grew older, they gradually retired from active labor, shifting into managerial roles. Meanwhile, aided by access to the settlers' large land-holdings, most sons eventually acquired land and families of their own, establishing themselves in the community as masculine household heads.

Boys learned to do male work and to behave like men primarily by assisting their fathers and older brothers in the fields. Birth order and the labor needs of the family influenced boys' degree of responsibility for adult work, as well as the age at which they began it—Louis Banks, for one, recalled: "Being the oldest boy, I became my father's assistant in the farm work, very early."[15] But even most younger sons were expected to be proficient with the plow by the age of twelve. Toward that end, Isom Cranfill built a small plow for his eleven-year-old son Rufus, whose older brother taught him to use it. The first straight row a boy plowed by himself was a major milestone in his life, and successful plowing represented his initiation into manhood.[16]

Boys between the ages of ten and fourteen made substantial contributions to the family's labor output, but unless their family was extremely needy, they were not yet fully committed to daily work. Most boys attended school at least occasionally, whenever their fathers could spare them from the fields, and because frontier needs were often intense, it was not uncommon for young men to attend school sporadically until they were in their late teens or early twenties. Many boys also took breaks from field work and studying to hunt or fish—activities that combined productivity and pleasure.[17]

By the age of fourteen, boys had learned most of the skills required to be a successful farmer. Yet, with the exception of a few who came west as teenagers and were able to claim land under the Donation Land Claim Act (DLCA), they did not immediately begin working their own land. Instead, adolescent boys either worked for their fathers or hired themselves out to neighbors by the day, month, or year, plowing, cutting wheat, and chopping wood.[18] They might also assist their mothers or sisters with husking corn, digging potatoes, and other tasks that lay in the borderland between men's and women's work. Although fathers remained responsible for making most decisions, by age twenty their sons shared their work on nearly equal terms. When sons took part in the neighborhood's informal labor exchange network—which they frequently did—payments would typically be credited to their father.[19]

While males who came of age in the 1850s were generally able to marry and claim land by age eighteen, those who grew up in decades when unoccupied land was more rare often had to delay their independence substantially. Some young men who wished to leave home right away migrated to the valley's growing cities in search of paid work, eventually making their own start in life. Others moved away to find free land in eastern Oregon or surrounding states, repeating their parents' frontier experience. Many young men, however, remained in extended relationships of semi-dependence as laborers for their fathers, waiting to inherit part or all of their parents' large landholdings. In fact, demographer Christopher Carlson found that in Lane County in approximately 1880, a majority of young men remained dependents in another's household past age twenty-five, and one-third still did not head their own household by age twenty-eight.[20] While articles in the *Willamette Farmer* urged fathers to give their sons more responsibility in operating their farms, providing an incentive for them to remain at home rather than seeking their fortunes elsewhere, most were loathe to follow this advice. Only as fathers aged did young men gain notable influence in their households and over the running of the farm.[21]

A close examination of settler Cyrus Locey's relationship with his sons helps to illuminate the male apprenticeship experience and the corresponding shifts in father-son connections over time. In addition, it illustrates the different paths that young men might take toward independence. In many ways, the ideal father-son relationship is represented in that which Cyrus developed with Julian, his eldest surviving son, who began assisting him with field work and ran errands for the family at age eleven. By age fourteen, Julian was a reliable field hand, working alongside his father to raise grain and livestock, and by age twenty, Julian's labor became so integral to the farm's operation that when he went to trade in town, his father complained to his journal that Julian's absence kept him busy with chores. Julian had become a man, trusted to make wise decisions when trading the family's produce and relied upon to carry a man's work responsibilities on the farm.[22]

In 1886, at age twenty-four, Julian Locey got married and purchased a nearby ranch, but he continued to work on his father's ranch as well, apparently dividing his attention between the two homesteads. Cyrus paid Julian to work on his ranch for a month while Cyrus was away taking the federal census, and he also assisted his son, staying with Julian for two days to help him slaughter his hogs. In fact, long after Julian had married and established his own ranch, father and son maintained familial ties of assistance. But as Julian was shifting his interest more and more toward his new home and developing family, Cyrus relied on hired laborers until his next oldest son, Ernie, began missing school to help with ranch work at age thirteen. When Julian's sisters married, Cyrus also incorporated his sons-in-law into the family network, exchanging work and parcels of land with them as he did with his own sons. Cyrus began to treat Julian and his sons-in-law as equals as they became household heads, joining the adult male community.[23]

It should be noted that, for reasons they rarely recorded in their farm journals, first-generation men did not always anoint their eldest sons as their partner or successor. In contrast to the Locey men, Lucien Davidson's sons moved off the family farm early and acquired their own land while Lucien's son-in-law, John Cox, rented his farm. Lucien and John Cox helped each other, trading roles as farmer and field worker—but it is not clear why a son-in-law, rather than one or more of Lucien's own sons, entered into such a close partnership with him. More typical was the situation of Seth Lewelling, whose daughter's new husband (one of his former field workers) returned to work for him following the marriage, but did not obtain the right to joint control of the farm (as John Cox had done with the Davidson property). In any case, Lucien Davidson and Seth Lewelling were similar in that they each chose to cooperate with and trust a selected son-in-law.[24]

By the time Cyrus Locey's younger sons, Ernie and Fred, were old enough to contribute to the household economy, Cyrus was already past fifty years old. Health problems forced him to reduce his workload, but he refused to relinquish farm management to his sons. Instead, he entered into a casual partnership with Ernie, who was in his early twenties. Shortly before Ernie's marriage at age twenty-five, Cyrus informed him that he intended to change the terms of their partnership the following year because he was "not satisfied with the present management." Apparently, like many adult sons who stood to inherit a substantial portion of their parents' land, Ernie had been drawn into a power struggle with his father. But despite Cyrus's dissatisfaction, their partnership continued, and Ernie, his wife, and their two children lived with his parents for the next thirteen years. Cyrus urged each of his sons and daughters to claim the 160 acres to which they were entitled under the 1860 Homestead Act as soon as they turned twenty-one, but when Ernie and Fred acquired land nearby through homesteading and purchase, the new acreage was simply added to the Locey family ranch. This arrangement strengthened Cyrus's position as the elder member of his partnership with Ernie, rather than enabling the son to gain authority within his father's household or to remove his family from his father's control.[25]

Although Cyrus's two younger sons shared labor fairly equally, he interacted with them each in very different ways. Cyrus often complained to his journal about power struggles with Ernie, questioning the wisdom of their partnership. On one such occasion, he wrote: "I had quite an unfriendly confab with Earnie as he finds fault with my management while he was away. I am not certain but it would be better for us to divide up and go it separate. I have no doubt we should be better friends by so doing." In contrast, Fred consistently pleased his father, making him confident that he was "going to make quite a careful farmer." In fact, Fred managed to avoid criticism even when he and Ernie both did things that Cyrus considered foolish. For example, when Ernie paid in advance for goods that he ordered from town, Cyrus wrote in his journal that it was a "poor plan to pay for goods before they are delivered." Yet just two weeks later, when Fred and Cyrus's wife similarly sent money ahead, Cyrus merely commented, "[H]ope these orders may go all right."[26]

The Locey family journals do not reveal why Cyrus refused to trust Ernie as he did Julian and Fred. It appears, however, that the sons' own expectations largely shaped their relationships with their father. As Ernie married and had children of his own, he became increasingly desirous of being a truly equal partner with his father, in decision-making power as well as labor contribution. Fred, who remained a bachelor, apparently accepted his subordinate role in the partnership and the household even after Cyrus died. While Cyrus and Ernie each battled to establish his own manly independence, Fred played a more feminine role in the family, assisting his mother with domestic work and submitting to the masculine authority of his father and older brother. For reasons that remain unclear, Fred apparently did not feel the same need to prove his masculinity through work roles and marriage that can be seen in most Oregon men of his generation.[27]

Cyrus Locey worked alongside his sons until his health finally gave way when he was in his mid-seventies. After about 1910, Cyrus turned over the daily working of his and his sons' combined ranches to Ernie and Fred. Yet Cyrus remained unwilling to give up decision-making power for the Locey family ranch—even to the favored Fred, who had attended a business college in Baker, Oregon. Cyrus continued to identify with the work of the ranch even when he was unable to take part, and he was determined to influence the ranch's finances. While "the men" (his sons and their hired hands) fed and vaccinated the cattle, Cyrus did paperwork and corresponded with the authorities regarding those vaccinations. When decisions were made or money exchanged hands, Cyrus used the word "we" to describe the party in control of the situation—whether or not he was personally involved. Well before his sons had fully taken over responsibility for the ranch, Cyrus bemoaned his loss of independence, writing, "How can I bear to be treated as tho' I was a child and have no part or lot in saying what shall be done on the farm or what we shall buy for our use? Blue, bluer, bluest." As he lost control of the Locey ranch, Cyrus also nearly lost hope, intimating to his journal: "I almost feel that I am in the way on my own farm." This man, like many Willamette Valley settlers, wanted his sons to become independent farmers. Yet in the end, Cyrus's desire to help his younger sons came into direct conflict with his own need to remain in control of his household. Ultimately, he was unable to relinquish his decision-making power in order to permit his younger sons to become real men in their families and community, and when infirmity finally forced him to let go of that power and begin to pass on his land to his sons, Cyrus lost his desire to live.[28]

Land ownership was one of the most important components of masculine power and independence in nineteenth-century Oregon, and had thus been one of male settlers' primary motivations for migrating there. Like Abraham Wigle's father, each man "wanted to go to Oregon that his children might secure homes and all settle near him."[29] Ironically, however, the generous terms of the DLCA left very little farmland unclaimed by the time most second-generation Oregon men came of age. Actually, in only twelve out of the thirty-nine families profiled for this study did at least one son claim his own land, and in most of these cases, only the older sons were able to do so.[30] Further, as this study shows, sons had little hope of inheriting land while their fathers were alive. Out of twenty-one first-generation men sampled, eighteen chose to maintain control of the family farm until death, no more than four of whom lacked substantial quantities of land to disburse. Only two fathers distributed land to their children during their lifetimes—and both of these men were extremely wealthy by Oregon standards, and thus were able to do so without risking their own financial independence. The remaining man in the sample sold his land and moved in with his youngest son, apparently using the proceeds to support himself in his son's home. This last circumstance, however, was uncommon. Like Cyrus Locey, the vast majority of first-generation men were adamantly unwilling to hand over control of their farms—even if they held far more acreage than they were able to farm in their lifetimes.[31]

Although only male offspring entered informal apprenticeships with their fathers, large donation land claim (DLC) grants encouraged many first-generation Oregon men to divide their estates among all of their children to an extent that was not possible elsewhere. In eighteenth-century New England, for example, farmers typically had only enough land on which to settle either their eldest or their youngest son, and among early Michigan settlers, historian Susan Gray found that fathers and sons or pairs of brothers commonly farmed together to avoid "spoiling the whole."[32] In the Willamette Valley, on the other hand, many farmers distributed their estates more or less evenly among their children; indeed, half of the first-generation men of interest in this study's sample did so. Most of these men owned significant quantities of land—one owned 2,900 acres of farmland and another about 1,760 acres; others held 300- to 700-acre DLCs or several valuable town lots. Isaac Bond, the only exception, owned just 20.93 acres, but he held a generous $3914 in cash and notes. And Bond's estate, too, was divided equally when he died intestate, as were the estates of almost all settlers who died under such circumstances. In any case, settlers who chose not to evenly divide their estates appear to have been motivated in part by informal apprentice relationships with their sons.

It is worthwhile to mention that even Oregon men who planned fairly even divisions of their whole estates did not simply subdivide their landholdings equally among their children. In keeping with their expectations that their sons would become farmers and their daughters would do domestic work, these men tended to give most or all of their land to their sons upon their death, while they gave cash or other moveable property to their daughters—sometimes while they were still alive, upon a daughter's marriage. If a father did give away part of his estate while still living, he would often explain in his will that certain offspring had received their inheritance at an earlier date. Of those sampled for this study, six men (or 28.6 percent) gave larger portions of their estates to their sons than they did to their daughters, predictably leaving primarily personal property to their daughters. Four other men were more generous to their youngest children, who did not already own significant amounts of land or other property. Like Cyrus Locey, these fathers probably sought not only to help their younger children but also to favor those who remained at home and assisted with the family homestead rather than forming households of their own. The choices made by this small sample of first-generation Oregon men suggest that while inheritance patterns varied in the Willamette Valley, most first-generation men were both able and eager to provide for all of their offspring in some way. When they did favor some of their children over others, that choice was based on need or interdependence.

Sons' informal apprenticeships to their fathers followed a fairly consistent pattern, at least until the second generation reached adulthood. However, as the Locey men illustrate, there were variations within and across families that depended on individuals' personalities, interests, and abilities. Although first-generation men gradually retired from active field work, many expected to continue making decisions for the household, and sons reaching maturity often became increasingly unwilling to simply accept their fathers' directions. Fathers and sons were therefore forced to negotiate their own degrees of independence as workers, providers, and household heads.[33]

Labor

Throughout rural America, farmers relied on their sons—and occasionally their daughters—to assist with field labor. But father-son apprenticeships were not possible for every Oregon family. Farmers who did not own sufficient land to support their families, or whose large family created a surplus of labor, might temporarily hire out one or more of their children to neighbors, and beyond casual labor exchanges within the neighborhood, a growing number of young men became more permanent hired hands. These hired hands grew to be part of the household in which they worked, providing labor in exchange for training, room and board, and perhaps a small wage. Although their work schedules were similar to others' on the farm, the power relations between them and their employers differed from those between fathers and sons.

First-generation men frequently failed to differentiate between the labor performed by sons and that done by hired hands. Edward E. Parrish was typical, writing in his farm journal that "The Boys"—Jackson (his thirty-five-year-old son) and Jim (an Anglo-American hired hand)—split rails while he rode around the farm with his dogs, "trying to chace away the Kioties" from his sheep.[34] Young men sometimes took on the household head's annual road-building and maintenance responsibilities, but in general, both teenage sons and hired hands did field work and lower-status tasks such as chopping wood, building fences, digging wells, and even assisting with "women's work" like laundry or churning. Assigning these low-status or feminine jobs to young field hands enabled fathers to focus on work that reinforced their positions as skilled masculine workers.[35]

The distinctions between paid laborers and apprenticed family members could also become quite blurred when farmers began to pay their apprentices. For instance, young William Chapman's father and uncle both paid him, often in cash, to work in their fields, just as neighboring farmers did. Most farmers maintained more careful records of wages and days of work performed when it came to their hired hands than when it came to their sons, but in general, they only occasionally mentioned work done by "the boys" in their journals.[36]

Notably, however, while the work roles and payment of hired hands and sons were similar, the relationships that developed between employers and hired men differed greatly from those between fathers and sons. For one thing, it does not appear that first-generation men were as concerned with training their hired hands as they were with grooming their sons to become careful farmers. At the same time, hired hands were probably more willing to accept their employer's authority than were sons like Ernie Locey, who sought to share power with his father over the lands that he would eventually inherit. Paid laborers' status as employees made them less able to challenge the household head's decisions, but it also insulated them from family power struggles.

Due to the ethnic homogeneity of the post-mid-century Willamette Valley, nearly all hired hands in the region were Anglo-American. American Indian men sometimes found work as casual laborers during the 1850s, but this became increasingly rare following the Rogue River War and the creation of reservations in the 1860s. In addition, a small number of Chinese men found their way from California's gold mines and railroads to Oregon, where they worked for white farm families, but by 1870 there were only 597 Chinese in the Willamette Valley.[37] Three decades later, 7,481 of the valley's 8,470 Chinese (92.6 percent) were living in Portland, home to a vibrant Chinese community.[38]

Although these American Indian and Chinese men never made up a significant proportion of the paid laborers in nineteenth-century Oregon, scattered references to non-Anglo hired help suggest that when interethnic employment did occur, race was a notable influence on social position. Whereas farmers consistently referred to both their sons and Anglo-American hired hands by first name or collectively as "the boys," they carefully recorded American Indian and Chinese laborers' ethnicity, in many cases appearing uninterested in learning these workers' names. Instead, a laborer's ethnicity became his or her primary identity in farm records. Thus Nathaniel Coe recorded that "Indian George and wife" were gathering apples to make cider in his orchard; similarly, in the 1870s, Seth Lewelling regularly described work done by Anglo field hand Willard, but only specified the names of his "Chinamen" workers when recording how much he'd paid each one.[39] And while Anglo-Americans were each hired by separate agreements, American Indian and Chinese men (and occasionally even women) were often hired in gangs, which further supported a lack of individual recognition and respect. References in farmers' account books thus suggest that Anglo-American hired laborers were substantially higher in status than their Indian and Chinese counterparts.[40]

Minority men—especially Chinese men—were also set apart by the work roles assigned to them, which were comprised of low-status farm tasks such as digging potatoes, grubbing fields, and—most significantly—often performing domestic labor. In contrast to settlers in California, where virulent anti-Chinese attitudes led to boycotts of Chinese laundries and servants, Oregon settlers appeared satisfied with Chinese domestics; although these workers were less desirable than Anglo-American women, they served as acceptable and available substitutes. Oregon wife Lucy Preston Peters recalled that domestic servants were more available in the 1870s than they were in later years, particularly if one was willing to hire a Chinese man to do women's work: "The question of household help in those days, was nothing like as strenuous, as it afterward became. We could always get good girls from the country, and before the Chinese were restricted from the country [in 1882], we generally employed a Chinese to cook."[41] Although laundering and cooking were women's work in China as well as in the United States, Chinese men accepted these jobs in Oregon because other positions were unavailable to them. Whether it was done intentionally or not, Anglo-American Oregonians hired Chinese and American Indian men for work that further emasculated them in the whites' eyes.[42]

New Possibilities

As second-generation Oregon men married and established households of their own, they worked hard to provide for their families as their fathers had done. However, the second generation came of age in a period of rapid economic change in Oregon. Although many continued to do field labor, their work changed as they adapted to changing conditions in the Willamette Valley.

First-generation men had cleared, plowed, and harvested enough acreage to feed their families, but their limited labor supply made it difficult to produce more than a little surplus grain. To achieve larger yields, the second generation relied on new technologies and a growing number of workers. As a result, Willamette Valley wheat production grew 150 percent in a decade, from 2.1 million bushels in 1870 to 5.4 million in 1880, and oats production doubled to 3.2 million bushels during the same period.[43] Men joined together to share expensive equipment, horses, and human labor, and some even hired large traveling harvesting teams in their quest to increase their production of marketable grain. Although the plowing and harvesting work itself changed little, social relations shifted in significant ways. Market-oriented farmers managed larger farms and moved into managerial positions at much younger ages than had been possible for their fathers' generation. Meanwhile, young men who lacked large land holdings were less likely to serve informal apprenticeships with neighboring farmers, instead becoming paid laborers increasingly divorced from land ownership. Whereas there were six times as many farmers as farm laborers in Oregon in 1860, there were only twice as many by 1900.[44]

During the last decades of the nineteenth century, as the prevalence of railroads reduced shipping rates nationwide, Willamette Valley farmers in-

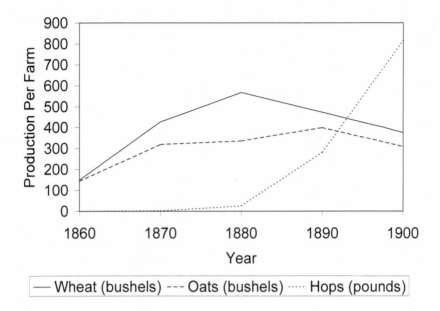

2.1 Willamette Valley grain production, 1860–1900

creasingly found themselves competing with wheat farmers elsewhere in the United States. In response, many Willamette Valley farmers adopted new cash crops such as berries and hops that flourished in the valley's unique climate. Harvesting methods for these crops remained unmechanized, requiring large teams of hired labor during the harvest season; nonetheless, hops production grew dramatically from less than 9,000 pounds in 1870 to 3.4 million in 1890 (fig. 2.1). By 1900, the Willamette Valley produced 14.1 million pounds of hops—more than one-quarter of all hops grown in the United States—while wheat production shifted to the Great Plains and Washington State, and farmers in California increasingly focused on citrus and viticulture. Although many farmers throughout the valley grew hops, not all areas did so at equivalent rates. In fact, in 1900, farmers in neighboring Marion and Polk counties produced more than half of all hops grown in Oregon (and one-sixth of those grown in the United States), averaging more than 2,000 pounds per farm (fig. 2.2). Meanwhile, other Willamette Valley farmers turned their attention to a variety of additional cash crops.[45]

Many second-generation farmers living near Oregon's growing cities chose to focus on producing fruits, vegetables, or dairy products for the

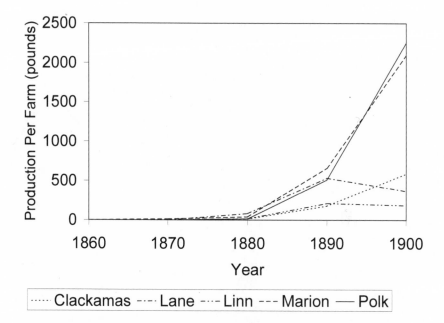

2.2 Willamette Valley hops production, 1860–1900

urban market. While they still raised grain and hay for home use, these farmers shifted their attention to goods that had traditionally been women's responsibility, often becoming increasingly involved in planting and tending vast gardens and large orchards. Farmers living near Portland—which nearly doubled in population during the last decade of the nineteenth century—largely abandoned grain crops to produce vegetables, milk, and butter for the growing city. Those in nearby Clackamas County emphasized orchards and fruit production, while the less-populous Lane, Linn, and Washington counties continued to emphasize grain farming but also began producing cheese, a less-perishable product, for more distant markets.[46]

The garden, barnyard, and orchard remained borderlands between men's and women's workspaces; however, while work roles in these areas had become more clearly delineated over the first decades of settlement, the second generation's emphasis on market production made the boundary between them murky once more. Men remained responsible for planting and tending the trees in the orchard and plowing the earth for the garden, yet as they shifted their attention toward garden and orchard production, they increasingly worked alongside their wives, sons, and daughters to pick and dry fruit, hoe the garden, or dig potatoes. Where formerly they had hired young men to work their fields and perhaps a young woman to assist with domestic work, second-generation farmers began to hire both men and young women to tend the growing garden and to harvest fruit. Whether they managed teams of male field hands or mixed-gender fruit pickers, however, men's management of these budding farm businesses marked them as masculine providers.[47]

Second-generation farmers also supplemented their income by taking on a variety of temporary employments. Many of these were jobs in field labor, similar to those performed by the first generation as part of an informal trade network in their neighborhood. But as Oregon's population grew and became more urban, opportunities to do various non-agricultural tasks for pay increased. Local and state government agencies hired men as tax assessors, census-takers, mail carriers, and other civil servants, and local companies hired both permanent and occasional workers for construction, to haul goods, or for similar projects. Some men also worked at skilled trades like surveying and carpentry—Lucien Davidson, for example, occasionally paid others to do field labor on his farm while he completed mechanical tasks for Oregon Iron & Steel Company. Another young man, Hamlin Smith, became a streetcar conductor. New employment opportunities enabled many second-generation settlers not only to make more money but also to balance their field work with other types of respected male employment.[48]

A significant number of second-generation men left farming altogether. In fact, by 1890, only one-third of Oregon men worked in agricultural professions; of these, 29,313 were farmers and 10,521 were agricultural laborers.[49] Some men left farming to enter the commercial world, opening a variety of small businesses in Portland or Oregon's smaller towns, or serving as clerks in larger companies. Others became teachers or attorneys or entered another kind of specialized vocation. For these second-generation men, education and professional skills permitted them to leave behind not only farm life but also the relatively flexible work roles their rural parents had been forced to adopt. Instead of striving to fulfill a masculine identity through farm labor, purposefully distancing themselves from "women's work" as much as possible, they were able to earn money for their families working exclusively outside the domestic sphere—just like their counterparts in eastern urban areas.[50]

Thus, for the younger generation of Oregon men, national changes and new financial opportunities were conducive to branching out from the subsistence-surplus farming existence that their fathers were devoted to. As they looked to cash crops or new professions to provide for their families' needs, these men adapted their work roles to match the requirements of their new economic strategies. While young men who focused on fruit and vegetable production redefined traditionally female tasks as masculine business strategies, those who left the farm to pursue other occupations enjoyed particularly distinct gender boundaries. Regardless, changing work roles helped to influence shifts in gender behavior as well.

Manly Men

During the early years of settlement in the Willamette Valley, physical needs such as food and shelter took precedence over enforcing refined social behavior. Cursing, heavy drinking, and violent behavior were tolerated—and at times even encouraged—among Oregon men. As communities grew, however, societal expectations for conduct became more clearly defined and more strongly enforced. Rough behavior came under attack by the 1860s and 1870s as women and men sought to establish more stable, refined communities. Like their fathers, second-generation men were expected to provide for their families, but in addition, they were held to a higher standard of genteel behavior. Control replaced physicality as a primary indicator of manliness.

First-generation Oregon men had brought with them from the Midwest and upper South a culture of male competition and adventure. These men's social interaction frequently centered on activities such as drinking, hunting, and wrestling, and they maintained order and proved their dominance over their families, employees, and peers through demonstrations of superior physical strength. Because men's work was crucial to their families' survival, and the use of limited force to maintain order within households was legally sanctioned, many women were forced to accept their husbands' occasional drunkenness or physical violence. However, as Oregon's gender ratio became more even in the 1860s, women began to exert a greater influence over male behavior, and many wives sought to curb such demonstrations of masculine prowess. Though they did not all succeed, men's physical power did begin to play a less prominent role than it had before.[51]

By approximately 1870, as the second generation came of age, settlers' acceptance of rough behavior such as drunkenness, cursing, and physical abuse had been replaced by expectations of refined conduct. Interest in temperance societies rose, and divorces were increasingly granted on the basis of abuse and "gross habitual drunkenness." When Mary Dinsmore, for example, sued for a divorce in 1869, her brother testified: Her husband "frequently grew angry at [Mary] for trivial affairs or without any excuse whatever so far as I knew, and cursed and abused her in a most ungentlemanly manner."[52] In the latter part of the nineteenth century, five Marion County women and three Lane County women sued for divorce from their husbands because of drunkenness, and another 36 in Marion County sought divorces for some combination of drunkenness, physical cruelty, verbal cruelty, and neglect during that same time period. Twenty-eight Lane County women likewise named drunkenness along with other causes for divorce, often implying that it was their husband's alcohol consumption that led them to abuse or neglect their wives.[53] Seeking to remedy situations like these and to leave the crudeness of frontier life behind, Oregonians grew to insist on men being as gentlemanly as women were ladylike. Men must provide for their families, it was believed, but they should also carry themselves in a decent manner.[54]

Mid-nineteenth-century temperance organizations were small, relatively few, and specifically directed toward men by men. Temperance proponent Edward E. Parrish, for instance, carefully aimed his sobriety message at his male peers, relying on them as heads of household to adopt his teachings and then share them with their families. By the 1880s and 1890s, however, temperance organizations such as the Women's Christian Temperance Union increasingly encouraged women to speak out against male drunkenness. Just as they emphasized their own good moral character, these women held their husbands to higher standards of genteel behavior.[55]

So it came to be that ideal second-generation men were polite, pleasant, modest and, like Oregonian Joseph Lane, they "always treated ladies with the greatest deference."[56] Yet they must balance that genteel behavior with a new kind of "manliness."[57] As one newspaper commentator explained, "If their is anything humiliating to a woman, it is to have a lover, whom she wishes to honor, weak and vapid, ever yielding and half afraid of her. She longs to tell him to 'act like a man!' "[58] One second-generation Oregon male highlighted the various aspects of manliness when he testified that his father didn't treat his mother "in a manly way before he left," abusing her verbally and failing to provide for her and the children.[59] By the turn of the century, Oregon men were expected to treat their families with kindness, at the same time demonstrating their masculinity by providing well for them and being a strong household leader. These expectations proved particularly difficult for young men—like Ernie Locey—who were forced to wait until their fathers' deaths to gain control over their land and households.

Another difficulty for second-generation men was that they were expected to provide for their wives and children even more than their fathers had been. Women continued to contribute to the household income as their mothers did, working in the home, garden, and dairy, but as they began to live out their domestic ideology, they sought to make their financial contributions invisible. These wives felt much like second-generation woman Ida M. Loughmiller when she wrote: "[I] done all I was able, but I think it is a man's duty to support his family."[60] In fact, just as many of the older female settlers had done, a number of second-generation women went to so far as to divorce their husbands for failing to provide for their families. To support their legal complaints, these women cited a variety of unacceptable behaviors displayed by their husbands, including drunkenness and physical and verbal cruelty—which we have seen were common reasons for divorce at the time. Yet they frequently referred to such cruelty or immoral behavior simply as aggravating circumstances that added to the primary complaint of non-support. Husbands' failure to live up to their responsibility as providers, or even their outright desertion, was often what finally persuaded women to divorce them.[61]

Most men understood and accepted their manly role as providers, as did George W. Lindsey when he "often said that he had no business with a wife as he was not able to support one."[62] Similarly, Oliver Jory, whose story opened this chapter, refused to marry fiancée Ella Hobson until he could provide for her financially. But those who did not embrace this type of thinking fell short both as spouses and as men. While many things had changed for these younger Oregonian males, the ability to support their families was still the primary factor in determining their gender identities.[63]

Conclusion

The masculinity of first-generation Oregon men revolved around the field labor that represented their families' primary financial support, providing food, shelter, and other necessities. During the first half of the nineteenth century, a man might drink or occasionally use violence to maintain his rightful position as household head, and this was acceptable as long as he consistently provided for his family. These first-generation men attempted to pass on their work skills and gender ideology to their sons through an informal apprenticeship system. But even as fathers successfully raised their sons to be good providers and wise decision makers, they increasingly found their own authority and ability to provide—and thus their masculinity—challenged by their sons. Men like Cyrus Locey struggled to come to terms with their decreasing ability to provide for their families as they grew older. They clung to their roles as leaders of the household, moving into more managerial positions as their sons or hired hands took over the bulk of the physical labor. While many fathers at least partially realized their dreams of settling their children near them in Oregon's farmland, they were not prepared for the conflicts that arose as their grown sons' desires to prove their genteel manliness brought them into competition for their fathers' masculine role.

CHAPTER 3

Love, Power, and Marital Choice

"I do need a wife no mistake," wrote a bachelor from the Oregon frontier to his parents in Ohio in 1853, "for I am geting most tired of doing my own cooking washing and mending."[1] A quarter-century later, an article in a Willamette Valley agricultural newspaper advised young men and women: "[I]f you do not love, then do not marry. Singleness is blessedness compared to marriage without affection."[2] As these differing perspectives on marriage suggest, by the close of the frontier era, motivations for Willamette Valley marriages had changed from the need for shared labor to demands for companionate relationships. Settlers' daughters grew unwilling to cook, wash, and mend in exchange for field labor and male dominance. They began to expect greater influence over household decision making and became less tolerant of physical and emotional abuse. In only one generation, economic and technological change spread a romantic, more egalitarian middle-class American culture from the East to the Willamette Valley. As it took root, this culture pruned patriarchal authority and planted seeds of companionship and love in the fertile soil of the American West.

Throughout the nineteenth-century United States, economic prosperity helped to transform the meaning of marriage. While family historians Karen Lystra and Ellen Rothman disagree about exactly when romance first became crucial to courtship, they concur that by the latter part of the century, "ideal love" remained the only chance for a happy marriage. The universality of these findings, however, is called into question when they are applied to early settlers: although John Mack Faragher found mid-nineteenth-century courtship rituals in the Midwest similar to those described by Lystra and Rothman, he argued that romance was not accessible to people raised on the frontier. Certainly, he believed, frontier men and women were glad to marry someone whose company they enjoyed, and many later bemoaned the death of their beloved spouses, but for Oregon settlers—unlike residents of more settled states—the financial necessity of a partner in labor superceded their desire for a romantic companion.[3]

This necessity was short-lived. Comparing these early Oregon settlers to their children—who benefited from large grants of productive farmland and the West's economic incorporation into the American nation—reveals how fleeting were the difficult conditions first encountered in the Willamette Valley. Analyzing interactions between the area's husbands and wives shows that the westward expansion of middle-class culture, aided by local prosperity, allowed the second generation to indulge in an "ideal" romantic love.[4]

Not only had frontier conditions prevented the early settlers from seeking romance; it also barred them from matching their daily lives to their class aspirations. Practical needs took precedence over settlers' emotional desires. Immediate labor requirements forced men and women to marry at relatively young ages and, once married, to remain flexible about their gender-based division of labor. And although husbands and wives valued one another as economic partners, men's land ownership gave them a great deal of patriarchal authority over their wives. This was particularly true of those men who had the advantage of the Willamette Valley's exceptionally generous land grants.

As the children of early settlers came of age, labor constraints eased and increasing prosperity enabled the second generation to set aside the practicality previously imposed by frontier conditions. Meanwhile, new employment opportunities for women combined with a shortage of available land to shift the balance of power between the sexes, and expanding railroad and telegraph networks carried modern household technologies and print media to previously isolated western farms and communities. Improved trade and communication networks tied the West to a national consumer culture that carried with it new expectations for men's and women's behavior.

Increasingly, the children of early settlers took on the cultural expectations of the eastern middle class, which included both an emphasis on romantic love and a marked distaste for forceful demonstrations of patriarchal authority. Inspired by advice pieces in local newspapers and emboldened by educational and occupational opportunities, second-generation women postponed marriage in search of a partner in life—not only in labor. When each of these women finally found a man who met her demands for romance and companionability, they expected their modern marriage to bring with it a greater voice in household finances and freedom from spousal abuse. Thus, by the late nineteenth century the children of Oregon settlers had abandoned the practical but highly patriarchal marriages common among their frontier parents, joining their eastern counterparts in embracing relationships based on shared feelings and authority more than shared labor.

Frontier Marriages

The chief purpose of early frontier marriages was to combine men's outdoor work with women's domestic labor to overcome chronic labor shortages. Despite the economic interdependence this implied, men maintained significant patriarchal authority over their wives. As historian David Peterson del Mar demonstrated, moving families from the male-dominated Midwest and upper South to distant Oregon—separating women from the protection and support of kin in the process—generally enforced male dominance.[5] And this power was enhanced still more by the availability of large land grants, which gave men legal and social authority while their wives were made more vulnerable by the additional isolation that vast farms created for women. As the initial frontier period passed, first-generation Oregon women gradually gained a degree of influence over their domestic products, but they failed to significantly challenge their husbands' roles as household heads.

Rural families throughout the United States—but especially on the frontier—relied primarily on the labor of family members to survive. Women needed a husband who would provide, in the words of 1832 Missouri bride Rhoda McCord, "ample support and [a] comfortable house," while men relied on their wives to supply labor and domestic expertise.[6] A wife was "an equal partner in every-thing," as first-generation Oregon settler Maria Locey proclaimed, but particularly in labor.[7] And as Willamette Valley bachelor William VitzJames Johnson remarked in a letter asking his sister in Ohio for advice on preserving berries: "If I had a wife I wouldn't have to ask, would I?" In addition to domestic labor, women bore and raised children, who would also contribute to the household economy by assisting in the

Table 3.1

Age at first marriage

	Men	Women
First generation	26.0	18.6
	(N = 47)	(N = 38)
Second generation	27.6	20.8
	(N = 62)	(N = 47)

Source: Family database.

field and home. For all of these reasons, marriage was a necessity, and frontier men and women lacked the luxury of searching for romantic love.[8]

To secure a partner in labor, as well as to claim available land, mid-nineteenth-century men and women across rural America married at relatively young ages. Uneven sex ratios and acute labor needs meant that they could not afford to postpone marriage in the search for a perfect mate. This was exceptionally true in Oregon: scholars Paul Bourke and Donald DeBats estimated that the median age of female settlers at first marriage in Washington County was only 17.4 years, far younger than the 1860 national norm of 23 years.[9] Among this book's own sample of thirty-eight women who migrated to Oregon prior to 1865, the average age at first marriage was 18.6 years (table 3.1), and more than two-thirds of those profiled were married before the age of twenty (tables 3.2 and 3.3).[10] Interestingly, this shows Oregon women's ages at first marriage to be comparable to those who first settled in Sugar Creek, Illinois, several decades earlier.[11] Oregon men also married at relatively young ages: in my sample of forty-seven men, the average age to wed was 26 years (table 3.1), and although only 8.5 percent of these men were married by age twenty, all forty-seven were married by age thirty (tables 3.4 and 3.5). Not only did these settlers need a partner in productivity; they needed one soon—thus their haste to find security made the romance of eastern middle-class courtship virtually impossible for them.

Neither did the ample land grants enjoyed by Willamette Valley settlers make finding romance any easier. On the contrary, the terms of Oregon's Donation Land Claim Act (DLCA) of 1850, which permitted married couples to claim twice as much land as could single men, appears to have encouraged teenage girls to marry at even younger ages than their counter-

Table 3.2

Age of women at first marriage

	Married by age 20	Married by age 30	Never married
First generation (N = 38)	78.9%	100%	0%
Second generation (N = 47)	57.4%	93.6%	0%

Source: Family database.

Table 3.3

Age distribution for women at first marriage

Age	First generation	Second generation
10–14	0	1
15–19	26	17
20–24	12	20
25–29	0	2
30–34	0	2
35 and above	0	1

Source: Family database.

parts in other frontier regions. Memoirs, like those of Lucy Henderson Deady, suggest that fifteen was a typical age: "[I]n those days the young men began wondering why a girl wasn't married if she was still single when she was 16."[12] In addition, female teenagers who migrated to Oregon with their families were sometimes pressured to marry significantly older men, and at least a few young women married men whom they hardly knew. For example, one fourteen-year-old married a man twice her age whom she had known only a week. As Oregon women's rights activist Abigail Scott Duniway averred, such relationships enhanced men's domestic authority at the expense of their young brides: "[W]hen a man of forty, thirty, or even twenty-five, marries a child of fourteen . . . the result is subjugation on one

Table 3.4
Age of men at first marriage

	Married by age 20	Married by age 30	Never married[a]
First generation (N = 47)	8.5	100	0
Second generation (N = 67)	0	76.1	7.5

Source: Family database.
[a]Excludes those who died before age 40.

Table 3.5
Age distribution for men at first marriage

Age	First generation	Second generation
10–14	0	0
15–19	1	0
20–24	21	22
25–29	18	23
30–34	4	10
35 and above	3	7
Never married[a]	0	5

Source: Family database.
[a]Excludes those who died before age 40.

hand and despotism upon the other."[13] Of course, not all single women married at such an early age; in fact, Jennie Stevenson Miller recalled: "I had my first offer of marriage when I was 13, and from then till I was 24 I had numerous proposals." However, Miller resisted these offers precisely because she "had a pretty strong suspicion that many of the men who wanted to marry [her] wanted the extra land they could get if they were married."[14] Financial opportunities offered by the DLCA thus exaggerated frontier pressures to marry for practical reasons, encouraging many who came to the Willamette Valley as pre-teen or teenage girls to marry with little or no attention to social compatibility.[15]

From the Willamette Valley to the Ohio Valley, most rural courtship lore and superstition cemented the trend toward practicality by focusing on whether a person would marry—and to whom—rather than on romance. Young people experienced significant anxiety about finding a mate because they recognized the need of a partner for success on the frontier, and popular midwestern songs reflected this, emphasizing that a happy, lasting marriage was characterized by complementary roles:

> *Here stands the loving couple,*
> *Join heart and hands;*
> *One wants a wife,*
> *And the other wants a man.*
> *They will get married,*
> *If they can agree;*
> *So it's march down the river,*
> *To hog and hominy.*[16]

Within the context of their economic reality, young midwesterners of the 1830s and 1840s did have some degree of choice in whom they married. Like Jonathan Keeney, who wed Sarah Ragsdale in Missouri in 1849 and migrated to Oregon two years later, these young people each sought someone who would make a "good industrious and agreeable companion for life."[17] They hoped to find a mate whom they found physically and emotionally attractive. However, their preference for a congenial relationship should not be mistaken for romantic love. Reciprocity, rather than romance, remained the foundation of a successful rural marriage.

While frontier marriages in both the Midwest and Oregon were based on economic reciprocity, pecuniary partnerships did not lead to equal power relations. Instead, mid-nineteenth-century rural men demonstrated their masculinity by directing the finances and relationships within their households, and their independence was defined largely in opposition to the dependence of their wives and children. Men controlled everything from small purchases to the decision to sell their farms and migrate more than 2,000 miles to Oregon, and a man who lacked such control risked calling into question his very manhood. Thus, if husbands and wives disagreed on major decisions, women ultimately had little recourse but to give in.

It is difficult to determine the precise nature of power relations within nineteenth-century families because men and women rarely wrote about them directly. Migration to Oregon, however, was one decision on which a number of women did candidly record their experiences. It is clear that for men—the decision makers—the journey to Oregon represented a masculine adventure and promised access to sufficient land to establish a significant patrimony. For their wives, in contrast, the move represented at least a temporary loss of their domestic role, as well as permanent separation from family and friends around whom their lives had centered in the Midwest. "While many women were just as enthusiastic and anxious to undertake the journey into this Far West as brothers and sons were," Mrs. Robert A. Miller recalled, "the majority of them came in obedience to a man's judgment, whether or not in accord with her own."[18] This is reflected in a 1982 study of women's trail diaries done by historian Sandra Myres, which shows that while one-third of the 159 women profiled ultimately came to favor the journey, 18 percent of the sample strongly opposed migration.[19] And notably, not one of the wives in John Mack Faragher's sample initiated the idea to move. But whether or not women wished to migrate, the vast majority eventually bowed to their husbands' decisions.[20]

For the small minority of women who did not, their only option was in outright refusing to follow their husbands to Oregon, remaining behind in the Midwest while their husbands migrated. Some of these husbands later persuaded their wives to join them in the Willamette Valley. But if a wife kept refusing, a man might seek a divorce on the basis of his spouse's "wilful desertion," for declining to "cohabit and live with him, as in duty bound she ought to do."[21] Significantly, while these husbands chose to migrate to Oregon without their families, it was the wives who were found guilty of desertion. The court clearly believed that women had a duty to live with and follow the decisions made by their husbands, no matter where their husbands chose to move.[22]

Upon their arrival in Oregon, men typically took control of household finances. Decisions over land and crop sales lay squarely within men's work and provider roles and were seldom challenged by their wives. Yet even more mundane decisions about household expenditures also remained largely under men's control during the early years of settlement, notwith-

standing that they were often directly related to their wives' domestic responsibilities. Settlers' account books indicate that men were typically responsible for maintaining their families' accounts at the local general store,
consistently purchasing groceries and dry goods as well as seed and plows in
exchange for the various goods their households produced.[23]

Over time, however, women gained influence over "women's" work.
They began to control the schedule, pace, quantity, and quality of labor
within the home. Furthermore, frontier women appear to have developed an
informal rural exchange network, trading small surpluses of vegetables, eggs,
and milk with other women. As they produced goods for exchange, they
increased their families' dependence on their own work and that of their
female neighbors. Unfortunately, the extent of this female-dominated rural
network is difficult to document because Willamette Valley women rarely
maintained written records of their exchanges, which remained separate
from the formal accounts recorded in men's farm and general store records.
Like Martha Ballard a half-century earlier, who did record extensive trading
of goods and labor among females on the Maine frontier, women in the West
controlled a domestic economy that remained largely invisible to their
husbands and relatively free from their husbands' control.[24]

Shifts in frontier women's work and their growing influence over
household finances are highlighted by changes in dairy and poultry production. Shortly after families first settled, work roles had been flexible, but
financial control lay squarely with men. In those years, when the nearest
neighbor might live several miles away, women's eggs, milk, and butter were
sold as part of their family's larger financial strategy. Within a decade of
settlers' arrival in Oregon, however, as farms became better established and
women were able to concentrate on domestic production, wives began to
exert more influence over the sale of their goods and the ways in which the
proceeds were spent—just as Mid-Atlantic women had done in previous
decades.[25] Husbands and wives worked out individual arrangements about
control over household products, which often reflected the labor that each
man and woman invested in the enterprise. For example, in her fourth
marriage, thrice-widowed Eleanor Shrum of Marion County controlled the
money earned from the sale of her chickens and eggs. However, her husband maintained the income from butter production, with which he frequently assisted her—an arrangement that Eleanor apparently chose. This
illustrates the way that over time, as men's and women's work roles became

separated, their relative influence over certain aspects of household finances came to be earned through their contribution to corresponding projects.[26]

Cyrus and Maria Locey provide a dramatic example of the ways in which wives gradually gained a say in financial matters. Early in their marriage, Maria Locey believed that she and her husband ought to be saving money steadily to give to the church. However, she confessed to her diary, "Sometimes I almost fear you [her husband, Cyrus] feel as though I had not the right to make suggestions on such matters if they differ from your opinion, but I hope you *will* not feel so in the future, for our interests are too closely interwoven for there to be any danger." Furthermore, Maria believed that a husband ought to treat his wife as "what she *is*, an equal partner in everything, money-matters and all, and ten to one she will be happy herself, and make you the *same*, by the very overflow of her love and gratitude."[27] Evidently, Maria's hopes were fulfilled, for eventually, she managed to acquire her own dairy cattle, maintaining separate accounts of her earnings. She used the proceeds for her personal expenses such as clothing, and she enjoyed giving as much as she wished to the church and to neighbors in need without having to beg the money from her husband. As Maria became more financially independent, she grew more outspoken toward her husband in her opinions on financial matters, and Cyrus apparently began to trust her more. He continued to go into debt to acquire land, contrary to Maria's wishes, but he did begin to consider her opinion on other significant economic decisions, such as whether to sell cattle in order to pay off those debts. As Maria became bolder in voicing her opinions and acting on her financial interests, her husband gradually began to take her views into account, although he continued to claim final decision-making authority.[28]

While the DLCA technically granted equal portions of land to married men and their wives, it failed in itself to enhance women's influence over household affairs because the government rarely recorded wives' names on donation land claim (DLC) titles. Men typically controlled the couple's combined landholdings and chose how to divide the acreage among their children. Nonetheless, the extent to which Willamette Valley women "owned" their land appears to have varied widely, and all women did hold at least some legal claim to their half of the DLC acreage, thanks to married women's property laws. In addition, a substantial minority of wives apparently gained some voice in the sale of the land, for when Oregonians sold portions of their DLCs, the titles recorded sale *by* and *to* the man in question "and Wife," and the deeds were signed by both husband and wife. Thus it appears that wives at least enjoyed more control over their family's land than was common in the Midwest and upper South, where it was owned almost exclusively by men.[29]

Despite women's somewhat greater influence, however, most Oregon land deals were still negotiated by men, who used a variety of methods to persuade their wives to agree to land sales or purchases. One second-generation Oregonian even testified in his parents' divorce suit that "when talking about deeding some land if he should want to sell it he said he would sign the deed with her heart's blood if she would not sign it."[30] While most Oregonians did not resort to violence, it is clear that first-generation men made use of their position of authority in the household to persuade their wives to agree, or at least sign off on, their decisions.[31]

Local divorce records highlight the extent of men's control over Oregon DLCs. Prior to 1870, property divisions were rarely discussed in divorce complaints, but after that date, a number of first-generation Oregon women who sought divorces requested in their complaints what they considered to be an equitable portion of their husbands' and their combined property. The terms sought by these women varied, but most wanted approximately one-third of the family land and household goods. These women did not usually indicate separate ownership of their half of the DLC, but instead referred to all of the DLC acreage as belonging to their husbands, effectively requesting the equivalent of the traditional widow's third of the estate. It is not clear whether women considered this one-third to be necessary for their support, in keeping with the tradition of supporting widows, or whether they believed that they had contributed one-third of the labor and resources used in developing the family farm.[32]

Also reflected in divorce cases of the time was the fact that Oregonians appear to have become increasingly concerned about the influence women exerted over men in the household. Whereas court documents from the early years focused on women's willingness and ability to work hard, in later years they were progressively more concerned with women's obedience to their husbands. One female settler, Maria Rhoades, understood this, and she "endeavored to conduct herself as an obedient and dutiful wife . . . never failing to adhere strictly to all his interests."[33] But a number of men sought to divorce their wives simply because they failed to submit to their husbands' authority. In one case, a witness testified that Pyra Rudolph also said that she wanted to let her husband know that "she intended to be 'boss' of that place, that she had been 'bossed' long enough"—and her husband's petition for a divorce was granted.[34] Another man complained of his wife asserting undue authority over his property, and of being arrogant and domineering. Whereas before men had rarely sought a divorce except on the grounds of adultery, as they became more established in Oregon, they became increasingly concerned with maintaining their masculine control. Although women had become more independent managers of their domestic affairs—a change that could potentially have increased their status within the household—their influence was not to extend over their husbands as family heads.[35]

Since most women did not directly confront their husbands regarding major household decisions, many tried to challenge their husbands' authority in subtle ways, such as by refusing to do small things that their husbands wished them to do, or by using manipulation to get things they desired. For example, Moriah Kelly appeared to be insulted when others suggested that her husband Albert should ask her opinion on decisions such as their 1849 move to Oregon. Nonetheless, once in Oregon, she persuaded Albert to provide her with the expensive refined white flour she craved while her neighbors made do with home-ground wheat. In a similar situation, Nathaniel Coe agreed to remove and relocate the split rail fences he built on his family's farm so that they would not obstruct his wife's view of the surrounding mountains and rivers. Perhaps Moriah Kelly and Mary Coe used the form of influence depicted in this humorous poem that was published in the *Oregon [City] Statesman* in 1851:

> A couple sat beside the fire,
> Debating who should first retire;
> The husband positively had said,
> "Wife you shall go and warm the bed"
> "I did so once and nearly died,
> And I will not," rejoined the spouse,
> With firmer tone and lowering brows;
> And thus a war of words arose,
> Continuing till they nearly froze
> When both grew mute and hovering nigher
> Around the faintly glimmering fire,

Resolved like heroes ne'er to yield,
But force each other from the field,
And thus, this once fond, loving pair,
In silence shook and shivered there,
When all at once the husband said,
"Wife, hadn't we better go to bed?"[36]

As we can see, some women found quite effective ways to influence the decisions that their husbands made.[37] Yet the efforts they exerted to do so—and the devious manner they often had to adopt—only underscore the fact that these wives had little power outside the sphere of the home.

In contrast to women's subtle effects on their spouses, men controlled their wives' conduct quite directly. For example, Maria Locey and her neighbor, Mrs. Derrick, had "only just settled down to do a little visiting when the old fellow [Mr. Derrick] brought out the carriage and took them off. Mrs. Derrick said 'he made her tired,'" but she did not challenge his right to decide when they would return home.[38] Mr. Derrick was not willing to accommodate his wife's desire to visit longer, and his responsibility for driving and attending to the horses only reinforced his authority. Tellingly, Mrs. Derrick admitted her dissatisfaction with the situation to her female friend, but did not openly challenge her husband's decision.

Maria Locey expressed frustration with neighbors who controlled their wives in this manner; nonetheless, she—like Mrs. Derrick—ultimately accepted male patriarchal authority. This can be seen through an event in which Maria and her husband Cyrus, in their positions as leading members of the local church, visited a couple who were fighting. After listening to the woman's concerns, Maria advised her to sacrifice whatever she could to achieve peace with her husband. Maria was gratified that the woman accepted her advice, and rejoiced when the couple eventually reconciled. Thus, while she boldly sought influence within her own marriage, Maria ultimately concurred with her female neighbors that they must submit to their husbands to maintain comity within the household.[39]

Oregon men took advantage of this power imbalance to ignore their wives' desires and valued their own magnanimity far more than that of their wives. When one woman chose to stay with her ill mother for a few days rather than travel with her husband, the couple's friend Edward E. Parrish recorded in his journal that "from the goodness of his heart [her husband] soon made up his mind to let his Deare wife remain & passed on to Salem without her."[40] Parrish was less impressed by the woman's selflessness in assisting her sick mother than he was by her husband's supposed kindness in allowing her to do so. Hence, while women joined together and commiserated with each other in their passive roles, men supported one another in their dominance.[41]

Some first-generation Oregonians sought marital power through physical force, and the unequal treatment of husbands' and wives' violence in divorce cases highlights the power differential between them. As might be guessed, a far greater level of violence was tolerated from men than from women, especially early on. Indeed, 1850s Oregon society and its courts were relatively accepting of men who physically dominated—and even repeatedly beat—their wives, so long as they did not cause permanent physical damage. Only when a man such as W. W. Coulton (who threatened to kill his wife if she left him) subjected a woman to such "cruel and inhuman treatment" that he "rendered it unsafe and improper for her to cohabit with him" was the court system likely to become involved.[42] In contrast, it took very little violence for a husband to complain. In 1860, for example, William Larkins sought a divorce because his wife challenged his patriarchal authority by refusing to meet what he considered reasonable requests in front of his friends, and she struck him once with her fist.[43]

As this section has shown, young first-generation Oregonians formed economic partnerships in which women eventually gained some degree of financial control within their households, and many did find small ways to influence their husbands or to voice their opinions to female friends. In the end, however, these women were expected to bow to their husbands as household heads. Much of this would change as settlers' children embraced changing economic and social conditions in post-frontier Oregon, modeling their lives and their marriages after urban middle-class men and women.

Marital Choice

Like their parents, second-generation Oregonians had good economic and social reasons to marry. Yet life in the Willamette Valley offered new opportunities to women during the 1870s and 1880s, even as a shortage of available land pushed young men into prolonged semi-dependence on their fathers. Although nearly all of the second generation eventually married, they waited longer to do so, seeking greater financial stability and a partner who met expectations that would have been unreasonable for their parents. Meanwhile, growing transportation and communication networks brought from the East new middle-class attitudes toward relationships and gender. Abandoning early settlers' frontier practicality, the next generation increasingly married for love and challenged the male authority that had previously been so established.

Several simultaneous societal changes—including postponed male independence, new female economic opportunities, and a new consumer culture—combined to encourage young Oregon men and women to join those throughout the United States who were marrying later. First, decreased land availability lengthened young men's residency with their parents. This meant that, from the first to the second generation, men's average age at marriage increased by approximately one and one-half years—going from 26 to 27.6 years of age (table 3.1). Furthermore, nearly one-quarter of second-generation men postponed marriage past age thirty, and 7.5 percent in this study's sample never married at all (tables 3.4 and 3.5). This reduction in young men's opportunities for financial independence coincided with an increase in young women's prospects for paid work. As Willamette Valley communities grew, so did demand for female workers in the fledgling service industry, as well as for schoolteachers—by 1880, in fact, 55.8 percent of Oregon's 1,018 teachers were female. In that same year, 4 percent of the state's female population reported occupations to federal census takers; of these employed women, 21 percent were teachers, 35 percent were domestic servants, and 21 percent were milliners, dressmakers, or seamstresses.[44] Inspired by fashion magazines and mail-order catalogs, many young women were all the more motivated to work outside the home because they sought to participate in new patterns of conspicuous consumption developing in eastern cities (see chap. 4), and earning money prior to marriage supported their fashionable lifestyles. In addition, it earned them a more powerful voice in deciding when and whom to marry. In fact, on average, the second-generation women in this study's sample married more than two years later than their mothers, making their median age at first marriage 20.8 years—comparable to that of second-generation women on earlier frontiers like Sugar Creek, Illinois.[45] Further, a noteworthy amount of Willamette Valley women—three out of forty-seven in this study's sample—married after age thirty (tables 3.2 and 3.3).

As economic opportunities simultaneously increased for young women and lessened for young men, it is perhaps not surprising that second-generation Oregonians recorded a broader range of attitudes toward marriage than had their parents. At one extreme was Nellie Hill, who wrote to her mother that, while each man "ought to try to get the best woman and make himself worthy of her," she believed that women ought not to marry at all.[46] In contrast, Linus Darling hearkened back to first-generation views when he emphasized in a high school composition the dangers of girls becoming "old maids," whom he characterized as physically unattractive gossips.[47] While these Oregonians came to opposite conclusions on women's proper course of action, both Darling and Hill clearly believed that marriage held the power to dramatically change young men and women, and that members of the second generation could—and should—decide for themselves whether or not to marry.

Ultimately, Darling, Hill, and nearly all of their peers did marry, but they felt less urgency about the issue than had their parents, embracing the middle-class belief that it was better not to wed than to marry the wrong person. They agreed with an 1875 article in the local weekly *Willamette Farmer* that "the maiden [is rich] whose horizon is not bounded by the coming man, but who has a purpose in life, whether she meets him or not."[48] Additionally, the new demand for more genteel male behavior—and particularly sobriety—made these women desire a more gentlemanly mate than their frontier fathers had typically been: as one young woman announced, "I would rather die than marry a man that was in the habit of drinking."[49] If few second-generation women died over such possibilities, some women, like Mary Eliza Buxton and her sister Nancy, actually preferred to remain single rather than to marry someone who was not ideal. As Mary Eliza reported, Nancy had remained single because "the men she wanted she couldn't get and the ones she could get the devil wouldn't have."[50]

Unlike the previous generation's midwestern folklore, which centered on finding a hard-working spouse, stories published in Willamette Valley newspapers during the 1870s and 1880s focused on navigating among conflicting desires for love, economic partnership, and shared power within a relationship. Young women like Mollie Hill clipped and collected a variety of short fiction and advice columns related to choosing a suitor, which encouraged those like herself to prioritize their own happiness above parental obedience, and which reflected second-generation women's growing efforts to protect their own interests. For example, the *Willamette Farmer* twice reprinted a *Christian Standard* article urging young women to "make [their] own match," and not to "marry for a home and a living." With all its authority, the paper counseled: "Do not let aunts, fathers or mothers sell you for money or position into bondage, tears and a life long misery, which you must endure."[51]

Instead, local articles emphasized, youths *must* seek out romantic love, for "married people who are not lovers, are bound by red-hot chains."[52] Even advertisements played on young people's anxiety about choosing a suitable lover, claiming to reveal "Why She Didn't Marry Him."[53] Likewise, humorous pieces reflected growing passion: in an 1877 story, a character named Dan told of kissing his beloved repeatedly, and "when I finally ceased," he said, "the tears came into her eyes and she said in sad tones, 'Ah, Dan, I fear you have ceased to love me.' 'Oh no, I haven't,'" Dan replied, "'but I must breathe.'"[54] Probably influenced at least in part by stories like these, in 1870, seventeen-year-old Anna Harris went so far as to desert her husband of one month, leaving behind a note explaining: "i have found the man that i love . . . i shall stay with him as long as i live."[55] Within a decade of Harris' desertion, it became common for men and women to describe themselves in divorce suits as loving spouses, or to complain about spouses who ceased to love them.[56]

Local publications' focus on love determining spousal selection also reflects the extent to which second-generation women sought to limit patriarchal power. In one popular story, "The Crack in the Door," the heroine overhears her suitor boasting to his male friends that when he marries, he will intentionally break his wife's will to his own as he would break a horse. He declares that he can write poetry or talk sentimentally to women while he is courting them, but once he marries he will have no more need for such things. The heroine of the story is determined to have control over her own life, and hopes to make romance last past her wedding day. She gladly withstands others' astonishment when she turns down his marriage proposal the following day.[57]

As the literature of the time advised—and like young middle-class men and women back east—most Oregon youth did not seek out parental guidance on whom they should court. Violet Ann Brown Kersey perhaps explained their attitude best when she recalled, "[My father] had good judgment and he thought he could pick out a husband better than I could, but as I had to live with the man who was to be my husband I decided to do the picking myself."[58] Thus, only after a couple reached an agreement between themselves did they typically approach the woman's parents for permission to marry, and men apparently did not find it necessary to seek permission from their own parents at all.[59]

Harry Denlinger, far from asking for parental consent, actually ignored his father's wish for him to marry for more than six years, until true love persuaded him to give up his bachelor status and even to abandon some of his relatively conservative expectations for his wife. This occurred when Denlinger fell in love via correspondence with progressive, twenty-six-year-old Stanford University student Nellie Hill, shortly after she herself had confided to her mother that she was "quite convinced that it is dangerous for women to marry," for they "have not been raised to find out life" and are "quite civilized enough without getting married." Although Hill's identity as a New Woman conflicted with Denlinger's traditional belief that women should be "Queen of the home," love won out in the end, and the two married after meeting in person only three times.[60]

Like many young men, a few second-generation women rejected parental guidance altogether, eloping with the man of their choice. Although they had openly challenged their fathers' power by running away with men who did not meet approval, these young women were eventually able to persuade their fathers to accept their husbands once the weddings had taken place. One young girl, Margaret LaFore, was only fourteen years old when she ran away a fair distance to Albany, Oregon, to marry Freeman Folsom, but rather than condemn her decision, Margaret's father purchased a claim near the couple on Howell's Prairie (east of Salem). Similarly, Cyrus and Maria Locey at first disapproved of their daughter Susie's marriage to their field hand, but following the ceremony they welcomed the pair by building a bedroom onto their house to accommodate them. Apparently, parents expected their daughters to accept their guidance in selecting a marital partner, but their dissatisfaction with a spouse was insufficient to ultimately break the familial bond between first-generation men and their willful daughters.[61]

If daughters could not find a suitable companion, they were usually content to teach school or continue assisting with domestic work in their parents' homes, cheerfully braving the derogatory label "old maid" and removing much of its former bite in the process. For instance, Mary Robinson Gilkey "was wedded to [her] profession," teaching school until age thirty-four.[62] Similarly, Maria Locey's oldest daughter Mary taught school for many years before finally marrying at age fifty-one, decades past the age of an old maid. In fact, by 1880, the *Willamette Farmer* had claimed that the term "old maid" was rarely heard, and seven years later, the paper admitted: "[The aphorism] 'any husband is better than no husband' had once a great deal of truth in it . . . Today . . . the scales tip the other way with a vengeance."[63] As second-generation women increasingly preferred to chance their neighbors' criticism rather than risk an unhappy marriage, communities began to accept their choice.[64]

Second-generation Oregonians who did marry generally believed that with love should come more equality between man and woman. Like their fathers, second-generation men were responsible for providing for their wives: as Harry Denlinger explained to his intended, "No man has a right to marry until he is reasonably certain of furnishing a decent support for himself and some one else."[65] Unlike their parents, however, these young men did not take for granted that the "support" they provided entitled them to control their wives. Thus Oliver Jory cautiously wrote to his fiancée about his neighbor, "I suppose now that he has become *if I may[ ]be excused for using the term* the head of a family, will be a very staid and steady boy[,] leastwise I hope so."[66] In this letter, Jory clearly associates responsible behavior with the position of household head, yet in his anticipation that his fiancée might be uncomfortable with assigning such authority to a young husband, he asks to be excused for using a term that would have caused no comment in his parents' generation. In addition, he sought to soften the blow of the expression by describing the neighbor as a "very staid and steady *boy*," rather than a man who might truly have dominion over his wife.[67]

As men's power was reduced, young wives fittingly expected a degree of economic and domestic control rarely enjoyed by their mothers. Second-generation men, like their fathers, still chose whether and whither to move, and their management of fields and crops gave them a significant degree of power over the family's finances. However, the authority they took on was as much a topic of criticism as an admired display of manhood, so that models of middle-class manly restraint increasingly replaced frontier men's patriarchal privilege as the standard for proper behavior. As the *Willamette Farmer* sought to teach: "Many a home has been happily saved, and many a

fortune retrieved, by a man's full confidence in his 'better half.' "[68] It followed that, rather than controlling all of the household finances, men began
to manage only the wealth derived from their own labor. In "ordinary
families," as the *Farmer* explained, it was the wife who regulated household
expenditures.[69]

Whether or not women ultimately devalued patriarchal authority,
second-generation men did begin to pay lip service to their wives' right to
make household decisions, and in some cases, women simply ignored men's
guidance—even when it came to major issues. The story of Oliver Jory and
his fiancée, Ella, is a good example. At first, while Oliver frequently encouraged Ella to make her own decisions regardless of his advice, he did not
acknowledge the power he held as he continually postponed their marriage
through an eighteen-year engagement, during which Ella continued to live
and work with her family in distant Coos County. Because Ella's letters did
not survive, her exact views cannot be known, but from Oliver's letters it is
apparent that she remained patient throughout their remarkably long engagement, waiting for his business to improve and for him to make good on
his promise of marriage. In 1901, however, when they finally had married,
the business had yet to fully develop and Ella had apparently given up
waiting for it to do so. Ignoring Oliver's request to remain at home until he
was able to travel, Ella took their son to visit her relatives and, having told
him they would be gone three to four weeks, stayed away with her son for a
year. Obviously, Ella had finally lost patience with Oliver's refusal to consider her priorities in his decision making. The frontier generation's acceptance of male authority had thus gradually eroded in the Jory household.[70]

For the Beesons in southern Oregon, contestation over patriarchal authority was so prominent that it gradually replaced romance. Early in their
marriage, the couple had a very loving relationship, and Kate Beeson entrusted her husband Welborn with most decisions affecting their household. Only when Welborn was away did Kate make decisions on her own,
and even then she feared that her actions would make Welborn cross. For
example, when Welborn's apprentice Logan Estes refused to do the work
assigned to him, she threatened to send him away, but soon regretted having
usurped her husband's authority and forgave Logan for her husband's sake.
Husband and wife continued to write one another love notes in Welborn's
diary, and Welborn followed Kate's wishes in naming their sons. Within a
decade, however, Welborn was complaining to his diary that Kate was "of

but little value," continually spending "mony as fast as [he could] make it."[71] Kate grew bolder as she and her husband grew older, inviting many guests for prolonged visits against Welborn's wishes, and his complaints gradually drowned out their earlier romantic musings.

Newspaper articles in local publications suggest that second-generation women sometimes resorted to indirect influence over their husbands, just as their mothers had done. However, these stories also center around new expectations for genteel behavior and a widespread focus on consumer goods that had been inaccessible to the first settlers. For example, a young woman in one story taught her husband not to grumble about every detail in their home by mimicking the crudeness of his behavior. Another author, in a piece appearing in the feminist weekly the *New Northwest*, claimed to prevent her husband from becoming a "domestic tyrant" by causing him to mistake her desires for his own: "[W]hen I want a new dress," she explained, "I tell him that Mrs. Brown has been terribly extravagant and bought a new velveteen, and I am sure she doesn't need one half as bad as I do, but I can't think of such an expense." Describing her husband's response, she wrote, "[He insisted that] he can afford to dress me as well as Brown can his wife, and I must go right down town and get a better dress than hers!"[72] These stories suggest that Willamette Valley women continued to subtly manipulate their husbands' decision making, but rather than emphasizing their domestic responsibilities, they won over their spouses by playing to the pressures of consumerism and new social standards.[73]

Building on the small gains their mothers had made, second-generation Oregon women took an active role in negotiating power relations within their families, so that control of household finances often created a primary fault line between husbands and wives. Some women gained a greater degree of influence over household matters by explicitly maintaining separate domestic accounts, since Oregon law granted women the right to hold property separate from their husbands—and since, after 1872, their separate property was protected from seizure for their husbands' debts. Nonetheless, some second-generation husbands considered women's separate property to be expendable, available for sale to raise cash for other purposes that fit within their own priorities. Several first-generation women loaned money they had inherited to their husbands and when, after a number of years, their husbands proved unable to reimburse them, these women had to accept repayment in personal property such as household goods or livestock. One Linn County resident, Ida Peterson, loaned her husband a total of $1500 over twelve years with the understanding that he would pay her back—which he did not. Although Peterson took legal action to protect her property from her husband's apparent economic difficulties, she did not challenge their economic partnership. Instead, she eventually accepted ownership of personal property in place of the cash that her husband owed her, agreeing, she said, "as long as my said Husband takes good care of said property [to] let him use the same but not to sell said property without my authority . . . and not to take or remove said property from our home."[74] Similarly, when W. E. Payne of Linn County was unable to repay the $2400 plus $1333 interest that he owed his wife Sarah, he sold her an assortment of livestock, field equipment, and grain to fulfill the debt.[75]

At least a few second-generation wives took legal action after their husbands appropriated their separate assets. In 1882, Laura Woodworth complained to the Marion County circuit court that her husband George had failed to respect the property given to her by her father. She said that George spent her cash for horse feed, sold her cattle, and kept the proceeds against her wishes, and he "never furnished any money with which to support the family."[76] Five years later, Selena Potter complained that her husband had sold her sewing machine and other belongings, stating, "[He] used the mony for his own use, and never gave me nothing, but abuse."[77] Both Woodworth and Potter sued for divorce on the basis of their husbands' cruelty, which they demonstrated in large part through their husbands' forced acquisition of their separate property. Thus, while many second-generation women gave in to their spouses by accepting loan repayments in less-than-ideal forms, those who got no repayment at all stood up for their rights. These settlers' daughters insisted on maintaining control over their portion of household finances, and they were ultimately more outspoken against abuse than their mothers had been.[78]

Women's changing views of marital property rights are also illustrated through the ways they wished to divide family estates upon divorce: after 1870, a substantial minority of Willamette Valley women began to request a larger-than-usual portion of the household's real and moveable property. Perhaps empowered by new married women's property laws passed during that decade, these women sought more than the one-third requested by the previous generation, some demanding a full half of the family's donation land claim. A particularly well documented illustration lies in the divorce proceedings for Malvina and Mitchell Whitlock, in which Malvina told the court that she owned a half-section from the Whitlock DLC, with about 60 acres "under fence & plough," worth about $1500. Her husband owned the other half-section, plus additional acreage he had purchased from neighbors' DLCs, including 150 cultivated acres and their house and barn, as well as a house and lot in the town of Silverton. Altogether, Mitchell's properties were valued at approximately $3500, and although Malvina held her half of the DLC, her husband had acquired sole title to additional lands purchased by their combined labors. Malvina initially demanded all of her own property plus one-third of her husband's, but realizing that the court would not support this request, she eventually agreed to accept $700 gold in lieu of a share of his land. Few women asked for a larger share of their husband's property than did Malvina Whitlock, but whatever the precise terms of their complaints, these second-generation divorce complainants demanded that the court recognize a greater female economic role within marriage than had been seen before.[79]

Although many second-generation men granted their wives greater influence over household finances, they still expected to maintain authority in other areas. John McCarl, for one, received a divorce in 1889 because his wife refused to obey him—despite what he saw as compliance with new guidelines for husbandly behavior. In his testimony, he claimed that he was a responsible provider and kind husband who "turned my pay over to her as good as anybody could do."[80] And yet, he complained, "[E]ver since we were married she would do nothing according to my wishes, but was contrary in every thing." McCarl detailed the ways in which his wife refused to do domestic labor, failed to adequately care for their children, and was unwilling to follow his direction in proper conduct. Furthermore, he asserted, "She would refuse to cook anything for me which I wished, unless it was something she wanted to eat herself."[81] Thus, his wife was guilty not only of failing in her role as housewife but also of refusing to obey him or prioritize his desires above her own. This proper second-generation man might be willing to give up control over the household accounts, but he still expected his wife to submit to his guidance and authority in other aspects of their lives.

In addition, even if second-generation men permitted their wives to manage certain minor expenses, they generally expected to control major purchases. This became a defining issue in marital power struggles as costly mechanical equipment became increasingly available to assist with women's domestic work. Like their fathers, second-generation Oregon men were hesitant to invest in expensive domestic equipment, instead favoring farm equipment that would enhance their own productive efforts. In contrast, Oregon women coveted domestic technology, a desire perhaps expressed best in 1875 by the *Willamette Farmer*, which quoted "a certain sensible woman" as saying that there were two things she would "never allow anybody to meddle with—her husband and her sewing machine."[82] For both mothers and daughters in Oregon, these machines represented both increased productivity and independence from drudgery. But they took on a special significance for younger women as they freed them to participate in New Women's voluntary organizations outside the home, as well as enabling them to decorate their dresses with the many tucks, frills, and bustles required by new middle-class standards for women's fashion. Because of sewing machines' great practical value—and because they granted women freedom to take part in new cultural trends and activities—second generation wives took sewing machine ownership very seriously, and many struggled to justify purchasing one to their more land-oriented husbands.[83]

Couples' disagreements over productive equipment such as sewing machines revealed those goods' symbolic importance to second-generation Oregonians. When Florence and S. T. Garrison fought a court battle over control of their property shortly after their 1873 marriage, Florence escalated their power struggle by purchasing, as S.T. described it, "a Sewing machine, and other articles to the amount of One hundred Dollars, without [his] knowledge for the purpose of involving [him] in debt, when the same might well have been avoided, as She herself afterwards admitted: Saying, she did it to punish [him], for that [he] would have to pay whether [he] wanted to or not."[84] In other words, Florence Garrison chose to "punish" her husband by purchasing a sewing machine, which would not only increase her own productivity and stylishness but also redirect household resources from the fields to the domestic sphere. Intriguingly, her husband also complained to the court that Florence had refused to do laundry for his hired hand, saying that that she had threatened to leave him and to burn down his house and barn, and that: "[She said] she would not help make money for as mean a man as I was or for my children." Like many other second-generation women, Florence Garrison insisted on setting her domestic priorities above the wishes of her farmer husband, seeking to obtain more control in her marriage without endangering the separate work identities hammered out by men and women of the frontier generation.

Since power relations within marriage were such a central issue for the second generation, it is helpful to examine the frequencies of various divorce complaints and how they differed from the first to the second generation. In the 1860s, more than one-tenth of divorce complaints in Marion and Lane counties included adultery, and an additional tenth in Marion County complained of fraud (table 3.6). Not surprisingly, men, who enjoyed greater economic power and freedom of movement, were more likely to charge their wives with adultery than with fraud, while women frequently complained of fraud, usually declaring that their husbands had knowingly abandoned their families and moved to new frontier areas to pose as single men and marry second wives. Such fraud complaints became less common among the second generation, as the settled society made it more difficult for men to abandon their wives and remarry in a new community, and as expectations for companionate relationships eclipsed financial contracts at the heart of marriage relationships. In addition, adultery complaints were proportionately fewer, perhaps a reflection of the second generation's increased appreciation for romantic love.

Another significant shift in common causes for divorce can be seen in Marion County as complaints of cruelty became more frequent than those of financial non-support (table 3.6). In this county, physical abuse grievances declined over the course of the late nineteenth century as expectations for manly restraint replaced frontier models of masculinity. This shift could be seen among the second generation as early as 1868, when Thomas Ward testified, "[I] cannot strike a woman . . . it is against my principles."[85] At the same time, however, complaints of verbal abuse increased dramatically. For example, six Marion County residents claimed verbal cruelty in divorce complaints between 1860 and 1869, representing only 7.7 percent of all divorce suits, but forty-eight Marion County residents made the same complaint between 1880 and 1889, representing one-quarter of those seeking divorces in the county during that decade. An additional 12 percent sought a divorce solely on the basis of verbal cruelty (table 3.6). This might suggest that second-generation marriages featured more verbal arguments than had previously been common because power conflicts played a more prominent role.[86]

Interestingly, although Lane County also experienced a significant in-

Table 3.6

Percentage of various grounds for divorce in Marion and Lane Counties, 1860s–1880s

	Marion		Lane	
	1860s	1880s	1860s	1880s
Adultery	12.8%	6.8%	10.9%	9.6%
Fraud	7.7	1.0	1.6	0
Felony	2.3	3.1	0	0
Desertion or financial non-support	52.6	55.2	73.4	60.9
All cruelty (physical and/or verbal)	43.6	54.7	56.3	66.1
Verbal cruelty (only cause provided)	2.6	12.0	4.7	9.6
Verbal cruelty	7.7	25.0	48.4	66.1
Physical cruelty	9.0	2.6	25.0	34.8
Total number of divorce complaints	78	192	64	115

Sources: Marion County Circuit Court Divorce Files, 1848–1900; Lane County Circuit Court Divorce Files, 1855–1891.

crease in cruelty complaints by the 1880s (table 3.6), residents of this south-ern Willamette Valley county were far more likely to include both physical and verbal cruelty in their divorce complaints as early as the 1860s, offering cruelty as an additional aggravating circumstance to more acceptable causes for divorce such as adultery and desertion. In fact, complaints of physical cruelty increased significantly in Lane County even as they decreased in Marion County. This may indicate that patriarchal abuse occurred more frequently in rural Lane County than in urbanizing Marion County. How-ever, the handful of attorneys working in Lane County during the 1860s were particularly savvy in providing as many causes as possible in divorce complaints. Based on referees' reports, it appears that most of these divorce applications were granted—primarily, if not exclusively—on the basis of adultery or desertion. The cruelty complaints may therefore have been an attempt to insure that the divorce would be granted if claims of adultery or desertion failed, or they may have been intended as an appeal for a more favorable settlement for the plaintiff.[87]

Besides holding their husbands to higher behavioral standards, young married women of the late nineteenth century also appear to have called for

greater male sexual restraint. It is difficult to study nineteenth-century sexuality because Victorian men and women were generally very reticent about
recording sexual behavior and attitudes—so much so that, in 1864, Edward
E. Parrish used euphemisms even to record livestock breeding: "I have in a
gentleman cow for Susa's comfort. All went off nicely."[88] However, second-
generation Willamette Valley women appear to have joined their counterparts throughout the United States in speaking more openly about sex and
gradually discarding the belief that women had a duty to submit to their
husbands sexually. Particularly, they began to reject frontier beliefs in men's
right to have sexual intercourse with their wives when those wives were
opposed or had delicate gynecological health. For example, on the fifth
night of Arnold and Mary Myers' 1870 marriage, Mary informed Arnold
that an injury had rendered her unable to bear children. Citing two doctors'
advice that pregnancy would kill her, she refused to have sexual intercourse
with Arnold and said she had not told him prior to their marriage because
"it was not the place of a young girl to tell such things." Mary later testified
that they only had intercourse on their wedding night, "and that was imper-
fect & got more by force than anything else & hurt her very much." After
two weeks of marriage, Mary deserted Arnold and moved to California to
live with her mother, while Arnold was granted a divorce on the grounds of
impotence and fraud. And yet, as to whether the defendant was "guilty of
cruel & in human treatment" towards the plaintiff, "rendering his life bur-
densome in refusing to have sexual intercourse with him," the judge was
"not prepared to find definitely, as that would depend much upon the
passion & inclination of the Pl[ainti]ff."[89] That is to say, although the verdict
was ultimately against Mary, the judge was not unsympathetic to her—and
the situation for women only improved with time. In fact, a quarter-century later, the Marion County court was far more compassionate in the case
of Cora Ramsden, who complained in her divorce case that, even after
excessive sexual intercourse had damaged her health, her husband had
continued to force himself upon her once or twice each week. Cora was
easily granted the divorce and received $1100 in lieu of claims against his
land. Thus, through the courts, we can see that societal expectations were
shifting in favor of protecting women and imposing upon their husbands a
more stringent code of gentlemanly conduct—both inside and outside the
bedroom—than had been present during the early years on the frontier.[90]

Local courts also began to reflect the second generation's belief that marriage should be initiated thoughtfully, and that financial necessity was not sufficient reason to enter or remain in an unhappy marriage. In 1880, the circuit court for Marion County heard a divorce complaint against Nancy Parker, who had deserted her husband because, as she stated, "I do not wish to live with any man[.] I do not wish to have [additional] children or be a married woman. I was married thoughtlessly when quite young, and as I grew older I . . . desired to leave married life."[91] The woman's desertion clearly justified granting her husband a divorce. Yet the court took unusual steps on her behalf because she openly regretted having followed the first generation's pattern of marrying young. Rather than granting custody of their six-year-old daughter to the husband, as was customary in the United States throughout much of the nineteenth century, the court gave custody to the wife, in keeping with a new middle-class emphasis on the maternal role. Nancy's maiden name was restored, and she was permitted to live with her daughter on her father's farm. Similarly, in an 1888 case, Rebecca H. Minto was granted a divorce after her husband, Sheriff John W. Minto, moved to a different part of their house and refused to cohabit with Rebecca. With the help of the court, the couple agreed that Rebecca and their two daughters would live in a house near her husband's father, State Representative John Minto Sr., and the younger John would give her $1000, a sewing machine, a carpet, and a set of bedroom furniture, as well as paying to support the two children until Rebecca remarried (or until their daughters married or reached age twenty). Thus, in the cases of both Nancy Parker and Rebecca Minto, the court failed to unreasonably uphold the institution of marriage when it was not beneficial. Furthermore, in granting a substantial financial settlement to Rebecca Minto—and in giving both women custody of their children—the court showed an increased respect for women's happiness and independence.[92]

In fact, argued an article in the *New Northwest*, it was only right that women had been given this respect, for it was not they who were responsible for Oregon's relatively high divorce rate. On the contrary, it was proclaimed, women actually considered marriage " 'a sanctified union, to be dissolved' not even 'at death's gate,' " and if men and legal codes reflected women's expectations for just, well-mannered husbands, wives would abandon divorce suits altogether.[93] While not all second-generation women supported the *New Northwest*'s rather radical call for changes in marital laws, many were taking steps in their own lives to prevent exposure to "drunkenness and brutality" through careful selection of their mates. At the same time, divorce became somewhat more available and acceptable for women whose husbands failed to meet rising standards of courteous behavior.

Conclusion

In the East, middle-class Americans embraced new expectations for romance as early as the mid-nineteenth century, but in both the Midwest and the Far West, difficult conditions long forbade the frivolity of love and compelled early settlers to marry primarily for practical reasons. In addition, although frontier women's domestic skills earned them a certain degree of autonomy within the home, they ultimately accepted their husbands' patriarchal authority. All this was brought into question when the second generation came of age.

As frontier conditions faded, a simultaneous postponement of young men's independence and an increase in economic opportunities for young women encouraged couples to wait longer to wed. At the same time, romantic concepts of marriage were brought westward to the Pacific Slope, and young women embraced the opportunity to search for the perfect union—one of companionability, refinement, and more balanced power relations. By adopting new standards of marital choice and post-marriage conduct, second-generation western settlers abandoned the constraints of frontier household formation and embraced an increasingly national middle-class lifestyle, which women sought to demonstrate through their participation in a new consumer culture.

CHAPTER 4

Refining the Domestic Sphere

Amid the hardships of frontier life in Polk County, Oregon, during the mid-nineteenth century, Zeralda Carpenter Bones Stone hoarded scraps of navy and brown cotton print fabrics, perhaps exchanging fabric scraps with women on neighboring farms to obtain the colors she most desired. Stealing time from her daily chores, Zeralda pieced these scraps into symmetrical blocks that resembled the paddle with which she churned butter each day. She, or more likely her husband John, traded a precious portion of their small agricultural surplus for several yards of a pretty pink calico to alternate with the pieced blocks, as well as a sturdy pink-and-brown plaid for backing. With its warm wool filling—or "batting"—held in place by long rows of quilting stitches, Zeralda's "churn dash" quilt would provide warmth and cheer for her one surviving son and eleven adopted children (fig. 4.1).[1]

As the new century approached, a widow in her early forties—whose parents had moved west from Kentucky while she was still an infant—left rural Washington Territory to marry a businessman in the bustling city of Portland. Perhaps it was her new life as a middle-class urban housewife that enabled and inspired Minnie Biles Brazee Knapp to embrace the new crazy quilt fad. Gathering together oddly shaped pieces of silk, velvet, moire, brocade, and satin ribbons left over from her most fashionable dresses, and purchasing a variety of manufactured appliqués and yards of braid to bind the edges of her handiwork, Minnie created a masterpiece of whimsy (fig. 4.2). Her highly decorative throw showed off her artistry with needle and paintbrush and displayed her membership in the urban middle class within her wonderfully cluttered Victorian parlor.[2]

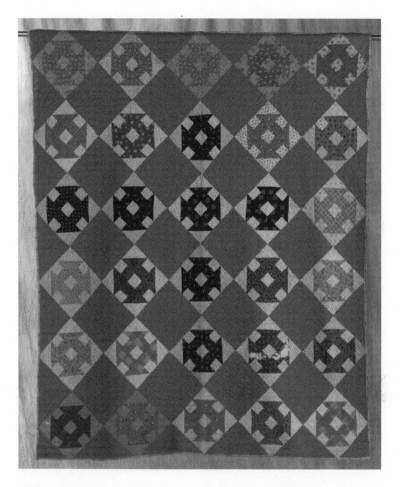

4.1 Zeralda Carpenter Bones Stone, churn dash quilt, circa 1860. This bed-sized quilt of "churn dash" blocks, made of blue, tan, and brown cottons alternating with squares of pink calico, is representative of mid-nineteenth-century patchwork quilting. (Scott Rook, photographer; courtesy Oregon Historical Society Museum, 67-368)

At the close of the frontier era, young women living in the Willamette Valley's rapidly developing communities had unique opportunities to gain a greater political voice and to move into a more public role than women could in the past. Yet, at the same time, greater economic security encouraged them to withdraw further into the private realm of the home. Women's

4.2 Minnie Biles Brazee Knapp, crazy quilt, circa 1890. This late-nineteenth-century "crazy quilt" throw was made from irregular pieces of various fine fabrics and ribbons, decorated with embroidery stitching, and painted with appliqué flowers. (Scott Rook, photographer; courtesy Oregon Historical Society Museum, 86-97)

work provides a unique window into the ways in which the daughters of Oregon settlers negotiated the conflicting social forces that simultaneously lured them into the world and drew them deeper into domesticity during the late nineteenth century. Most notably, these women replaced their mothers' faith in separate work spheres and female morality with new standards for middle-class belonging, patterning their lives after their fashionable contemporaries in eastern cities and redefining the private domestic sphere as a place of conspicuous consumption. In this way, women's homes—and their very bodies—became showcases of their middle-class identity.

Reinforcing Domestic Boundaries

Even more than their mothers had done, second-generation Oregon women set aside the frontier's flexible work roles to concentrate on domestic labor. Taking advantage of the border their parents had constructed between men's and women's spheres, most young women accepted that the boundary of their workspace fit closely around the walls of their home. For some settlers' daughters, however, necessity weakened that boundary, and for others, it made them feel limited rather than freed. These women crossed the line separating them from the larger world to pursue teaching or other work—but often only until they married and established their own domestic space.

During the early days on the Overland Trail and the Oregon frontier, children had been forced to be flexible about their work roles. Those who came overland as teenagers received only a rudimentary formal education, missing school when they were needed to do housework or field labor. Upon their marriage at an early age, young women "went to housekeeping" with their husbands and took responsibility for the domestic tasks they had learned from their mothers. One of these women, who came overland at age thirteen, recalled that she "was married at 15, and was not only a good cook and housekeeper, but . . . knew how to take care of babies, from having cared for brothers and sisters." Yet like members of her mother's generation, this young woman also had to take on male tasks at times—she told journalist Fred Lockley: "When my husband was away I could rustle the meat on which we lived, for I could handle a revolver or rifle as well as most men."[3] Thus, in their early years of marriage on the frontier, these women used both the domestic skills and the adaptability they had learned from their settler mothers.[4]

However, second-generation girls who grew up after their families' farms were well established had far more distinct work roles than had been possible for their mothers or older sisters. This can be seen in the way that second-generation couples, once married, renegotiated and refined the boundary that their parents had established in the barnyard. Photographs

4.3 Backenstos' Ranch, Marion County, Oregon, circa 1889. This typical Marion County farmhouse is surrounded by a garden and yard. However, the woman pictured has crossed the boundary surrounding her domestic sphere to join her husband and sons in a field behind the barn, where they stand with assorted livestock. (Courtesy Oregon Historical Society; OrHi 60677, no. 719)

from the early period reveal that, in reality, this border had never been as neatly drawn as it was in the idealized illustrations that appeared in local histories (compare figs. 4.3 and 4.4). As has been discussed, settlers often crossed the line separating men's and women's work, especially in borderland areas such as the barnyard. But while second-generation men and women continued to cooperate in dairying to some extent, most women began to expect their husbands or male hired hands to do the milking. In 1886, one "Farmer's Girl" asserted that "Few women would object to do the milking [during] busy times if there were conveniences about the farm, so that it could be done without soiling clothes and shoes."[5] She argued that Willamette Valley families had left frontier work role flexibility behind, and that women deserved appropriate shelter to protect their fancy clothing and shoes—items that had been unavailable during the early years on the frontier. Increasingly, second-generation men took over responsibility for milking even in "busy times."

4.4 Farm and residence of R. A. Belknap. In this idealized image of a Benton County farm, women do not stray beyond the protection of the spacious clapboard farmhouse's broad porches. Their domestic sphere is clearly demarcated by a picket fence; rougher split rail fences separate the garden, orchard, livestock, and fields tended by men. The man rides a horse, prepared to journey to the distant regions of the family farm and beyond. (From "Farm and Residence of R. A. Belknap," *History of Benton County* [D. D. Fagan, 1885], 40; courtesy Oregon Historical Society; OrHi 39941)

In fact, as butter-making became highly profitable on some second-generation farms, many men took almost complete control of dairying in general, mirroring a change that had occurred on Mid-Atlantic farms in the first half of the nineteenth century.[6] Like farmers in the Philadelphia hinterland during the 1820s and 1830s, Oregon men of the late nineteenth century shifted their focus to dairying because cities were growing rapidly and the railroad brought them into competition with wheat farms on the Great Plains and elsewhere. As Willamette Valley milk production increased dramatically during the last two decades of the century—going from 121,392 gallons to 23,397,602 gallons—butter production nearly tripled to 4.3 million pounds.[7] Some Oregon farms, particularly those close to Portland and those nearest the Pacific Coast, began to use dairying as their primary source of income. On these farms, men supervised dairy work, sold their cream to a creamery, and hired younger men to milk the cows—effectively replacing women in their traditional churning role with a mechanized cooperative business. By 1890, more than 90 percent of the 184 Oregonians employed as dairy workers were men.[8] Only two of the twenty-four students enrolled in a turn-of-the-century dairying course at Oregon State University were women, while many more female students received training in home economics courses like sewing and cooking. As men began to take over dairying in Oregon, as they had done in the Mid-Atlantic a half-century earlier, Willamette Valley women turned their attention to other traditionally female market products.[9]

As had occurred with butter-making, attitudes toward gardening and poultry raising also changed as profitability rose, but these enterprises remained in women's hands at least to some extent. By the 1870s, eggs and garden produce no longer provided mere "pin money" for extravagances, and local newspapers began to encourage women to produce these goods for market, just as their mothers had done during earlier years. The *Willamette Farmer* suggested that young women who lived far from town could raise fruits and preserve them as jam or produce flower seeds for sale. Similarly, an 1876 *Oregon Cultivator* article promoted women as poultry raisers, viewing this industry as an extension of women's maternal role: "The special capacity of women for caring for pets is so well established that it is a matter of surprise that a larger number do not make their natural inclination a matter of profit in the raising of poultry." The writer of this article argued that men should build the coop, however: "After the hennery or coop is built there is no department of the work that a woman cannot perform without exhausting labor or too heavy demands on her time."[10] Men appear to have heeded this advice, constructing chicken coops in their barnyards. Yet not all second-generation men were content to have their wives take over control of this profitable business once the coops were built.[11]

Actually, as the growth of cities like Portland and Eugene improved the market for eggs, many young men took a decided interest in poultry raising. In the mid-1880s, the *Willamette Farmer* began to feature a regular column on poultry alongside columns about grain crops and other traditionally male farm products. Egg production rose 600 percent in Multnomah County between 1880 and 1900—a 180.7 percent increase per farm—to meet the growing demand in Portland, and it increased more than 400 percent in neighboring Clackamas and Washington counties, as well as in Marion County (home to the state capital of Salem). In all, by 1900, Willamette Valley farmers were producing more than 52.5 million eggs each year.[12] But unlike second-generation men in the growing dairy industry, who entered into dairying as a full-time career, male poultry raisers did not adopt the enterprise to the exclusion of field work. Instead, they typically shifted some labor into a cottage poultry industry to raise cash with which to acquire land and farming equipment, later returning poultry responsibilities to their wives. Perhaps because poultry raising had been less of a shared activity in previous generations than had dairying, second-generation men viewed the poultry business as an opportunity to raise capital for other, more masculine ventures. It is also possible that Willamette Valley men set aside poultry raising because it was less lucrative than other agricultural projects. Unlike the men who focused solely on turkey raising in Idaho during the 1920s and 1930s, Willamette Valley farmers were enabled by the area's rich soil and ample rainfall to raise crops in addition to taking the notoriously risky step of investing in poultry.[13]

As men gradually took more control of work like dairying and poultry raising, second-generation women expected to be freed not only from field labor but from physically demanding domestic and barnyard tasks as well. Emma Simmons, for instance, complained that her husband refused to provide for her, forcing her to milk the cows, carry and chop firewood, and feed the hogs. When he was away, she did his regular work as well, tending the larger livestock. Apparently most damning, however, was that in addition to all of this work she had "done [her] own cooking for threshers and work hands, without any help."[14] Similarly, Jessie Parkes complained to the court in 1898 that, while she "was in exceedingly delicate health"—advanced pregnancy—and had the care of her two small children, her husband "compelled her to cut and carry the wood, and carry the water necessary for family use, a distance of about one eighth of a mile, and to go after the cows and milk them."[15] First-generation women had regularly done all of this work and more, including helping their husbands in the fields, even while pregnant and caring for several young children. But for the second generation, these tasks were well beyond what was acceptable to demand of women, particularly those in "delicate health."

Just as fathers taught young men about field work through informal apprenticeships, the mothers of second-generation women laid the groundwork for their daughters' future occupations as housekeepers. Yet not all young women were content to remain within the domestic workspace that had been carved out for them. Although few sought to compete with men for careers outside the home, many more began to rethink the meaning of women's paid and unpaid work in relation to their gender identity. In the process, they redefined the boundary their mothers had constructed around the domestic sphere.

Genteel Consumption

Oregon settlers toiled to relieve their daughters from field labor and trained them to be proper housewives. However, second-generation women dreamed of becoming middle-class ladies not through their mothers' standards for refined behavior, but through participation in a growing national culture of consumption. Rather than using new technologies solely to reduce domestic drudgery, these younger women took advantage of their less tedious lives to enhance their social status through fashionable apparel.

Second-generation wives were first introduced to consumer culture through the new presence of household conveniences. Following the completion of the first transcontinental railroad in 1869, trains brought an ever-increasing number of mechanized inventions to western markets, including the rural Willamette Valley. Larger and more efficient butter churns, operated by a hand crank or even a dog-powered treadmill, replaced older dash-style churns. Crank-powered tabletop models such as G. A. Wickerson's patented Stoddard churn enabled a housewife to produce butter more quickly and more comfortably than her mother had done. In addition, new cookstoves were more efficient and easier to control, and by the 1890s, items such as preserved fruits, vegetables, and meats—as well as prepared foods such as brandied peaches and condiments—became widely available through national mail-order catalogs. By 1895, a washing machine could relieve a woman from scrubbing her family's laundry on a washboard for the cost of a basic barrel butter churn. Together with treadle sewing machines, new churns, cookstoves, and washing machines reduced the amount of time and physical strength required to do daily domestic work.[16]

However, new domestic conveniences did not necessarily reduce middle-class women's workload. As cookstoves and convenient foods became available, expectations for women's cooking kept pace. New cookbooks offered more complex recipes and suggestions for preparing decorative as well as delicious meals. And while second-generation women could purchase china teacups and roasted coffee—unlike their frontier mothers, who had substituted parched peas for coffee—they were expected to provide tasty treats prepared from new recipes along with that pre-roasted coffee. Likewise, as washing machines became available, standards of cleanliness rose to counterbalance savings in labor, and the more complex women's fashions that evolved in the late nineteenth century required significantly more effort to clean and press. Thus, rather than freeing women from domestic toil, these labor-saving devices enabled full-time housewives to meet growing expectations for complexity in both cuisine and attire.[17]

The advent of practical home sewing machines coincided with a dramatic expansion in industrial production of cloth goods in the eastern United States. Beginning in the 1820s, northeastern mills turned out increasing quantities of cheap cotton cloth, and the development of cylinder printing enabled factories to quickly and easily print continuous patterns on fabric. By the mid-1830s, American mills were producing about 120 million yards of printed cotton cloth each year.[18] However, this development at first had a very limited impact on the Oregon frontier because its distance from eastern factories made their goods prohibitively expensive for most families. During the gold rush era, when women's labor was needed in the fields, some families purchased ready-made men's clothing and many bought used clothing and other goods from neighbors or local estate sales, but most first-generation men purchased only a limited quantity of new woolen cloth, calico, muslin, needles, and thread, which their wives used to make simple clothing and bedding for the home. With both cloth and women's labor at a premium, frontier families made do with only two or three sets of clothing per person, wearing and repairing them until they were rags (which could then be cut down for other uses). Clearly, the growth of the American textile industry in the antebellum era failed to help first-generation Oregonians match new standards for neat personal presentation.[19]

While frontier families had all they could do to keep themselves clothed, Victorian Americans in growing eastern cities were becoming extremely concerned with appearances, as well as with hiding, disguising, and controlling their bodies. Beginning in the 1830s, it was largely the urban middle classes' complex set of rules for dress and behavior that distinguished them from poorer people. These rules were less important in small rural communities, where individuals' social status and personal reputation were well known, so it is not surprising that etiquette was relatively unimportant on the Oregon frontier. But by the 1880s, as Portland grew into a substantial city and the Willamette Valley became increasingly tied to urban areas, second-generation Oregonians began to adopt or adapt eastern standards for behavior. Men and women began to display their class and gender identity through their public appearance, and particularly their style of dress. When women wore fancy dresses, therefore, they were using their bodies to demonstrate their status as genteel middle-class women.[20]

Limited evidence makes it problematic to study frontier women's clothing. Most frontier women could afford only one or two dresses for daily wear and one for "best," which they would use and occasionally make over until it was worn out. Due to heavy wear, very few everyday dresses survived intact, so museum collections tend to be skewed in favor of women's best dresses and those of the wealthiest women. The few surviving daguerreotypes and ambrotypes also depict women in their best clothing. Therefore, scholars are restricted to studying women's most valued attire. But this attire can be quite revealing in itself.

First, it shows us that while first-generation Oregon women sought to make their best dress as fancy and fashionable as possible, frontier life tended to favor more durable fabrics and patterns. At mid-century, frontier women also had limited access to information about the latest styles, even though they regularly exchanged descriptions of new fashions and swatches of cloth with family and friends back east. Thus, Laura F. Burr Bushnell's black-on-white cotton two-piece dress was probably similar to many other Willamette Valley frontier women's "best." Its decorative features—including an overskirt, flounces, matching decorative cotton tape, and piping at the shoulder and neck—set it apart from dresses intended for daily wear, yet it was sturdily made, with a practical, muslin-lined bodice.[21]

Some wealthier Oregon women were able to afford finer silk gowns. Ester Lockheart, in fact, owned several silk garments, and was pleased on reaching Oregon in 1851 to find that they had survived the journey and that other frontier women shared her appreciation for the "niceties of life."[22] But even most wealthy women had only one silk dress, which was often first created as a wedding dress and worn on special occasions for many years afterward. For Sarah Finley's 1866 wedding to the president of Corvallis College (now Oregon State University), she wore a drop-shouldered black silk dress with a full hoop skirt and silk ruching (a kind of ruffled trim) (fig. 4.5). Another well-off woman, Dr. Mae Whitney Cardwell, owned a fine chocolate-brown striped silk taffeta gown with black jet beads and black lace, which her medical career may have enabled her to afford. This dress included similar design elements to Bushnell's black-and-white cotton, with piping at the drop shoulders and a box-pleated skirt, but the very fine hand-stitching and detailed work suggest that it may have been made by a professional seamstress rather than by Cardwell herself. Its pagoda sleeves, delicate fabric, lace, and silk-covered buttons made it unsuitable for domestic labor, but it does show signs of wear, and it was fully lined with brown cambric and trimmed with horsehair braid to protect the hemline. Hence, for Dr. Cardwell and the other early Oregon settlers, it is apparent that even fine dresses balanced beauty with practicality in construction, so that they would last for several seasons.[23]

By the time second-generation Oregonians came of age in the 1870s and 1880s, improvements in transportation had fueled the rise of mail-order houses, which made available sewing machines, a wide variety of cloth, and mail-order catalogs and periodicals featuring the latest fashions. Oregon women in the early 1870s continued to sew their own clothing, occasionally hiring skilled seamstresses to sew dresses for them, but in addition to calico, they were now able to choose from a wide variety of fabrics. It is clear from local advertisements that as the affordability of a large selection of dry goods rose, so did Oregon women's expectations for finer "best" dresses and a wider array of everyday attire. Laura Woodworth, for one, certainly had these expectations—in her 1882 divorce suit, she complained that her husband bought her only "one worsted dress . . . also two calico dresses, some shoes, but not all the clothing [she] needed."[24] Newspaper articles, photographs and surviving textile pieces suggest that while Woodworth wore her worsted, increasing numbers of Oregon women dressed in elegant silk.[25]

Because second-generation women's stylish gowns indicated their class aspirations, sewing became not simply a productive activity, but also a performance through which to display genteel handiwork and refined taste. Wealthier second-generation farm wives might have owned a richly decorated silk gown like those worn by Portland's "belles of the 1870s" (fig. 4.6) or made richly ruffled white dresses for their high school graduation, as did the 1877 class of the growing city's St. Helen's Hall. Less-affluent women might wear simpler two-piece suits with ruffled accents such as that worn

4.5 Sarah and W. A. Finley as bride and groom, 1866. Sarah Finley wore a typical black silk dress with hoopskirt, pagoda sleeves and silk ruching accents for her 1866 marriage. Not until the 1880s did white wedding gowns become common in the Willamette Valley. Throughout the nineteenth century, many brides wore serviceable black silk dresses that could be re-worn and made over for years to come. (Courtesy Oregon State University Archives, Harriet's Photographic Collection, HC 224)

4.6 "Belles of the 1870s," Portland, Oregon. In the early 1870s, wealthy urban women attending social events in the Willamette Valley wore fashionable silk gowns. The dresses pictured here still feature the pagoda sleeves and bell-shaped skirts that had been popular in the eastern United States in the 1860s, but by the mid-1870s, styles in Oregon began to change. (Courtesy of Special Collections and University Archives, University of Oregon Libraries)

by Louisa Gay in approximately 1875 (fig. 4.7). But wealthy or not, by the 1880s, many young Oregon women posed for photographs in the latest styles. The bell-shaped ball gowns of the previous decade were replaced by straighter, heavily ruffled or draped skirts and rear bustles, like those featured on Ida Humphries' fitted dark velvet dress, which she wore for an 1888 portrait taken by a Salem photographer (fig. 4.8). Such photographs show that as second-generation women grew up, the use of fine fabrics and fashions borrowed from eastern urbanites emphasized the wearers' financial success.[26]

Fashion columns and "chit-chat" in the women's suffrage organ the

4.7 Louisa Gay, circa 1875. Louisa Gay wore the latest fashions at about age nineteen. By the mid-1870s, hoopskirts gave way to straighter, loosely gathered skirts covered by a polonaise, typically worn with fitted jackets and throat ruffles. (Courtesy Oregon Historical Society; OrHi CN 017711)

4.8 Ida Humphries, Salem, 1888. Ida Humphries wore a fashionable fitted dark velvet dress with a large brocade bustle over a stiff corset, all of which helped to define her figure and accentuate her small waist. (Courtesy Oregon Historical Society; OrHi O195G073)

New Northwest reflected rural women's eagerness to keep up with the latest fashions. Beginning in the early 1870s, the paper published descriptions of all the newest styles and how to make them, reporting on displays in Portland millinery shops for women living in rural areas. A decade later, advice columns began to give more explicit counsel on proper dress; the second installment of the 1881 series "What to Wear and How," for example, announced that those who traveled in "cities and cultivated circles" unconsciously learned the appropriate attire for each social situation. "But in country places," it warned, "where the limit of rustic range is compassed by village balls and rural meetings in secluded churches, there is often a conspicuous lack of fitness in the selection of apparel."[27] One column in "Fashion Notes," a regular feature of the paper, advised women on what to select if they could only afford one new gown, declaring that, while sateen might still be popular in the East, it was not suited to the damp Oregon climate and was "losing favor" there.[28] Other columns in the series gave guidance on selecting fashionable bonnets and dresses and advised women to wear cotton flannel underclothes and "well-fitting" corsets.[29] Briefer features announced which fabrics were fashionable for the coming season. By subscribing to the feminist *New Northwest*, even women in rural areas could keep up with eastern styles.[30]

Ironically, as the American middle class lost interest in women's morality as an indicator of class status, they embraced elaborate wedding gowns that symbolized the bride's purity. Throughout the United States after the Civil War, the serviceable dark silks or good cotton or wool dresses in which antebellum women had married were replaced by fine white or light-colored wedding gowns. One of the most magnificent examples of these was a princess-line dress worn by Louise Chamberlin and later altered for her granddaughter and great-granddaughter, featuring panels of ivory brocade separated by draped cream satin and trimmed with manufactured lace and hundreds of small cultured pearls. While the pearls had been hand-sewn on the dress by the bride, the rest of the garment was likely made by one of the dozens of professional dressmakers working in the Willamette Valley in 1880. This reveals the extent to which women were willing to invest their resources in a single outfit.[31]

But although many Willamette Valley brides adopted the new fashion of white wedding dresses, not all could afford one as fancy as Louise Chamberlin's. Many others were likely married in gowns similar to that worn by

Alice Jacobi on New Year's Day in 1882—a dress made of sheer ivory wool, with a fitted bodice, a shirred tiered skirt, and a slight bustle in the back. This dress was primarily machine-sewn but featured many hand-sewn gathers, and Jacobi probably made it herself by copying its drapes, gathers, and bustle from descriptions in local periodicals such as the *New Northwest* or from eastern fashion magazines such as *Ladies' Home Journal*. The reattached sleeves and alterations to darts in the bodice suggest that this dress was mended and adapted so that it also could be passed on to another bride. Although not nearly as fine as the Chamberlin gown, Jacobi's wedding dress demonstrated her eagerness to emulate other young American women by adapting the most recent styles to her financial constraints.[32]

As trade networks improved and fabric prices dropped, many second-generation Oregon women—especially the wealthier ones living in Portland, Salem, and Eugene—built extensive wardrobes by adopting rapidly changing styles. It became more common for women to wear special white gowns for formal occasions such as marriages or high school graduations without ever adapting them to other uses. Some women documented their many fashionable dresses in formal portraits. For example, Salem-area resident Addie Burdett wore a light-colored gown of softly draped material, accented with a dark ribbon belt and dark velvet trim, in a May 1890 family portrait—but just over two months later, she returned to the portrait studio wearing a dark plaid dress with a clearly defined waist, ruffled bodice, and gathered polonaise (overskirt).[33] Addie's mother's generation could not have imagined the luxury of sitting for such frequent portraits or wearing such an impractical light-colored gown, let alone owning such a variety of fine dresses.

Photographs of Salem-area residents Ida and Ella Burley likewise reveal how rapidly Willamette Valley fashions changed during the 1890s. These two sisters had full-length portraits taken at the beginning of the decade that showed Ida already embracing the fuller skirts and cleaner lines of eastern fashions of the time. Ella, meanwhile, posed in a more transitional style similar to that worn by Addie Burdett in May of 1890: a dress of delicate floral-print fabric draped at the hips and then falling more vertically through the skirt, reminiscent of 1880s bustles and decorated hiplines. As can be seen in a later portrait of the sisters, by 1894, they had both adopted the simple A-line skirts and heavily ruffled shirtwaists (blouses)—complete with eye-catching "leg-of-mutton" or gigot sleeves—that swept the nation in the mid-1890s (fig. 4.9).[34]

4.9 The Burley sisters—Ida and Ella—holding cherry blossoms, 1894. Puffy gigot sleeves dominate the Burley sisters' 1894 costume. While Ella (right) wears a typical white shirtwaist and dark A-line skirt, Ida appears to be wearing a two-piece dark silk dress that borrows similar style elements. (Courtesy Oregon Historical Society; OrHi 0178G017)

Despite wider availability and reduced prices for dry goods, poorer women still struggled to keep up with the latest styles. Even in the latter 1880s, some Salem residents continued to pose for portraits wearing plain plaid dresses reminiscent of the frontier era, or bell-shaped silk gowns with drop shoulders that had gone out of fashion a decade earlier. Attempting to help, women's columns in local newspapers and national magazines advised women in making over old dresses to appear more fashionable and recommended less-expensive alternatives to the latest fashions. Each installment of the *New Northwest*'s series "What to Wear and How," for instance, suggested inexpensive substitutes "for those of moderate means."[35] Similarly, L. Nina Hazelton's 1876 ode to "My Striped Silk Dress" illustrated less-wealthy women's efforts to remain fashionable, describing the author wearing her first silk dress to every social occasion for several seasons. She eventually made it fashionable once more by replacing grey piping with bands of black velvet and combining a leftover piece of fabric with the overskirt to form a polonaise. Although Hazelton's article no doubt was encouraging to women who struggled to afford stylish attire, it also revealed the relentless speed with which fashions were cast aside as she wrote of cutting up the altered dress for rags: "It is only a year and a half since [my silk dress] came to me fresh from the shop window; and now [its] short but busy life has just ended."[36] Like their wealthier counterparts, those of "moderate means" displayed their gender and class identities on their bodies, so these women felt perhaps even greater pressure to replace or remake their clothing every few months.[37] But thanks to commercially-produced dress patterns, cheaper fabrics and sewing machines, and the advice of the *New Northwest*, even poorer Willamette Valley farm wives could afford at least one stylish dress by the late nineteenth century.[38]

Lower prices for sewing machines and shipping also encouraged the manufacture and retailing of ready-to-wear clothing, particularly men's fashions. This shift is reflected in newspaper advertisements and directories for the growing city of Portland, as well as in second-generation Willamette Valley account books—in which men recorded purchasing more and more ready-made suits, shirts, handkerchiefs, coats, and "overhauls" beginning in the 1870s. Throughout the last quarter of the nineteenth century, while women continued to make most of their own clothing at home, men's ready-to-wear sack suits displaced homemade or tailored suits as custom tailoring and retail clothing businesses grew apace in Portland. Unsurprisingly, with this shift toward off-the-rack men's attire came language indicating a growing separation of men's and women's apparel. For example, the 1873 Portland directory included the category "tailoring and repairing," and the listing for retail "Clothiers" included a cross-reference to general dry goods stores, which accommodated both men and women. But by the mid-1880s, "tailoring and repairing" was renamed "Tailors," and retail clothing was referenced with male-only merchant tailors rather than with female-dominated general merchandise department stores. By the 1890s, local clothing retailers and national mail-order catalogs such as Sears, Roebuck & Company, and Montgomery Ward & Company had made a wide variety of ready-to-wear men's clothing available to rural families throughout the Willamette Valley and across the United States.[39]

Of course, both sewing machines and the new availability of ready-to-wear clothing greatly reduced the labor required to complete a simple garment. However, just as cookstoves brought with them more complex cooking demands and the advent of washing machines called for more cleanliness, these changes failed to substantially decrease households' labor burdens as standards for clothing appearance kept pace with women's increasing ease in making it. Rural journals and account books suggest that women continued to sew most of their families' clothing, and particularly their own dresses, at home. Furthermore, as sewing machines reduced the time required to sew each seam, "the call came for tucks, more flounces, and fashion requires that double the amount of sewing is required for finishing a garment than before the advent of machines."[40] Instead of liberating women from manual sewing, technological advances offered them an opportunity to shift their attention away from their husbands' clothing needs and toward dressing themselves and their homes in the trappings of Gilded Age middle-class life.[41]

All of this shows that, by embracing new products such as sewing machines and fancier clothing styles, second-generation women tied themselves into a national trade network and a developing consumer culture that their parents had rejected. Settlers had first migrated to Oregon with a conservative goal: to limit their market participation, and to participate only on their own terms. They hoped to meet most of their daily needs on the farm and to be selective in trading for other necessities and perhaps a few treats. In contrast, second-generation Oregonians, like their midwestern counterparts, grew confident that they could participate in the market in ways that were meaningful to them. They relied on developing trade routes to provide them with the comforts and finery of middle-class life, and they used the proceeds from market-oriented production to easily purchase consumer goods that had largely been out of their parents' reach. If second-generation Oregon women could not window-shop at large eastern department stores like Wanamaker's, they could nonetheless admire the increasing array of goods in their local dry goods store, and by the last decade of the century, they could also pore over the pages of goods offered by Sears, Montgomery Ward, and other mail-order retailers. While still making substantial contributions to the household economy, they were more able to think of themselves as consumers, like those in New York or Boston. Throughout their lives, however, these increasingly consumption-conscious women remained enmeshed in a rural network of female production.[42]

From Practical Comforts to Conspicuous Consumption

Second-generation Oregon women, who grew up learning the distinct gender roles and genteel behavior that signified their mothers' middle-class membership, did not wholly leave behind the domestic sphere. In fact, they continued to engage in many quite traditional female pastimes—most notably, quilt making. Yet at the same time, once new expectations for consumption were carried westward, frontier daughters began to perform old activities in new ways and for new, blatantly consumeristic reasons. As young women who grew up safely within the boundaries of settlers' homes embraced crazy quilts and fine parlor furniture, they transformed their own homes from private retreats into public displays of their membership in the *new* middle class.

Frontier women taught their daughters to sew at an early age—often before they could read—making it a formative activity for all second-generation females. Settlers' daughters first learned to sew by piecing quilt tops in simple patterns such as a checkerboard pattern known as "nine-patch," and completing one's first quilt was a highlight of a young lady's youth. As a child on the Oregon frontier, Marianne D'Arcy often traded pieces of cloth with neighbor girls, and she recalled that they were always "eager to hear the history of all the pieces" in her mother's quilts and would in turn "tell of the wonderful patchwork quilts they had at their home."[43] A number of rural girls received praise from the local newspaper's children's column editor for writing letters about quilting accomplishments—one ten-year-old girl proudly wrote of having pieced two quilts the previous winter, and another girl bragged of piecing seven quilts by age thirteen. By the time of these young girls' marriage, they would have each pieced a number of serviceable comforts and a few finer decorative quilts.[44]

The fact that girls consistently wrote of merely *piecing* quilts suggests that quilting their completed quilt tops remained a communal activity. Indeed, we know that quilting helped to initiate second-generation girls into the informal network of trade, friendship, and mutual assistance that their mothers and older sisters had built on the frontier. Quiltings (also known as quilting parties or quilting bees) provided opportunities for women of different ages and generations to share their labor and their lives—even young children could contribute to these events by threading needles or fetching things for their mothers and older sisters gathered around the quilting frame. Gaining a seat at that quilt frame indicated acceptance as an equal member into the adult female community, and attending one's first quilting party—as second-generation newlywed Laura Woodworth did with her mother and seven other married ladies—marked a woman's inclusion in a common female bonding ritual. One turn-of-the-century photograph of an Oregon quilting (fig. 4.10) makes obvious the sense of intergenerational female community fostered at these events, depicting Mary Stout Milkey, three of her sisters, her mother, her sister-in-law, and seven other women of varying ages all posing around a quilting frame. Miral Milkey, who was probably Mary's niece and about ten years old, can be seen standing between two of the women sitting at the frame. Although she was too young to contribute skillful quilting stitches, Miral's elders are shown to have both literally welcomed her into the quilting circle and symbolically welcomed her into their intimate circle of female friends.

Through quilting, nineteenth-century women of all classes and regions united beauty and practicality within their accepted sphere. The mid-nineteenth century is typically thought of as the apex of American quilting, a time when eastern middle-class women embellished their homes with fabric masterpieces and recorded important events and relationships in cloth. Settlers carried quilting traditions with them to the Far West, and some women even pieced quilt tops as they walked beside their wagons on the Overland Trail. Yet not many women had time for piecing or appliquéing

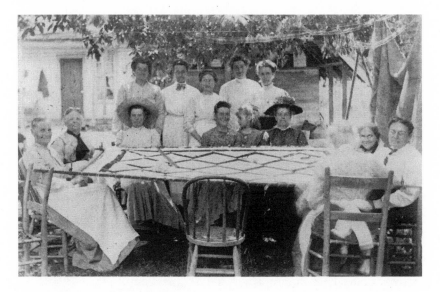

4.10 Quilting bee, Mehama, Oregon, circa 1900. Three generations of women attended this quilting bee, working on a patchwork quilt that was already old-fashioned. Most of the women wear fashionable, heavily pleated shirtwaists and A-line skirts with light-colored aprons, while others wear older styles of simple, dark, printed cotton dresses. (Courtesy Oregon Historical Society, Ray Stout Collection; OrHi 21876, no. 739)

complicated quilts during the early years on the frontier. Whereas many eastern ladies favored intricate Baltimore album quilts, characterized by their bright red flowers and green leaf patterns appliquéd on a clean white background, frontier women were more likely to produce a number of practical comforts from scraps of worn-out clothing. A few were able to construct more complex patchwork quilts, which emphasized order and created beauty out of something practical. Like Zeralda Stone's churn dash quilt (fig. 4.1), pieced quilts generally repeated a simple geometric pattern and were made from pieces of fabrics such as calico or the woolen cloth used to make men's pants and shirts. Quilting stitching accented the geometric designs created by the patchwork, and ideal quilting stitches were tiny (twelve or more stitches per inch), straight, and regular, so that the pieced design could be seen in relief but individual stitches were only visible on close examination. These traditional quilts fit well with mid-nineteenth-century middle-class women's desire to demonstrate their accomplishments within a carefully ordered domestic sphere—even if their home was a rough log cabin.[45]

As second-generation women reached adulthood, they did not abandon their mothers' dedication to the needle. Instead, they used sewing machines to devote their time, energy, and creativity to making more complex and ornate types of clothing, quilts, and other needlecrafts. Since showcasing decorative needlework indicated a woman's status as a middle-class consumer rather than a frontier producer, many western women adorned their homes with embroidered samplers, and local newspapers increasingly included complex patterns for knitting lace and other fancy work along with guidance on more mundane chores. In 1888, one young Oregon woman wrote that she had been busy "carding wool and knitting lace and doing other works too numerous to mention."[46] While she and her peers continued to card wool to knit into socks and sweaters as their mothers had done, for this young woman, fine handiwork was part of a daily work routine instead of a treat to be indulged in. Needlecrafts that had been luxuries for the first generation became just one of the many regular occupations of the next generation as their creations' decorative role became integral to the household.[47]

With more time to devote to crafts and access to a wider array of materials than was ever present before, the second generation adopted new forms of self-expression through quilting, largely abandoning the order of their mothers' patchwork patterns. Enabled by new trade networks that made rich fabrics available and affordable—and perhaps emboldened by their increasing involvement in organizations outside the home—late-nineteenth-century western women embraced the crazy quilt fad of the mid-1880s. In striking contrast to the carefully ordered, symmetrical, and repetitive block-style patchwork quilts popular among the first generation, crazy quilts used a variety of rich velvets and silks pieced in irregular shapes to create a disordered or "crazy" appearance, and they were decorated with a variety of whimsical embroidered designs. These crazy quilts emphasized seemingly random shapes, fanciful decorations, and complex embroidery, suggesting that their makers—like the quilts themselves—had lost the restraint of the early frontier days.[48]

But despite their seeming lack of order, crazy quilts were built on foundations of simple squares, rectangles, or diamonds. While some quilters disguised this underlying logic by adding odd-shaped pieces that bridged sectional divides, others, such as Minnie Knapp, carefully fitted each asymmetrical piece of fabric within symmetrical quilt sections or contained the entire quilt top within a consistent border (fig. 4.2). Although these women intentionally created a degree of disorder that was foreign to mid-century quilting, their crazy quilts were not "manifestos that rejected the neat little geometric compartments of daughter, housewife, and mother," as quilt scholars such as Ellen Fickling Eanes suggest.[49] Instead, these quilts show that the second generation's more secure domestic lives freed them to decorate their quilts in less overtly controlled ways, showing off not only great domestic skill but also the ability to afford the expensive materials and the leisure time required to produce such masterpieces. Since crazy quilts were too delicate and too small to be practical as bedding, their sole purpose was to display their makers' refined taste to audiences within the domestic sphere. Thus, although the daughters of Pacific Slope settlers did often reject the repetitive geometry of traditional patchwork quilts, in doing so they supported the orderly domestic consumption patterns of which wild crazy quilts became an important part.[50]

The crazy quilt trend could not have spread to the Willamette Valley without the economic and technological changes that took place there during the late nineteenth century. Nationwide, companies produced a wide variety of flowers and other decorative items that found their way onto the highly decorative crazy quilts, and women were encouraged to take part in the fad by local retailers, who recognized an opportunity to profitably market their remnants and various notions. Even individuals took economic advantage of the fashion—in fact, one enterprising woman and frequent *Willamette Farmer* correspondent advertised in that paper that she was selling pieces of rich fabrics and embroidery thread, ready-cut for making crazy quilts.[51]

While not all Willamette Valley women could afford to immerse themselves in making these elaborate quilts, less-wealthy women and those living in more remote locations could adapt quilt fashions to their tighter budgets and schedules. Actually, during the 1890s, rural women in the Willamette Valley and throughout the United States began to make crazy designs from more practical fabrics such as woolens. Ellen Wright and Annie Wright Reynolds, for example, created a serviceable crazy quilt throw from a vari-

ety of men's shirt goods, cotton twill, calicoes, heavy woolens, cotton towel-
ing, and even incorporated salvaged "tumbling blocks" from a previously
pieced quilt top. This quilt is filled with cotton batting and an old woven
bedspread, tied with blue, green, and red yarn, and shows heavy wear
despite its durable fabrics. Although the Wright-Reynolds women did not
create a masterpiece like that of Minnie Knapp, they chose to incorporate
elements of the crazy quilt fad into a throw that met their physical and
cultural needs. Like those women who mimicked elaborate dress styles with
cheaper fabrics, rural quilters found ways to participate in the latest fads
without devoting large amounts of money.[52]

Late-nineteenth-century women expanded upon the crazy quilt to produce many varying quilt styles, all of which were a significant departure
from those they were taught by their more conservative mothers. Using
sumptuous scraps of silk, taffeta, and velveteen from stylish clothing,
second-generation women often incorporated the bright colors and elegant
fabrics characteristic of crazy quilts into otherwise conservative patchwork
patterns, emphasizing their quilts' impracticality as they turned even the
most traditional designs into displays of modern luxury. Popular fan patterns such as those in the "grandmother's fan" quilt made by Maria Anne
Pease Warner, Harriet Griffith Wise, and Laura Etta Warner (fig. 4.11) drew
on dramatic imported Japanese design elements rather than on the familiar
inspirations of their mothers' garden and butter churns. Thus, for quilt-
makers of every economic status, the ostentation of quilt styles in general
showed that conspicuous consumption had truly replaced pious frugality in
Oregon women's domestic sphere.[53]

The evolution of quilts, however, is not the only reflection of second-
generation women's tremendous interest in consumption and the way it was
manifested in their domestic lives. In fact, possibly even more can be revealed through many married women's property registers, which openly
declared ownership of all the accouterments of middle-class life. While many
young wives declared productive goods such as dairy cattle or tools—just as
their mothers had done—ten out of sixty-seven Linn County women declaring separate property listed household furniture or musical instruments
between 1862 and 1912.[54] In 1874, Elizabeth L. Myers of Marion County
declared a detailed list of goods that she had "acquired by purchase with
[her] own money," which her father had left to her in his will for her "own
personal use."[55] The items on this list, contrasting sharply with the simple

4.11 Maria Anne Pease Warner, Harriet Griffith Wise, and Laura Etta Warner, grandmother's fan quilt, circa 1890. Women in the Willamette Valley and throughout the United States incorporated Japanese design elements such as brightly colored fan motifs into their quilts in the years following Philidelphia's 1876 "International Exhibition of Arts, Manufactures and Products of the Soil and Mine" (better known as the Centennial Exhibition). This silk-and-velvet fan quilt was made with the stiff muslin base (rather than batting) and embroidery stitching characteristic of crazy quilts. (Courtesy Oregon Historical Society Museum, 71-186.84; Scott Rook, photographer)

homemade furniture that the early settlers had squeezed into cramped log cabins, included a bedstead, a bureau, a wardrobe, a heating stove, a carpet, a commode, three chairs, a wash stand, bed and bedding, and assorted pictures and trinkets—all recorded as belonging to the master bedroom alone. As for the rest of Myers' home, it featured a fully furnished and decorated dining room, kitchen, and spare room on the first floor, plus four additional bedrooms upstairs. Perhaps most telling, however, is that she owned furnishings for both a comfortable sitting room—with a piano and sewing machine—and a formal parlor full of furniture that she would only have used when callers came to call.

Because nineteenth-century parlors were rarely occupied except during formal visits, they comprised one of the foremost symbols of high class status. Sitting rooms, in contrast, were places of productive labor and casual interaction, where women might sew, knit, or perform other work. Wealthy families maintained both a parlor and a sitting room, enabling them to hide women's productive work from outsiders while displaying their collection of fine goods to visitors. Many Willamette Valley women—wealthy or not—sought to *appear* as if they did not do any productive labor, so they, like middle-class men and women striving after refinement in the eastern United States, transformed a portion of their domestic sphere into a public display of gentility. In fact, Elizabeth Myers' property list could have just as easily described the contents of a middle-class home in New York, Boston, or Philadelphia.[56]

While few second-generation women, particularly those in rural areas, enjoyed a home as large and well appointed as that maintained by Elizabeth Myers, many did own at least a few middle-class consumer items. For example, Myers' fellow Marion County resident Mary Hoyt decorated the parlor of her two-story home with a set of furniture, a mirror, two marble-top tables, a carpet, and eight-and-one-half yards of "stair Carpet."[57] Margaret B. Frink of Polk County owned an organ, three carpets, and three looking glasses in addition to basic furniture, a sewing machine, and a small collection of livestock and farm equipment. Unlike Myers, who probably lived in the state capital of Salem, Frink lived on a working farm and valued raising hogs and dairy cattle like her mother's generation, yet she also owned luxurious home accessories that would mask her productive activities for visitors to her well-furnished sitting room.[58]

In fact, Frink's sitting room was so nicely furnished that she might have boldly called it her parlor if it were also filled with crazy quilts, embroideries, and other knick-knacks. Decorating a woman's sitting room with such consumer goods converted this center of domestic life into an elegant parlor meant for public display—just as clothing a woman in the latest fashions made her body a display of her economic success. Thus, whether women were embroidering samplers, adopting changing clothing styles, purchasing furniture for formal parlors, or joining the nationwide crazy quilt craze, they announced their membership in a national middle-class culture based on women's adherence to fashion rather than on their positions as laborers. As second-generation women's primary role shifted from producer to consumer, they blurred the boundaries that separated the public and private spheres and redefined women's place within each.

Conclusion

Building on their parents' hard work, second-generation Oregon women were able to draw the domestic boundary even more closely around the home than their mothers had done, letting their husbands adopt responsibility for barnyard tasks such as milking and poultry raising. They generally accepted their parents' belief in separate spheres for men and women, but although many no doubt took pride in housework well done, they were not willing to be completely defined by that labor. Like the quilting stitches on old patchwork quilts, first-generation women's work remained largely invisible to the outside world. They contributed many daily tasks that were crucial to the household economy while placing their husbands' more celebrated economic achievements in greater relief. In contrast, second-generation women's work was more like the embroidery they stitched onto crazy quilts—it appeared to be only decorative, but in fact it, too, was central to their household, acting to materially manifest their middle-class status. As women enthusiastically adapted their homes to fit the new consumer culture, they developed a national consciousness that would have important implications for their role in the world beyond their domestic sphere.

CHAPTER 5

New Roles for "New Women"

Through the voice of a fictional character, novelist Mary Murdoch Mason divided young American women of the 1870s into three classes: the "giddy butterflies," the "busy bees," and the "women's righters." "The first," Mason wrote, "are pretty and silly, the second plain and useful, the third mannish and odious. The first wear a smile at you while waltzing; the second wear aprons and give you apple dumplings, and the third want your manly prerogatives, your dresscoat, your money and your vote."[1] These divisions resonated with second-generation Willamette Valley residents, sparking discussion in a local newspaper.[2] Many second-generation women, like Mason's "busy bees," sought to live out their mothers' gender ideal, becoming virtuous homemakers and reinforcing their parents' boundaries around the domestic sphere. A smaller number of "giddy butterflies" redefined middle-class womanhood, spending their time and energy on being fashionable, socializing with female friends and male beaux, and participating in the new consumer culture. Finally, an even smaller minority of second-generation women moved in a very different direction, seeking greater equality with men in the public sphere through paid employment or political rights. Mason failed to acknowledge that women might demonstrate characteristics of more than one of these categories, or that they might shift from one identity to another as they reached maturity. Nonetheless, applying Mason's categories to second-generation Willamette Valley women helps to illustrate the various ways in which settlers' daughters accepted, adapted, or abandoned their parents' gender ideology.

Busy Bees and Giddy Butterflies

Regardless of whether second-generation women embraced or rejected traditional female roles, they agreed that men and women were different, and that those differences should influence their work and social functions. Pursuing educational, occupational, or political opportunities led progressive "New Women" to question the proper boundaries of "woman's sphere," but did not challenge their belief in the fundamental distinction between the sexes. Whether women sought to be moral helpmates, bourgeois ladies, or political equals to men, they defined their proper place in relation to the domestic sphere.

As has been made clear, for first-generation Oregon settlers, the boundaries of the middle class were marked not only by a gender division of labor but by morality and refined social behavior. Their class aspirations could thus be achieved, in part, by raising their daughters to be proper ladies rather than domestic drudges or frontier tomboys. As the "umpires of society," settlers believed, women's "first duty" was to be a lady. Not only should women be restrained, but they should not even "have the impulses that need restraint."[3] By the age of eleven or twelve, daughters were expected to exemplify purity, modesty, kindness, and gentleness. Increasingly, parents also relied on local schools to turn their daughters into ladies.[4]

Oregonians made many sacrifices to furnish educations for all of their offspring, but they did so with very different goals in mind for children of each sex. Sons were sent to school to learn the reading, writing, and mathematical skills they would need to become successful farmers, and a significant number of those who came of age later in the century went on to high school or to business college, learning to adapt their families' farming strategies to changing market conditions. In 1890, in fact, 229 Oregon boys (1.5 percent of the male population ages fifteen to nineteen) were enrolled in professional schools, and many more attended secondary schools.[5] Meanwhile, settlers' daughters were sent to school to become young ladies, thereby fulfilling their parents' hopes for social improvement. Like small businessmen in cities such as Boston and New York, Willamette Valley parents hoped that as their daughters gained refinement, it would reflect positively on the rest of the family and help to secure their membership in the middle class.[6]

Private female academies and public schools went along with parents' wishes as they sought to turn little frontier girls into proper middle-class women. As early as 1851, female academies offered training in domestic and other arts as well as academic subjects, preparing their pupils to create the ideal middle-class homes longed for by their families. For example, one "Young Ladies Boarding and Day School" advertised that girls would take part not only in an academic English course but also in a class in the formation of the heart and female virtue; refinements such as piano, vocal music, drawing, and painting were available for additional fees.[7] Like eastern secondary schools in the mid-nineteenth century, Oregon schools taught girls to write graceful compositions in English and to avoid speaking extemporaneously in public, while their brothers learned Latin, Greek, and elocution. Some girls learned to be ladies even when not in school—in 1876, for example, a nine-year-old girl from The Dalles devoted an entire summer to a daily regimen of long division, sewing patchwork quilt blocks, letter-writing, and constitutional walks under the guidance of her teacher. It was a routine quite similar to those of businessmen's daughters in Boston's fashionable suburbs.[8]

Parents' hopes for their daughters to become fine young ladies combined with an older belief that women should be able to raise successful sons who would be good citizens—and this, too, required education. Many first-generation women were actually illiterate: in the typical town of Sublimity, Marion County, 37 percent of women over eighteen could not read in 1860. But while it was common for first-generation women to sign legal documents with an "X" mark, nearly all second-generation women in Marion and Linn counties were able to sign their names, and by 1880, less than 5 percent of females ages ten and over were illiterate. Although second-generation women did not enjoy political equality with men, they were at least able to read and sign legal documents, as well as to read publications such as the *New Northwest* that kept subscribers abreast with the latest ladies' fashions and advocated greater political rights for women.[9]

As daughters pursued refined ladyhood, older Oregonians warned them against inattention to the domestic arts, fearing that new opportunities outside the home had spoiled young women's focus on more proper pursuits. Advice columnists in the *Willamette Farmer*, for example, insisted that a wife and housekeeper's usefulness was more important than her physical attractiveness or feminine accomplishments. Rather than women "boasting of their ignorance of all household duties," one columnist wrote, "as if nothing would so lower them in the estimation of their friends as a confession of an ability to bake bread and pies, or cook a piece of meat, or a disposition to engage in any useful employment," they should take pride in domesticity because any husband would be far happier to eat good food than to sit and gaze on his wife's beauty.[10] Another *Willamette Farmer* writer declared that there were "a hundred young ladies who can [s]trum a piano to one who can make a good loaf of bread." Domestic tranquility, this author argued, could be maintained if only wives would prepare proper meals for their husbands, for "[e]ven the lion may be tamed by keeping him well fed."[11] At least one young second-generation woman agreed with these warnings, proclaiming that "Woman is the natural companion of man. . . . It is her joy and pride to give her love worthily and yield with exclusive devotion all the sweetness of her life."[12] According to this line of thinking, feminine beauty and accomplishments such as playing the piano might be appealing during courtship, but to have a happy marriage and fulfill their proper roles as wives, women must learn to be "busy bees."

Indeed, most second-generation men did want to marry "busy bees," whom they felt would fulfill the domestic role idealized by their frontier mothers. These young men agreed with Harry Denlinger that women's "sphere is in the home" and that wives ought to be the "Queen of the home."[13] Like Denlinger, Oliver Jory desired a life anchored in a cozy home, in which the husband went out to work and returned each day to a domestic haven maintained by a housewife "of a very domestic turn." "Truly," Jory proclaimed to his fiancée, "that is much the better way for people to pass their existence."[14] Local newspapers reinforced this lesson for Willamette Valley women, arguing that the "better, the pleasanter, the more attractive, the happier [that women] make the home, the more will they contribute to the force of goodness in the world."[15] Jory, Denlinger, and many other young men shared their fathers' feelings that through domestic work—and only through domestic work—second-generation women could make the world a better place.[16]

First-generation women certainly tended to agree, worrying that not only might their daughters abandon the domestic sphere in favor of socializing and dressing fashionably, but they might also lose sight of morality in the process. On behalf of concerned Oregon mothers, the *Willamette Farmer*'s "The Home Circle" editor attempted to save second-generation Oregon women from becoming selfish "giddy butterflies" by publishing advice on such fundamental household tasks as baking bread. "Aunt Hetty" described visiting a household in which the nearly grown daughters helped with light housekeeping, washing dishes, making beds, and sweeping. After completing a few simple tasks, the girls would rush off to picnics and parties, dressed in fancy clothes their mother had washed and ironed for them and carrying culinary treats their mother had prepared for them— while their mother remained at home doing more taxing housework. The author reported that the girls were transformed after "Aunt Hetty" pointed out their abuse of their overworked mother. They learned more substantive domestic tasks, including doing their own baking and fine ironing, and resolved to help their mother more in the future. Through advice columns and morality tales such as this one, some Oregon women sought to pass on their domestic skills to the second generation. It was an uphill battle, how- ever, because economic changes and farmers' middle-class aspirations had reduced the second generation's responsibility for helping their mothers. Although they, too, were ultimately destined to become homemakers, the second generation gave this role new meaning.[17]

This occurred largely because, freed from work on their parents' farms, young Oregon women of the 1880s and 1890s developed a peer culture similar to that which appeared in eastern secondary schools during the same period. Many second-generation Oregonians—both men and women —stepped outside of their homes to join their parents in the Grange, local pioneer organizations, fraternal orders, or groups such as the Hillsboro Firemen's Coffee Club. Some "busy bees" formed local chapters of the Young Women's Christian Association (YWCA), which enabled them to serve others while remaining within their mothers' domestic sphere. How- ever, the first generation's emphasis on women's domestic roles was often challenged by "giddy butterflies" that joined purely social organizations such as Salem's "High Five" club, whose members were "noted for good looks, pretty dresses, fascinating styles, and becoming ways of wearing their hair."[18] The emergence of these latter organizations reflected and helped to further the rise of style and sociability among the second generation. As a consequence, a number of women rejected their mothers' belief that a strict moral code and skillful domestic labor were the primary indicators of middle-class status. They relied on fashion and flirtatious behavior—rather than morality—to earn men's approval, patterning their behavior and ap- pearance after young urban women in the eastern United States, whose very freedom to pursue such impractical pursuits marked their families as above those in which women had to toil in the home.[19]

Predictably, a backlash developed against young "giddy butterflies" as many Oregonians mourned the wane of good moral character, selflessness, and frugality. But critiques of these fashion-minded young ladies revealed a deep ambivalence to women's changing roles because, in many ways, the second generation's superficiality fulfilled first-generation dreams of freeing women from the domestic grind. While slighting mastery of the domestic arts, the second generation learned to be gracious, beautiful queens of the home, albeit in ways that their parents never anticipated.[20]

In any case, while many first-generation Oregonians feared the influence of fashion and conspicuous consumption, they appear to have more readily accepted new opportunities for second-generation women to expand their minds. As an 1877 article in the *Willamette Farmer* cautioned, women would soon be required to "give their opinion on important topics which interest intelligent people" rather than "depend on their beauty and dress for attention."[21] Similarly, a local columnist declared that she would "be thankful to return to the habits of our grandmothers," who were much more prudent and sensible when it came to clothing. If young women adopted older generations' practicality, she argued, they "should then have more time for reading and study and more money to spend in books and traveling, to say nothing of the unlimited time and money for doing good."[22] It is clear that, although this author certainly seems to have longed for a simpler time, her desires reflected not her mother's respect for domesticity but her own generation's dreams for expanding their minds and experiences through service organizations, education, and travel—activities more closely associated with the *fin de siécle* New Woman than with midwestern frontier farm wives.[23]

This mindset was furthered by new educational opportunities that significantly broadened women's horizons. Literary and debate circles became a popular forum to discuss the role of New Women and women's suffrage, and an increasing number of Oregon girls attended secondary or normal schools, or even coeducational universities. Nearly half of all Oregon women ages fifteen to nineteen attended school in 1890, and approximately one-third of the students enrolled in Oregon professional schools that year were women.[24] Although the majority of female students at the University of Oregon and Oregon State University studied "domestic economy" and "cookery and the household arts,"[25] some young women pursued academic degrees alongside their male peers, and a few female graduates went on to take up traditionally male careers or to seek political rights for women. Only a handful of second-generation women actually became suffrage activists, but many pursued social or intellectual opportunities that challenged the old understanding of women's sphere.[26]

Votes for Women

Western states led the Union in granting voting rights to women. Beginning in the 1850s, Oregon law permitted some women to vote at public school meetings, and in 1872, under pressure from Abigail Scott Duniway and other activists, Oregon's legislature passed significant women's property legislation and very nearly gave women the right to vote. Why, then, did Oregon fail to grant women county and state suffrage until after the turn of the century? Examining changes in Oregon gender ideology over time helps to explain why Duniway's efforts failed in the 1870s and 1880s, and how Oregon's suffrage movement finally won over the public by 1912. Notably, throughout the women's suffrage debate, both proponents for and opponents of suffrage fundamentally believed that women were uniquely suited to housework and child rearing, and that they had an inherent moral sensibility that men lacked. However, women's suffrage supporters initiated a dialogue about the *meaning* of women's uniqueness and its implications for their political role.[27]

Soon after the nation's Woman's Rights movement formally began in Seneca Falls, New York, Oregon's territorial and state governments granted a few very limited suffrage rights to women. Although women were explicitly denied the right to vote in county and statewide elections, Oregon gave its few existing female taxpayers the right to vote in school board elections beginning in 1853, and when the state's 1857 constitution gave married women the right to separate property, more women were able to meet the property requirement for participation in these small elections. Two years later, the state legislature extended school board voting rights to widows, declaring: "[W]omen who are widows, and have children and taxable property in the district, may vote, by written proxy or in person, at such meetings, if they choose."[28] Further, in 1889, property requirements were removed for widows living in small school districts, and they were permitted to vote on local education issues based solely on their dual roles as mothers and heads of household. At the same time, the state offered these women protection from the supposedly corrupting influence of political life by permitting them to vote without physically entering the male sphere of elections.[29]

During the 1890s, Oregonians contested the constitutionality of distinct voting laws for school districts before the state supreme court. The first of these cases challenged Nellie M. Stevens' right to become school superintendent for Union County in Eastern Oregon after she received a plurality of votes in a countywide election. J. L. Carter, the previous superintendent, refused to surrender the books and papers associated with that position, averring that Stevens' gender made her ineligible to hold the office. In *Stevens v. Carter* (1895), the Supreme Court upheld the lower court's decision to require Carter to surrender the office and materials to Stevens,[30] but the following year in *State Ex Rel. v. Stevens*, the district attorney sought to oust Nellie Stevens from that office and reinstate J. L. Carter. While Stevens argued that an 1893 law allowed her to hold the office of school superintendent, the county court found that the state constitution permitted only male citizens to be elected or appointed to county offices. The Oregon Supreme Court affirmed this decision, declaring the 1893 law void.[31]

Soon after *State Ex Rel. v. Stevens*, Willamette Valley resident Laura A. Harris sued for damages against the Lane County judges of election for denying her the right to vote for the district school director. Like the Union County district attorney two years earlier, these election judges argued that a law extending the franchise in school elections to female citizens was null and void. Ignoring the laws of the 1850s, their counsel declared that prior to 1889, "none but male citizens exercised the privilege of suffrage, even in the most limited degree." He further asserted that "[i]n the early history of our state none but manhood suffrage was even talked about or thought of," editorializing parenthetically that the "'new woman' had not then appeared" and adding: "All honor to the 'old woman.' May her tribe never grow less."[32] Although acknowledging the logic contained in the defendants' contention, the court apparently disagreed with their counsel's argument against New Women as it upheld the jury's assessment of $50 damages to Harris. In contrast to *State Ex Rel. v. Stevens*, this case concluded with the finding that it was not unconstitutional for women to vote in local school district elections, even though they were denied the right to vote in county and state elections. Thus, although Oregon women were forbidden full participation in the political sphere, the Supreme Court ultimately affirmed that they could at least enjoy the opportunity to vote for the leaders of their children's schools.

By the turn of the century, Oregonians remained divided over the issue of female suffrage. Deeply held beliefs in women's maternal role gradually earned them some political influence over their children's education, but Supreme Court cases reveal that views of even this small gain varied widely. Rhetoric used in Oregonians' various interpretations of women's proper public role illustrates women's changing relationship with the domestic sphere.

Women's Righters and the Domesticity Debate

Opponents of women's suffrage argued that women belonged in the home because they were either too easily influenced or too morally pure to become embroiled in the masculine realm of electoral politics. Yet even "women's righters," who directly challenged the boundaries of women's sphere, discussed women's political situation using the language of domesticity. Ultimately, the suffrage question became part of a wider debate about women's proper place in society.

Many Oregon men and women continued to oppose women's participation in politics throughout the whole of the nineteenth century. Some argued that women were too gullible to vote for the best candidate, and even those who supported the freedoms available to the New Woman often believed that giving her the vote would be going too far. "I am not afraid of woman's rights," proclaimed a typical letter to the editor of the *Willamette Farmer*. "[I]n fact I believe in their having rights to a certain extent, but when it comes to their going to the polls and voting, I believe it will do more harm than good."[33] Likewise, poet Susan Coolidge thought it best to rejoice in her inherent "rights as a woman" without demanding the ballot, rhapsodizing: "[God has] made me a woman / And I am content to be / Just what he meant."[34] Oregon's New Woman might be educated and even temporarily self-supporting, but many Oregonians insisted that she did not belong at the polls.[35]

Most people who voiced opposition to women's suffrage focused on its potential to harm wives' domesticity and femininity, fearing that the home would be disrupted by women's political participation. Authors frequently reminded women of their responsibilities to their families, and that it was their "business to please."[36] In addition, local newspapers warned that women's suffrage would wreak havoc on the domestic sphere: "[W]hen they have the right to vote there are some who are more ambitious who will want to hold office, then who is to fill her place at home?"[37] Because women's morality was thought to be far superior to men's, it was crucial to many that women not abandon their maternal and wifely role. Moreover, if proper ladies were distinguished by their purity and domesticity, it was thought, then participating in the rough-and-tumble world of politics would defile them. As one self-described "mere girl" (presumably a young second-generation woman) explained: "[B]y stepping into a rough set of men of *every class* to cast a ballot, [a woman] is falling from the high position on which man has placed her."[38] In other words, by venturing out of their proper sphere, women would lose the special treatment and respect that gentlemen afforded ladies. "I claim then for her that it is her 'right' to be treated with the utmost love, respect, honor, and consideration in her sphere," announced the *Oregon Cultivator*. "She has a 'right,' then, to be exempted from certain things which men must endure."[39] If true women were pure and moral, then they must stay at home, where they would not be corrupted by the coarse influences of the manly world of professions and the ballot box.[40]

An 1877 debate in the pages of the *Willamette Farmer*'s "The Home Circle" feature reveals an interesting interconnectedness in Oregonians' thinking about social class, gentility, and women's rights. In April of that year, a woman writing under the alias "Susan Jane Cauliflower" shared an anecdote about manners that showed her opposition to the suffrage cause. When a "lady" entered a full train car, Cauliflower wrote, a "man asked her if she believed in woman's rights; her answer was: 'Yes sir, I do.' 'Very well, then,' [he responded], 'you have the right to stand as the rest of the men do.'" Cauliflower editorialized that this incident showed "how much respect men have for such women."[41]

Regardless of their opinion of "woman's rights," respondents to Cauliflower's story tended to react to the behavior of its characters rather than to the suffrage issue itself. For example, "Rose Hopvine" argued that "anyone who is worthy [of] the name of gentleman" would assist a lady traveling—"whether she believes in woman's rights or not."[42] Although Hopvine was willing to grant New Women a greater role in the world outside the domestic sphere, she clung tightly to the codes of refined behavior through which the first generation had distinguished between proper men and women. With a similar focus, another respondent calling herself "Jenny Squash" came to the opposite conclusion, approving of the man's behavior and declaring that the "woman's righter" was incredibly impudent to enter "a car filled with womanly women and manly men" and expect this man to relinquish his seat. Squash was confident that the ladies in the car had admired him, and that the gentlemen "must have honored him for his manly courage!"[43] Clearly, Squash believed that a "woman's righter" could be neither a womanly woman nor a manly man. Regardless, the reactions of both Hopvine and Squash, revolving so firmly around etiquette, highlight a shift from middle-class identity defined by proper decorum to one that accepted newly public roles for women.

A few participants in the Cauliflower debate confronted the issue of women's rights more directly, revealing a belief in changing social mores that allowed for more equal interactions between men and women. One woman who supported "equal rights" called into question the first generation's assumption that women deserved or required special treatment due to their physical limitations or moral superiority, arguing that the man in Cauliflower's anecdote "had a perfect right to his seat in the car because he had paid his money for it, and no woman had a right to expect him to give it up."[44] While few Oregonians were willing to openly challenge the widely held belief in women's inherent difference from men—or the social norms dictated by that difference—more and more second-generation females began to seek greater public role for women, as well as gender equality in certain aspects of society.

Like others throughout the United States in the late nineteenth century, many Oregon activists used the idea of innate gender differences as the basis of their quest for more voting rights for women, arguing that women should be able to vote on certain issues *because of*—not despite—their moral superiority. This angle first became popular with temperance workers like Mary Cartwright, who wrote a letter to the editor of the *Willamette Farmer* in 1876 "praying" that the legislature would grant women the right to vote on the licensing of alcohol sales. While assuring her readers that she was not a " 'woman's rights woman' in the common acceptation of the term," she confessed her desire for women to share men's responsibility for enforcing morality, at least in the area of temperance.[45] Although not necessarily arguing for political equality between men and women, Oregonians like Cartwright argued that women's moral superiority uniquely suited them to vote on issues such as temperance and education. Soon, advocates of full political rights for women adopted temperance supporters' strategy, arguing that women would provide a civilizing influence to politics. Abigail Scott Duniway became one of the most outspoken proponents of women's suffrage in the Pacific Northwest. The roots of Duniway's activism lay in her first-hand knowledge of the hardships women faced on the Illinois and Oregon frontiers, for although at first she played the housewife's role well enough to suit early settlers, she quickly grew discontented with the burden of household labor, agitating for hired help for farmers' wives at a time when families were only beginning to afford paid field hands. In 1859, before she had fully developed her philosophy, Duniway wrote that she wanted "to see ladies content . . . to use *cradles* for ballot-boxes, in which they have a right to plant, not votes, but *voters*."[46] But the more suffering she observed on the part of Willamette Valley women, the more convinced she became that women could not rely solely on their indirect influence as mothers. She began campaigning for female suffrage through public speaking and in the pages of her weekly paper the *New Northwest*, and her message gradually gained recognition among Oregonians of all ages.[47]

Indeed, Duniway's success is largely due to the fact that she promoted women's suffrage within the context of both first- and second-generation Oregonians' domestic ideology. To the frontier generation, she argued that women's moral influence was needed at the ballot box, and that political participation was consistent with middle-class ladyhood. As aging settlers sought to memorialize their own achievements, she added that women deserved the vote due to their equal role in civilizing the frontier. Meanwhile, Duniway published articles in the *New Northwest* addressed to "The Girl of the Period," encouraging her not only to excel as the "keeper of the home" but also to achieve meaningful accomplishments rather than slaving over the laundry or wasting time on fancy handiwork.[48] Perhaps most important of all, features in Duniway's newspaper reassured New Women that supporting female suffrage would not challenge their femininity. In fact, in an 1876 article, she challenged Mary Mason Murdoch's conservative formulation of females as either "giddy butterflies," "busy bees," or "women's righters." "Read it again, women," Duniway urged, "and see if after all there is much more credit attached to being members of one of these classes than to another. Rendered in plain terms, it means that you must either be the servant, the tool, or the dictator of men, and you know full well that you desire to be neither."[49] Thus, while persuading first-generation women that suffrage would assist them in their work as civilizers, Duniway reassured their daughters that their desire for the vote would not cost them their modern womanly ideals.[50]

Duniway's newspaper published articles that sought to debunk men's arguments against women's suffrage while simultaneously validating their belief in separate gender spheres. "Your vote we do not want," one *New Northwest* writer reassured male readers, "but we do want a vote of our own." Also playing on Mason's critique of "giddy butterflies" and "women's righters," this author promised, "[I]t won't take us all day to deposit a ballot, either, by hastening home to tie on aprons and dish up the family dumplings in good time and excellent style."[51] Another author claimed that it was hard-working farm wives rather than "idlers and butterflies" who sought women's suffrage; therefore, granting women the vote was in fact in farmers' best interest—since most farmers were married, suffrage would give farming regions proportionately larger representation. "Woman not only needs the ballot," *New Northwest* authors asserted, "but the State needs woman."[52]

Oregonians' political views did not change overnight—after all, even Abigail Scott Duniway had come to her radical views gradually. But little by little, beliefs about women held by Oregon settlers and their children evolved—much as Duniway's had—in favor of more rights and a more public role for women. For example, in 1859, first-generation settler Maria Locey wrote an essay on women's rights that agreed with Duniway's early view that women's purity and moral influence belonged within the domestic sphere. In this essay, Locey argued that women were too pure to be involved with politics and should instead influence less-moral men using their pens and the press. Yet fourteen years later, Locey reread this essay and penciled a note negating her earlier opinions. Perhaps influenced by second-generation women's pro-suffrage arguments, she commented that the 1859 essay "was written by an enthusiastic *girl* of eighteen. The same *woman* at the age of thirty-two adds 'Fiddlesticks!' "[53] Like Duniway, Locey gradually became convinced that women could not rely on indirect influence to improve society. Over time, more and more Oregonians of both generations came to accept the same idea.[54]

A few of the more liberal second-generation Oregonians went further than acceptance to fully embrace Duniway's call for female participation in the public sphere. Nellie Hill, for one, had learned to think independently at an early age, and with her family's encouragement, she studied at Stanford University, where she became very involved in the Women's Rights movement. She even corresponded with Duniway regarding lectures such as "The Moral Responsibility of Womanhood" and "The Ideal and the Real Girl."[55] Nellie Hill believed that women should exhibit strong moral character, but she challenged the prevailing wisdom that women should remain in the home, influencing the world indirectly through their husbands and children. As she explained to her mother in 1894, Nellie believed that all boys should marry because their wives would inspire them to become better men. In contrast, she was "quite convinced that it is dangerous for women to marry" because "[t]hey have not been raised to find out life." Unlike men, she declared, women "are quite civilized enough without getting married."[56]

Many second-generation Oregonians disagreed with Nellie Hill's conviction that women should not marry, including Harry Denlinger, the man with whom she eventually fell in love. Although he claimed that he did not object to women voting if they desired to do so, Harry firmly disagreed with Nellie's adamant call for suffrage and for a career on par with men, stating: "[F]or the life of me I do not see why woman should want to do everything that men do simply because they can."[57] While paying lip service to women's abilities, Harry clearly believed that women should remain within the domestic sphere.

Nellie tried to persuade Harry of her feminist views and remained reluctant to marry him. As their debate continued, Harry insisted: "I do not think it is natural for women to be in the business and rush of life. I do not think *as a class* they are fit for it. There are physical hinderances which prevent." Under duress he admitted that there might be exceptions to this rule, if women *chose* to participate in the masculine world of business. In addition, in response to apparently strong arguments from Nellie, he confessed that whereas she appeared quite knowledgeable about the New Woman, he had not given the subject much thought. Still, he insisted,

"[N]ot enough importance is given to the work that women do already."[58] Harry apparently hoped that Nellie would be willing to be a housewife if men sufficiently valued her domestic work.

Despite their differing views, Nellie and Harry eventually married. Nellie—who wished to be a lawyer—was far more passionate about the law than her husband—who *was* a lawyer. But Harry's commitment to traditional gender roles prevented Nellie from pursuing her intended profession. In fact, Nellie fell victim to the very dangers she had cited when arguing that women should not marry. In the end, ill health and her husband's resistance cut short Nellie's dreams of a career in the world of men. She did not live long enough to vote alongside Abigail Scott Duniway in 1914.[59]

Duniway, Nellie Hill, and a handful of other second-generation settlers illustrate the passion that developed for many around women's political rights, as well as the preference some women had for careers over families. These progressive young people rejected their contemporaries' desire for women's lives to be purely decorative, believing that their morally superior influence should extend into the wider world outside the home. Yet, as their faith in women's inherent morality shows, even the most outspoken suffrage advocates did not ultimately challenge their society's belief in fundamental differences between men and women. These second-generation women redefined—but ultimately failed to reject—the domestic ideology brought west by their mothers and refined by their less-radical peers.[60]

Conclusion

Second-generation women accepted their mothers' teaching that women were morally superior to men and specially suited to domestic work. However, changing economic conditions and increased access to education changed the ways in which many lived out their domestic ideology. Some young women built on their conventional role to become "busy bees," maintaining the family home and providing a moral influence for their entire families. Others, while not abandoning their status as housewives, pursued middle-class social activities that highlighted their participation in the growing consumer culture. For a minority of second-generation women, though, the family home became stifling. Those like Abigail Scott Duniway and Nellie Hill sought to expand women's sphere far beyond the barnyard to permit female participation in the male realm of work and politics. But even these New Women never questioned their parents' philosophy that women were fundamentally different from—and more ethically advanced than—men. Whether they were busy bees, social butterflies, New Women, or some combination of the three, second-generation Willamette Valley women adjusted, but did not eliminate, the boundary that surrounded their domestic sphere.

CHAPTER 6

Remembering and Reinventing Oregon Pioneers

At a 1901 meeting of the Elizabeth Thurston-Odell Cabin No. 8 of the Oregon Native Daughters (OND), guest speaker Mrs. Minto "gave a vivid picture of the past, a glimpse of her own pioneer life" as an early settler woman, "reminding us of the noble, silent women who helped to sow Oregon to the Union." At the group's next meeting, Mrs. Minto urged members to collect "historical incidents and experiences of domestic life from pioneer women," so that a record of their "heroic lives" might be preserved.[1] In following Mrs. Minto's urging, second-generation women at the turn of the twentieth century would carry on the memories of the early settlers—while at the same time actively shaping and redefining them.

First-generation Oregonians had worked hard to establish the farms, communities, and domestic spaces that symbolized white "civilization." By 1893, they could join historian Frederick Jackson Turner in celebrating the passing of the frontier and unite with Americans throughout the nation in devotion to the ideal of Progress. As they did so, however, these settlers anxiously struggled to define their own place both within their nation and within their individual communities. The anxiety was particularly intense for those watching the ease of modern life rapidly displacing the hard work they had known in earlier times.[2]

Put simply, midwesterners had migrated to Oregon in search of economic opportunity. Yet they had also come seeking better versions of themselves, intending to participate in the market on their own terms and use their new prosperity to live out their conservative dream of becoming manly providers and true women. Most who came to the Willamette Valley did establish successful farms with clearly defined men's and women's spheres, and many families even produced masculine farmers and feminine home-makers in the second generation. Despite these accomplishments, however, the first generation was not content at the turn of the century because a variety of changes had challenged their gender ideology throughout migra-tion and settlement. Frontier conditions opposed women's status as proper ladies, economic changes ended men's dreams of settling their descendants on their donation land claims, and advanced age weakened the boundaries between men's and women's roles. Meanwhile, rather than continuing the behavioral gentrification begun by these early settlers, the younger genera-tions embraced modern conveniences and new fashions that directly chal-lenged the first generation's feminine ideal. All the first generation's hard work seemed to be slipping away.

Reacting to these changes, early settlers sought to build solidarity with other men and women of their generation. Utilizing new railroad and communication networks, they gathered with other aging settlers to remi-nisce, developing new identities for themselves in the process. As they proudly pronounced their many accomplishments as hardy pioneers, these Oregonians also developed distinct vocabulary and imagery to maintain separate spheres for male and female settlers. Frontier farmers became Indian fighters and community and nation builders, while their wives were subsumed under a single iconic pioneer mother.[3]

As members of the first generation reminded themselves and their off-spring of their deeds as brave pioneers and self-sacrificing mothers, they effectively rewrote their life stories. Amid declarations that the American frontier had closed, these early Oregon settlers developed a declension nar-rative that highlighted their bravery on the trail and frontier. In addition, this narrative partially united them with their immediate descendents as it emphasized the lack of morality and work ethic that both the first and the second generation saw in their successors—the third generation. After struggling to alter their place within Willamette Valley society, early settlers and their children failed to fully embrace the latest social mores that were the ironic fulfillment of early settlers' decades of hard work. Instead, they clung to symbolism that underlined women's domesticity and developed rhetoric that resisted or disguised changes in social roles. These symbols and words, steeped as they were in early settlers' gender ideology, were adopted by generations to come in Oregon and across the United States as they memorialized the accomplishments of the pioneers.[4]

Generational Differences

In their reminiscences, many first- and second-generation settlers commented on perceived differences between themselves and their children. Like people of many other ages and places, they became convinced late in life that the younger generation's existence was much easier than their own had been.[5] In the case of late-nineteenth-century Oregonians, however, these complaints also highlighted significant changes that occurred over the first half-century of settlement in the Willamette Valley. Older women, who sought to establish their class status through devoted homemaking and ethical behavior, were particularly concerned about what they perceived as laziness and loose morals in the third generation. They failed to appreciate the extent to which their grandchildren's behavior was made possible by their own efforts to separate men's and women's work spheres.

Just as first-generation women were highly critical of the greater freedoms experienced by their daughters during the 1870s and 1880s, by the early twentieth century, many second-generation women joined their mothers in complaining about the next generation's prospects. For one thing, while some settlers' daughters had worked as teachers prior to marriage, there were even more employment opportunities for third-generation women. A few entered male-dominated professions such as law and medicine, and many more worked in clerical positions or entered more "feminine" professions such as nursing. These women also appear to have either postponed marriage or to have worked during marriage—in 1910, only half of Oregon women under the age of twenty-five were married, and nearly one quarter of women aged twenty-one to forty-four were employed.[6] Along with greater mobility aboard trains and automobiles, new professional openings and delayed marriages exposed third-generation women to greater social freedoms and a more significant public role than even the New Women of their mothers' time had experienced.[7]

A number of second-generation women commented in their reminiscences on how much easier they thought things to be for members of the third generation, whose lives they believed were ruled by comfort and pleasure. Looking back on their own childhood, the older women wistfully recalled working in the fields as well as doing domestic work. "When I was a girl," Sarah Elizabeth Kinney Laighton remembered, "we had no movies, no joy rides in autos, not very many parties, but plenty of housework and mending and taking care of babies and nursing and things of that kind. It seems to me that the young women of today have a much easier time than when I was a girl."[8] Laighton and her peers implied that the younger generation was less motivated to work hard than they themselves had been. Further, they saw younger women's greater freedom from labor as a sign of slothfulness or even moral failure.[9]

But these second-generation women failed to acknowledge that, to the extent that they were freed from toiling in the fields and the kitchen, the third generation was actually living out their mothers' and grandmothers' dream. Clearly, the first generation had worked hard to ensure that their daughters would not become field hands, and the second generation, in turn, had embraced greater material comfort and social refinement for themselves as well as for their daughters. Yet in later years, the second generation criticized these same daughters for failing to appreciate their comfortable existence. Rather than interpreting their daughters' relative ease as a symbol of their own accomplishments, these aging New Women reverted to the rhetoric of the first generation, who believed that women should be the moral guardians of their homes and society.

Reinforcing older women's concern for young ladies' morality were the changing sexual mores of the "Roaring Twenties." Just as the second generation had eagerly embraced eastern consumerism in the 1880s and 1890s, their children enthusiastically took part in the 1920s youth culture embodied in the flapper, causing mothers to worry when their daughters donned shorter skirts or shingled their hair. One second-generation woman, whose parents had forbidden her to attend dances in her own youth, spoke out against the "flappers of today" and their "necking parties." Comparing old pastimes to these new, wild parties, she said: "[O]ur play games, as we young folks used to call 'Drop the Handkerchief', playing 'Postoffice', and other kissing games, were innocent."[10] The second generation failed to recognize that, in reacting against their girls' activities, they had adopted the same controlling manner they had themselves rebelled against when young —when they were actually paving the way for the third generation's supposed moral turpitude.[11]

Gendered Roles in Pioneer Organizations

From their formation, Oregon pioneer organizations established distinct roles for men and women that were shaped by the first generation's gender ideals. Even these culturally conservative pioneer organizations were not immune to women's changing social roles, ultimately enabling second generation women to move into leadership positions. However, the first-generation settlers who made up the dwindling ranks of the Oregon Pioneer Association (OPA) and other groups remained attached to the roles they had painstakingly carved out on the frontier.

The primary stated goal of the OPA and other pioneer organizations was to remember the contributions and accomplishments of the early settlers. Unlike many Oregon groups, such as the Grange, fraternal orders, and women's coffee clubs, pioneer associations explicitly set out to celebrate the first generation's ideology as well as their actions. Since, for this reason, it is likely that these organizations' members were more conservative than those in progressive clubs, the gender ideology reflected in their membership should not be thought to fully represent that of the Oregon population as a whole. However, because activists such as Abigail Scott Duniway participated in the OPA, neither should its members' perspectives be too quickly dismissed as only reactionary.[12]

Early on, the OPA sought to open its membership to women, but they held a distinct and subsidiary place within it. The organization's initial constitution stated: "All persons may become members of this Society, who arrived upon the coast, or were born in this country, prior to January 1st, 1851, and are twenty-one years of age."[13] This was amended in 1875 to clarify that "[a]ll immigrants [i.e., white settlers], *male or female*, who reside[d] within the bounds of the original Territory of Oregon" were welcome.[14] Despite the gender equality this language suggests, however, the OPA dictated differing duties for male and female members—for one thing, perhaps in recognition of men's traditional control over household finances, only male members paid membership dues. In 1876, several female members requested that the constitution be amended to eliminate this disparity. "[T]hey argue," explained the recording secretary, "that they wish to be placed on equal footing with male members." But even though the organization had limited financial resources, it did not adopt the proposed amendment. As late as 1887, when a significant number of Oregon women were participating in paid work before marriage, they still did not pay dues to the OPA.[15]

The active roles each gender took on within the OPA further highlight the different meanings of membership for males and females. Throughout the nineteenth century, the organization's board of directors was consistently male, while women served on arrangement committees, providing meals and decorations for the annual reunions. In 1891, in fact, a group of "pioneer ladies were appointed to take entire charge of" a lunch to be served on Pioneer Day.[16] Thus, while men took control of decision making within the OPA as they did in Oregon politics—and in their own households—they entrusted complete responsibility for all the more domestic tasks to their female peers.[17]

As its founding members passed away, the OPA gradually loosened membership requirements to permit settlers' descendants to join the organization, but older members expected these newcomers to adopt conventional functions. Although many second-generation women had taken on more prominent roles in Oregon society by the 1880s and 1890s, their position within the early-settler-dominated OPA remained fixed within the first generation's gender boundaries. For example, first-generation ladies served refreshments at the 1895 reunion, and "[p]ioneer daughters assisted in serving."[18] These daughters were thereby accepted into the social world of the early settlers, but not on their own terms.[19]

Other, smaller pioneer organizations drew gender distinctions very similar to those of the OPA. One group, the Polk County Pioneers, emphasized distinct social roles in the prizes they awarded to the oldest settlers at their 1901 reunion: a rocking chair went to the oldest "[p]ioneer lady," and an easy chair went to the oldest "pioneer gentleman." While the rocking chair might very well have been valued as a comfortable place in which the female prize-winner might rock her grandchildren or do the fine needlework popular among elderly first-generation women, it also identified her symbolically as a "pioneer mother." Meanwhile, the easy chair presented to the oldest pioneer man emphasized his retirement from an active life providing for his family, and at the same time gave him a stately seat from which to supervise his household.[20]

Various competitions hosted by the Polk County Pioneers likewise emphasized the lingering differences in male and female roles among their children. "Native sons" competed in bicycle races that recognized second-generation men's growing interest in sports, an embodiment of the new manly man. In contrast, despite women's growing interest in active leisure throughout the United States, Polk County "native daughters" competed in the categories of "best looking" and "best dressed," thereby reinforcing perceptions of second-generation women as "giddy butterflies." Thus, the accomplishments for which each sex was rewarded served to emphasize the persistent distinctions between men's and women's social roles even for young people at the turn of the twentieth century.[21]

The fact that some shifts *did* occur in women's place within these conservative organizations indicates the extent to which women had gained a greater voice in Oregon society by this time. In 1895, Mrs. Robert A. Miller— unlike her peers who bemoaned social change—marveled to OPA meeting participants that "[T]he last 25 or 30 years has wrought a wonderful [i.e., remarkable] change in the status of women. Do any of you pioneers of 1840 or '50 or even '60 remember that there were many women doctors, women lawyers, women preachers, women lecturers or speakers, during those years?"[22] Yet perhaps even more remarkable than the handful of women who became doctors or lawyers was the fact that a woman like Mrs. Miller had been invited to speak at an OPA annual reunion in the first place. Mrs. Miller's speech represented a significant change in women's visibility within an organization that had traditionally relegated women to domestic labor.

In fact, when Mrs. Miller made her speech, it had been only thirteen years since Abigail Scott Duniway had been the first woman to request a platform at an OPA annual reunion. Before a predominately male audience in 1882, Duniway read an address written by Judge Chenoweth, who was too ill to attend the reunion. Following this reading, Duniway received the president's permission to represent Oregon's pioneer women in her own words. The OPA secretary recorded in the official reunion minutes that Duniway's speech was "accepted the more cheerfully" by those in attendance "because she had already demonstrated the fact in reading Judge Chenoweth's address that a woman could sometimes represent a man."[23] It was this general acceptance of Duniway by her audience that encouraged her to go further, lecturing her fellow pioneers on the importance of enfranchising women. She argued that the leading men of the state, including those in the Oregon Pioneer Association, must give women the vote. Only in that way, she contended, could they protect their wives and mothers "from the proscriptive ballots of the lawless, ignorant and wicked hordes who presume to dictate our destiny."[24] Duniway thus relied on her accepted role as an expert on women's experience to gain the right to teach her political beliefs, playing to early settlers' insecurities about their class identity in an effort to win enfranchisement.

As the years passed, Duniway's confidence in speaking before the OPA grew, suggesting that some degree of change was indeed occurring within it. In 1896, making no excuses for being a female speaker at a meeting, Duniway took the initiative to submit a resolution in favor of equal rights for men and women based on a common pioneering experience.[25] In a departure from her 1882 speech, Duniway claimed *for herself* the right to speak and even to offer resolutions, skillfully proving women's equality to men using her audience's desire to commemorate the efforts of Oregon pioneers. While Duniway's women's rights resolution was not approved unanimously, it was "adopted by a rising vote," representing a marked change from the mere tolerance of her less boldly stated claim to suffrage rights fourteen years earlier. Thus, while Oregon would not grant women the vote for another sixteen years, Duniway's changing tactics, and her audience's increasingly positive response, indicate a growing acceptance of a public role for women in the late nineteenth century—both in Oregon's political system, and within the OPA itself.[26]

Still, despite having gained the right to speak at OPA meetings by the 1890s, women's places within the organization remained largely unchanged even as the early settlers' children and grandchildren came of age. In fact, perhaps in reaction to second- and third-generation women's growing equality with men (symbolized by their gaining suffrage in 1912), women's persistently distinct role in the OPA was formalized with the creation of a Woman's Auxiliary in 1913. The stated purpose of this offshoot was to provide "an entertainment at the annual reunions ... and to assist in promoting good fellowship among the members of the association by such other means as may be considered proper."[27] Yet its actual effect was to grant women control over the organization's "women's work" and to highlight this work's feminine nature, in the process reinforcing the differentiation of men's and women's places within the group. Utilizing skills that Oregon women gained through participation in other clubs at the turn of the century, the auxiliary maintained an independent budget and its own association records. Yet, as its name implied, members of the Woman's Auxiliary *served* the male members of the OPA rather than seeking greater equality within it.[28]

Second-generation men and women acted in keeping with their parents' gender ideology when they formed pioneer organizations of their own, some of the most prominent of which were the Native Sons of Oregon (NSO), the Native Daughters of Oregon (NDO), and the Sons and Daughters of Oregon Pioneers (SDOP). Although the SDOP was explicitly a coeducational organization, like the OPA it was apparently led by its male members, who adopted the complex language of business or fraternal organizations as it gathered "for social, literary and other purposes of mutual benefit, and the development of the physical and mental capacities of the membership of this corporation individually and collectively and to perpetuate . . . the memories of Pioneers of Oregon."[29] In contrast, the goals of the NDO were described in more casual and domestic terms, harkening back to the ideal of its members' mothers. Like the OPA, the NDO sought to preserve the history of Oregon and its pioneer men and women, but those within it also sought "[t]o help each other as members of one family, as did [their] ancestors, the sturdy pioneers, in the early years of Oregon."[30] Hence, while both organizations gathered for the same general purpose, the different styles used to state this purpose revealed distinct social roles.[31]

The ways in which the NSO and NDO operated and cooperated reflect their expectations for each gender as well as the continuing constraints on women's participation in the public sphere. Like the OPA, the NSO drew on men's greater financial resources, initially charging a three-dollar initiation fee, which they soon raised to five dollars. In contrast, the NDO charged only one dollar at initiation, contributing more labor than money to their historical cause as they helped the Native Sons with tasks like building their float for a July Fourth celebration. The NDO also presented the NSO with a silk banner to represent their organization—a gift presumably made by NDO seamstresses but, notably, financed in part by a loan from the Native Sons' richer coffers. In fact, the NSO had so little money that financial limitations made it difficult for them to function at a statewide level and for local chapters to find places to congregate. For example, after the organization's Portland headquarters disbanded in June 1904, members of the Tabitha Brown Cabin No. 24 had to give up their meeting space in the Odd Fellows' Hall. But, dedicated to studying Oregon history, they voted to continue their meetings and gathered instead in members' homes. Lacking the financial and organizational resources of second-generation men, the NDO thereby returned to their own social space, the domestic sphere.[32]

The extent to which native daughters clung to their mother's gender ideology can be seen quite clearly in the NDO's formal rituals. New initiates to the organization learned that its symbol was a log cabin, "the sacred abiding place of those who have gone before, and who have left us a heritage to be enshrined in our hearts and the hearts of our descendants."[33] (In fact, chapters within both the NDO and the OND were designated "cabins" and named in honor of prominent pioneer women.) During the NDO initiation ceremony, an organization member read a text purportedly from a woman pioneer, entrusting to the new members the legacy of first-generation females' work on the frontier. In this text, which relied more on the late-nineteenth-century "age of homespun" myth than on reality, the fictional pioneer woman professed: "We toiled and spun for you . . . our children, and you have now loyally taken up the work so laboriously begun by us in early days in Oregon."[34] The fact that few early settlers truly spun wool or flax was unimportant—what mattered was perpetuating the domestic ideology held by first-generation women settlers. By joining the Native Daughters of Oregon, second-generation Oregon women were incorporated into the legend of the self-sacrificing pioneer mother.[35]

Those belonging to second-generation pioneer associations adhered to their parents' ideology more than did others their age; however, even more than the OPA, the NDO and the SDOP were gradually influenced by the twentieth century's changing ideas about gender. This becomes apparent through comparing the activities in which the first- and second-generation pioneer organizations engaged. For example, as we have seen, in 1913 the OPA created a Woman's Auxiliary to continue women's work in planning—and presumably cleaning up after—banquets at the annual pioneer reunions. In contrast, at least one NDO cabin voted to hire a woman to wash the dishes following a pioneer supper for elderly pioneers as early as 1903. Although they had limited financial resources, these younger women did not expect such selfless service as that provided by female members of the OPA, so they hired another woman to take on the domestic chores that they were unwilling to complete themselves. In addition, the SDOP gradually accepted greater female power, ultimately electing third-generation Nancy Drain Singleton president in 1927. Thus even among these particularly backward-looking children of Oregon, women were to some extent freed from domestic toil in favor of greater leadership in their pioneer organizations as well as in their own homes.[36]

Pioneers and Pioneer Mothers

By the 1870s, early settlers recognized that their numbers were thinning with each passing year, and that their economic, political, and social dominance within their families and communities was beginning to wane. They sought to prevent this loss of their legacy by writing their memoirs and joining organizations such as the OPA, which was established "to perpetuate the history and incidents connected with the settlement on the Pacific coast" and to "promote social intercourse and collect from living witnesses facts worthy of preservation."[37] But after the turn of the century, another method of preserving settlers' achievements became available as second- and third-generation Oregonians joined their contemporaries across the nation in erecting monuments to their pioneer ancestors. Both in their memoirs and through monuments, first-generation Oregonians unconsciously shaped the ways in which they would be remembered.

It is not surprising that when early settlers sat down to record their memoirs, passing time and their desire to honor their achievements colored their depictions of themselves and their fellow settlers. Yet the adjectives and anecdotes they chose to use did not simply glorify early pioneers—they also consistently emphasized gender differences. Oregon pioneers described their generation, as in the words of prominent settler John Minto, as "Self-reliant, determined men; devoted, loyal, bravely enduring women."[38] This type of language called attention to men's most masculine characteristics and honored them for their independence and achievements, while it re-membered women as loyal and devoted wives and mothers whose status was derived more from their relationships to men than from their own accomplishments. More specifically, settlers remembered, while pioneer men had courageously journeyed to Oregon, opened the Far West to settle-ment, and established the political and economic basis for the State, pioneer women's sole important role, like republican mothers a half-century earlier, was to raise future sons and daughters of Oregon. In memory, even more than in daily life, Oregonians erased women's productive work by hiding it behind the rhetoric of their domestic ideal, and all of women's less "femi-nine" accomplishments—from traveling the Oregon Trail to battling fires and wild animals to toiling on their families' land claims—were absorbed by their role of protecting and nurturing future Oregon leaders. The ideal first-generation woman thus became the iconic "Pioneer Mother."[39]

Pioneer mothers were quite revered by their descendants during the early twentieth century, as can be seen in the fact that the Native Sons and Daughters of Oregon annually honored a "Queen Mother of Oregon." Mary Ramsey Lemons Woods was crowned "Mother Queen" in 1907, at the age of 120 years, and twenty years later, the tradition still held strong as Mary Dunn proudly accepted the same designation.[40] While these women were certainly honored for their various achievements as early settlers, the title given to them primarily emphasized their maternal role in birthing Oregon's future, both literally and figuratively.[41]

Perhaps the most striking manifestation of young people's admiration for their pioneer mothers can be seen in the monuments built by organizations in Oregon and throughout the United States after the closing of the frontier. As early as 1883, W. Lair Hill urged "some capable hand" in the OPA "to gather up the scattered materials and erect a monument to the pioneer mothers of Oregon,"[42] and while no statue builder came forward at that time, a pioneer monument movement had taken hold across the nation by the early twentieth century. In 1915, for example, the Pioneer Mother Monument Association raised $25,000 in popular subscriptions to place Charles Grafly's bronze statue *The Pioneer Mother* in front of San Francisco's Palace of Fine Arts. The pedestal's inscription summarized the traits for which pioneer mothers were honored throughout the country: "To an assemblage of men busied with the perishable rewards of the day," it declared, "she brought the three-fold leaven of enduring society—Faith, Gentleness, and the Nurture of Children."[43] Other groups erected similar monuments in the two subsequent decades. Between 1928 and 1929, the National Society of the Daughters of the American Revolution (NSDAR) erected twelve identical granite amalgam statues of the *Pioneer Mother/Madonna of the Trail* as part of the organization's "Pioneer Mother Movement." As sculpted by August Leimbach, this iconic pioneer mother carries a baby in one arm and a rifle in the other, prepared to protect that baby and the small boy who clings to her apron (fig. 6.1). Future president Harry Truman dedicated each NSDAR statue along the National Old Trails Road, from Bethesda, Maryland to Upland, California, in honor of the 800,000 "intrepid women" who participated in the nation's westward expansion.[44] A similarly sun-bonneted pioneer mother sculpted by Bryant Baker won the widely publicized "Pioneer Woman" competition promoted by oil tycoon Ernest W. Marland. Bearing the Bible rather than a rifle, this *Pioneer*

6.1 August Leimbach, *Pioneer Mother/Madonna of the Trail*, 1928. This statue is one of twelve identical granite amalgam statues erected by the National Society of the Daughters of the American Revolution's "Pioneer Mother Movement" in the years of 1928 and 1929. (Photograph by the author)

Woman of Ponca, Oklahoma, strides confidently toward the southwestern horizon, gently leading her young son—and, by extension, American society—by the hand. Like the Leimbach and Grafly mothers, this statue represents emotional strength and determination, and her defining characteristic is her relationship to the children she carries or leads westward. As the "Pioneer Mother" title suggests, although pioneer women were confident and might even carry a weapon, their purpose is to protect rather than to conquer.[45]

A quieter domestic image of the Oregon pioneer mother appears in bas-relief in a large marble plaque in the main lobby of the Oregon State Library. Gabriel Lavare's pioneer mother is seated, holding a book in her hand while she imparts knowledge to her son, who literally learns at her knee. According to a 1939 article announcing the completion of the building, the plaque symbolized "the continuity of knowledge and learning, handed down from one generation to the next."[46] This plaque celebrates a nurturing mother safely bounded within the domestic sphere and freed from the dangers of the Overland Trail depicted in many other pioneer mother statues. Yet examined in the context of early-twentieth-century pioneer mother imagery, it is not surprising that this knowledge and learning is passed down from a maternal figure to a young boy, who would go on to lead the next generation.[47]

Not all Oregon pioneer monuments were exclusively devoted to women, but they all embraced a similar pioneer iconography in which women appeared gentle, acting boldly only if necessary to protect their children, while frontiersmen were depicted as bravely and independently conquering the West. Leo Friedlander's marble sculpture *The Covered Wagon*, for example, which guards the entrance to the 1938 Oregon Statehouse (fig. 6.2), shows a family group, and both its caption and its imagery make clear that "Valiant *Men* Have Thrust Our Frontiers to the Setting Sun."[48] Dressed in fringed buckskin, the man stands confidently, with one hand at his hip and the other shading his eyes, as he gazes off into the setting sun and the future. Meanwhile, his demure wife kneels beside their son, her arm entwined with his to restrain him as he seeks to step boldly forward in imitation of his father. Another monument, Avard T. Fairbanks' 1924 *The Old Oregon Trail*, depicts a pioneer woman seated in a covered wagon clutching a baby in her arms, while her husband drives their oxen over a rocky stretch of trail. While Fairbanks' work accurately portrays men's and women's separate work roles on the trail, its dominant message is that men were brave and hard-working,

6.2 Leo Friedlander, *The Covered Wagon*, circa 1937. The caption of this massive marble sculpture, which guards the entrance to Oregon's 1938 Statehouse, declares that "Valiant Men Have Thrust Our Frontiers to the Setting Sun." The man in this family grouping gazes boldly into the future; his wife kneels timidly beside their son, attempting to protect him. (Photograph by the author)

while women were timid and maternal. In each of these Oregon sculptures, the pioneer mother's role, like that depicted in the pioneer women statues erected across the country in the 1920s, is to protect her young son and ensure that he grows up to be a valiant man like his father.[49]

One of the most skillful portrayers of gender-specific pioneer iconography was Oregon sculptor A. Phimister Proctor, who completed many well-known works. His famous *Pioneer Mother*,[50] which was dedicated in Kansas City, Missouri, in 1926, depicts a seated woman proudly gazing ahead with a sunbonnet dangling down her back and an infant in her arms—imagery that mirrors that of Fairbanks' woman in the covered wagon, Baker's *Pioneer Woman*, and Leimbach's *Madonna of the Trail*.[51] All of these maternal images contrast sharply with Proctor's 1918 depiction of a heroic male *Pioneer*, who is shown with a rifle thrown over his shoulder and an ox whip in his hand as he strides purposefully into the future (fig. 6.3). When Frederick V. Holman, Oregon Historical Society president and former president of the OPA and the SDOP, unveiled this latter work on Eugene's University of Oregon campus in 1919, he declared that the "statue symbolizes and immortalizes in a remarkable way the Oregon pioneer and his qualities—his courage, his determination, his instincts and his high ideals and those . . . of the people of which the Oregon pioneer is a fine specimen and example."[52] Like Ulric Ellerhusen's *Oregon Pioneer*, which later came to dominate the tower of Oregon's statehouse, Proctor's *Pioneer* appears ready to conquer nature, American Indians, or anything else that might stand in his way. The artist's *Pioneer Mother*, on the other hand, joined other monuments to female pioneers in emphasizing their placid motherhood.[53]

New York attorney Burt Brown Barker was familiar with Proctor's *Pioneer Mother* and Baker's *Pioneer Woman*, but he had something else in mind when he asked Proctor to create another *Pioneer Mother* for the Eugene campus to complement Proctor's earlier *Pioneer*. Rather than memorializing the hardships of the Overland Trail or the "battles and sorrows of pioneering" portrayed in other pioneer memorials, Proctor's new sculpture would remember pioneer women as "they sat in the evening glow resting from their labors."[54] The University of Oregon *Pioneer Mother*, which was dedicated on Mother's Day in 1932, depicted an elderly woman who sat gazing contemplatively at the partially-open book resting in her lap (fig. 6.4).[55] This statue, which conformed closely to Barker's specifications, depicts pioneer women quite differently than does the iconic young pioneer

6.3 A. Phimister Proctor, *Pioneer*, 1918. (Photograph by the author)

mother with babe and rifle in hand. In fact, only the bas-relief on the statue's marble base makes reference to the hardships faced by early settlers. However, like Lavare's bas-relief plaque of the bookish female pioneer, this memorial still emphasizes the pioneer woman's domesticity, putting her in marked contrast to her brave male complement.

6.4 A. Phimister Proctor, *Pioneer Mother*, 1932. In contrast to Proctor's earlier male *Pioneer*, this bronze sculpture depicts an elderly pioneer mother at rest within her domestic sphere, the book on her lap representing her piety and her role in protecting the future of Oregon civilization. (Photograph by the author)

Conclusion

In 1928, Catherine Thomas Morris, who had traveled overland to Oregon with her family at age eight, told interviewer Fred Lockley: "I cannot help thinking that, as busy as they were, the pioneers of Oregon had more time to be kindly, thoughtful, and considerate than the people of today."[56] Morris' tendency to look backward and to idolize the early settlers was a common one in the early twentieth century, when Oregonians formed organizations expressly to celebrate pioneers' accomplishments. However, the state's collective memory was shaped by individual experiences of *fin-de-siècle* Oregon life as well as by gender ideology. Forgetting the first generation's struggles to separate men's and women's work, later generations honored brave pioneer men who provided for their families in the wilderness, while women who had actually worked both in the fields and at home became a universalized pioneer mother, who gave birth to a civilized country in the midst of savagery.

CONCLUSION

The Willamette Valley was settled by farming families who carried with them a conservative dream of escaping the pressures of the market, fulfilling middle-class gender expectations, and settling their children—and their grandchildren—on self-sufficient farms. However, the same conditions that lured these conservative men and women westward offered opportunities for their descendants to embrace new markets and develop new gender identities. On the Overland Trail, for example, young Mary Ellen Todd learned to use an ox whip and enjoyed unusually flexible gender roles, while after settlement, Fred Locey never married, devoting himself instead to field labor and raising chickens. In an even more significant departure from tradition, Nellie Hill attended Stanford University and foreswore marriage for much of her life. Todd, Locey, Hill, and thousands of others who grew up on the Oregon frontier made decisions that challenged their parents' domestic ideology. How, then, did second-generation Oregonians develop a shared memory of monolithic brave pioneer men and maternal pioneer women?

In part, the answer lies in the second generation's diversity. For every Fred Locey and Nellie Hill, there were dozens of more conventional people like Harry Denlinger or Susan Coolidge, who shared their parents' belief in distinct roles for men and women. Many young men, like Oliver Jory, followed in their father's footsteps both professionally and socially, and even for Nellie Hill, romance eventually took the place of her radical views and led her to take a conservative husband. As for Fred Locey, while he himself was never established as an independent landholder, his brothers both married and embraced traditional male work. In fact, each of his siblings chose different life paths, including his sisters—Addie married at age eighteen, incorporating her husband into the family labor network; Susie failed to find happiness when she finally married at age thirty-four, dying a year later after premature childbirth; and Mary—the youngest— earned a Bachelor of Scientific Didactics degree and taught school for many years before finally marrying at the age of fifty-one. Differing personalities, as well as varied abilities and life experiences, led all of these children of Oregon settlers to engage in different behaviors and adhere to different values.

While growing cities offered second-generation men alternatives to farm labor, their wives and sisters faced potentially more radical choices. For them, frontier conditions passed particularly quickly. Yet few settlers' daughters wholly rejected marriage or committed themselves to Abigail Scott Duniway's call for activism and woman's rights. Instead, a number of them married good providers and became "busy bees," enthusiastically taking over the domestic sphere prepared for them by their hard-working mothers. Many others struck a middle course, sharing the responsibility for economic decisions with their spouses, participating in women's clubs or pioneer organizations, and applying their domestic skills to creating fashionable bustled silk dresses or crazy quilts. In these and other ways, the second generation sought to balance their parents' instruction with new realities in the Willamette Valley as they developed their own gender identity.

The rapid changes taking place throughout the United States at the turn of the twentieth century were particularly significant in Oregon, where favorable farming conditions enabled many to achieve their dreams of separate gender spheres within a single generation. But as the second generation stood poised to achieve their parents' middle-class aspirations, they discovered that middle-class identity was a moving target. Even as they separated gender spheres and learned refined behavior, consumerism replaced these things as markers of the American middle class, and companionate relationships replaced practical marriages. But while the second generation embraced a changing domestic ideal and raised their daughters to become modern women, they still managed to cling to memories of a seemingly simpler frontier past. Thus by merging older, gender-based standards for middle-class membership with a modern myth of frontier heroism, second-generation Oregonians simultaneously responded to rapidly changing gender roles and remembered their old-fashioned parents as mas-

culine pioneers and feminine pioneer mothers. In the process, they sought
to define and defend their own, more complex gender and class identities.

The image of the pioneer mother remains powerful in Oregon to this day. In
1987, in fact, the state legislature borrowed from the Native Sons and Daughters of Oregon's (NSDO's) tradition of naming queen mothers, honoring
Tabitha Moffat Brown as "Mother of Oregon" because she "represents the
distinctive pioneer heritage and the charitable and compassionate nature of
Oregon's people."[1] Despite this seemingly inclusive identification of Brown
with the state's "pioneer heritage," her biography reveals that, nearly a
century after the NSDO began crowning queen mothers, the gender-specific
expectations for pioneer women remained. Indeed, throughout her life,
Brown maintained a quite maternal and domestic image: after bringing her
family to Oregon Territory as a widow in 1846, she completed one of her
most honored accomplishments—the establishment of an orphan asylum,
which she supported through domestic work by selling buckskin gloves she
had sewn, and which she later served as "house-mother." In addition,
"Grandma Brown" worked with two ministers to establish Tualatin Academy
and Pacific University. Motivated by her care for her family and for those less
fortunate, then, this "Mother of Oregon" utilized her domestic skills to build
institutions that would educate future generations of Oregonians.[2]

As second-generation Oregon settler Catherine Thomas Morris observed, "Each generation thinks that it is a great improvement on past
generations."[3] Thus, like many aging people, first-generation Oregonians
sought to record their experiences and achievements for posterity, and their
descendants followed suit by constructing monuments to the pioneers that
celebrated both generations past and, through the ties of heritage, their own
generation. Yet these memorials, erected everywhere from Bethesda, Mary-
land, to Seaside, Oregon, subtracted from the true complexity of history as
it collapsed those remembered into two distinct types defined by gender.

Today, the organization calling itself the Sons and Daughters of Oregon
Pioneers claims more than 1,200 members worldwide, all of whom are
descended from men and women who settled in the Oregon Country prior
to Oregon statehood in 1859.[4] No doubt their numbers have grown with
recent interest in genealogy—interest perhaps sparked by new questions of
meaning in the new millennium, and encouraged by decreased transportation costs and improved communication via the Internet. Meanwhile, the

few surviving World War II veterans—part of what journalist Tom Brokaw dubbed the "Greatest Generation"[5]—have, like their frontier forefathers, worked to insure that their accomplishments and sacrifices will not be forgotten. Like second-generation Willamette Valley settlers, members of the Baby Boom generation have found themselves caught in the narrative written by their aging parents. They are torn between honoring the sacrifices of their elders and celebrating their own accomplishments and changing values. Whether the Boomers' children will embrace monument-building like second- and third-generation Oregonians did a century ago—or will instead focus on carving their own path—remains to be seen.

ABBREVIATIONS

The following abbreviations are used in the notes and the Selected Bibliography.

BCDR   Benton County Circuit Court Divorce Records, Oregon State Archives, Salem

CCHS   Clackamas County Historical Society Library, Oregon City, Oregon

CCWSPR   Clackamas County Women's Separate Property Register, 1859–1909, Oregon State Archives, Salem

ISAW   Institute for the Study of the American West at the Autry National Center, Los Angeles, California

LCDR   Lane County Circuit Court Divorce Records, Oregon State Archives, Salem

LCWSPR   Linn County Women's Separate Property Register for 1862–1912, Oregon State Archives, Salem

MAW   Museum of the American West, Autry National Center, Los Angeles, California

MCDR   Marion County Circuit Court Divorce Records, Oregon State Archives, Salem

MCHS   Marion County Historical Society Library, Salem, Oregon

MCMWPR   Marion County Married Women's Property Register, 1859–1897, Oregon State Archives, Salem

OHS   Oregon Historical Society Research Library, Portland

OHSM   Oregon Historical Society Museum, Portland

OSA   Oregon State Archives, Salem

OSU   Oregon State University Archives, Corvallis

PCMWSPR   Polk County Married Women's Separate Property Register, 1859–1897, Oregon State Archives, Salem

UO   Special Collections, Knight Library, University of Oregon, Eugene

WCHS   Washington County Historical Society Research Library, Hillsboro, Oregon

WCWSRR   Washington County Women's Separate Rights Records, 1881–1882, Oregon State Archives, Salem

NOTES

Introduction

1. Adrietta Applegate Hixon, *On to Oregon! A True Story of a Young Girl's Journey into the West*, ed. Waldo Taylor (Weiser, Idaho: Signal-American, 1947), 45–46.

2. Fabritus Smith Papers, UO A191; "Salem Pioneer Cemetery Data," http://www.open.org/pioneerc/qls (18 August 2006).

3. John Mack Faragher, *Women and Men on the Overland Trail* (New Haven: Yale University Press, 1979); Julie Roy Jeffrey, *Frontier Women: The Trans-Mississippi West, 1840–1880* (New York: Hill and Wang, 1979). By 1850 Anglo-American settlers seeking farmland greatly outnumbered the remaining American Indians and British fur traders present in Oregon, making the Willamette Valley a "frontier" of community development rather than a "borderland" of multinational and intercultural interaction. Jeremy Adelman and Stephen Aron, "From Borderlands to Borders: Empires, Nation-States, and the Peoples in Between in North American History," *American Historical Review* 104, no. 3 (June 1999): 814–41.

4. Lillian Schlissel, *Women's Diaries of the Westward Journey* (New York: Schocken Books, 1982); Sandra L. Myres, *Westering Women and the Frontier Experience, 1800–1915* (Albuquerque: University of New Mexico Press, 1982).

5. For example, see David G. Gutiérrez, *Walls and Mirrors: Mexican Americans, Mexican Immigrants, and the Politics of Ethnicity* (Berkeley: University of California Press, 1995); George J. Sánchez, *Becoming Mexican-American: Ethnicity, Culture and Identity in Chicano Los Angeles, 1900–1945* (New York: Oxford University, 1993); David K. Yoo, *Growing Up Nisei: Race, Generation, and Culture among Japanese Americans of California, 1924–49* (Urbana: University of Illinois Press, 2000); Judy Yung, *Unbound Feet: A Social History of Chinese Women in San Francisco* (Berkeley: University of California Press, 1995). Paula Petrik similarly identified a shift in gender roles between the first and second generation of middle-class white women in the mining town of Helena, Montana. She found that the first generation were involved in maternalist social reform, while their daughters campaigned for suffrage. Paula Petrik, *No Step Backward: Women and Family on the Rocky Mountain Mining Frontier, Helena, Montana, 1865–1900* (Helena: Montana Historical Society Press, 1987).

6. Frederick Jackson Turner, "The Significance of the Frontier in American History," *Annual Report of the American Historical Association for the Year 1893* (Washington, D.C., 1894), reprinted in John Mack Faragher, *Rereading Frederick Jackson Turner: "The Significance of the Frontier in American History" and Other Essays* (New York: Henry Holt and Company, 1994), 31–60. Building on the insights of the "New Western History" (e.g., Richard White, *The Middle Ground: Indians, Empires, and Republics in the Great Lakes Region, 1650–1815* [Cambridge: Cambridge University Press, 1991]; Patricia Nelson Limerick, *The Legacy of Conquest: The Un-*

broken Past of the American West [New York: W. W. Norton & Company, 1987]), gender historians have emphasized that, despite myths of rugged masculine individualism, western intercultural power relations were often negotiated on gender terms. See, for example, Sarah Deutsch, *No Separate Refuge: Culture, Class, and Gender on the Anglo-Hispanic Frontier in the American Southwest, 1880–1940* (New York: Oxford University Press, 1987); Elizabeth Jameson and Susan Armitage, eds., *Writing the Range: Race, Class, and Culture in the Women's West* (Norman: University of Oklahoma Press, 1997); Susan Lee Johnson, *Roaring Camp: The Social World of the California Gold Rush* (New York: W. W. Norton & Company, 2000).

7. *Census Reports: Compiled from the Original Returns of the Ninth Census (June 1, 1870)* (Washington, D.C.: Government Printing Office, 1872), 1:57.

8. *Ninth Census*, 1:57; *Population of the United States in 1860; Compiled from the Original Returns of the Eighth Census* (Washington, D.C.: Government Printing Office, 1864), 401, 405; *Report on Population of the United States at the Eleventh Census: 1890* (Washington, D.C.: Government Printing Office, 1897), 1:36, 426, 448, 488, 513.

9. *Ninth Census*, 1:57; *Population of the United States in 1860*, 401, 405; *Population at the Eleventh Census*, 1:36, 426, 448, 488, 513; Kristofer Allerfeldt, *Race, Radicalism, Religion, and Restriction: Immigration in the Pacific Northwest, 1890–1924* (Westport, Conn.: Praeger Publishers, 2003), 7.

10. William A. Bowen, *The Willamette Valley: Migration and Settlement on the Oregon Frontier* (Seattle: University of Washington Press, 1978), 25, 43.

11. Bowen, *The Willamette Valley*, 53.

12. Bowen, *The Willamette Valley*, 55.

13. Richard White, *"It's Your Misfortune and None of My Own": A History of the American West* (Norman: University of Oklahoma Press, 1991), 303.

14. Bowen, *The Willamette Valley*, 22–42.

15. On California, see Robert L. Griswold, *Family and Divorce in California, 1850–1890: Victorian Illusions and Everyday Realities* (Albany: State University of New York Press, 1982); Albert L. Hurtado, *Intimate Frontiers: Sex, Gender and Culture in Old California* (Albuquerque: University of New Mexico Press, 1999); Johnson, *Roaring Camp*; Carey McWilliams, *California: The Great Exception* (New York: Current Books, 1949); Malcolm J. Rohrbough, *Days of Gold: The California Gold Rush and the American Nation* (Berkeley: University of California Press, 1997).

16. On domesticity, see Nancy F. Cott, *The Bonds of Womanhood: "Woman's Sphere" in New England, 1780–1835* (New Haven: Yale University Press, 1977); Jane H. Hunter, *How Young Ladies Became Girls: The Victorian Origins of American Girlhood* (New Haven: Yale University Press, 2002); Mary P. Ryan, *Cradle of the Middle Class: The Family in Oneida County, New York, 1790–1865* (New York: Cambridge University Press, 1981); Barbara Welter, "The Cult of True Womanhood, 1820–1860" *American Quarterly* 18 (1966): 151–74. On manners: Karen Halttunen, *Confidence Men and Painted Women: A Study of Middle-Class Culture in America, 1830–1870* (New Haven: Yale University Press, 1982); John F. Kasson, *Rudeness & Civility: Manners in*

Nineteenth-Century Urban America (New York: Hill and Wang, 1990); Lawrence W. Levine, *Highbrow/Lowbrow: The Emergence of Cultural Hierarchy in America* (Cambridge: Harvard University Press, 1988). On moral standards: Paul Boyer, *Urban Masses and Moral Order in America, 1820–1920* (Cambridge: Harvard University Press, 1978); James Marten, "Bringing Up Yankees: The Civil War and the Moral Education of Middle-Class Children," in *The Middling Sorts: Explorations in the History of the American Middle Class*, ed. Burton J. Bledstein and Robert D. Johnston (New York: Routledge, 2001).

17. Gustavus Hines, *Voyage Round the World* (Buffalo, N.Y.: George H. Derby, 1850), 335–36, quoted in Peter G. Boag, *Environment and Experience: Settlement Culture in Nineteenth-Century Oregon* (Berkeley: University of California Press, 1992), 69. See also Boag, *Environment and Experience*, 4–38, 66–73; Bowen, *The Willamette Valley*, 6–21; John Mack Faragher, *Sugar Creek: Life on the Illinois Prairie* (New Haven: Yale University Press, 1986), 11.

18. Boag, *Environment and Experience*, 4–38; Bowen, *The Willamette Valley*, 6–21.

19. Boag, *Environment and Experience*, 10–11.

20. Bowen, *The Willamette Valley*, 59.

21. Bowen, *The Willamette Valley*, 6–59.

22. Despite an 1852 territorial law that granted up to 320 acres to the wife of each white male DLCA recipient, and later confirmation that land donated to a married woman under the DLCA "should be secured to the sole and separate use and control of the wife" by the Oregon Supreme Court (Leah Linnville *v.* Green B. Smith, 14 Or. 284), the extent to which women gained practical control over their shares in their families' DLCs remains unclear.

23. Quoted in Paul Bourke and Donald DeBats, *Washington County: Politics and Community in Antebellum America* (Baltimore: Johns Hopkins University Press, 1995), 64. See also: Richard H. Chused, "The Oregon Donation Act of 1850 and Nineteenth Century Federal Married Women's Property Law," *Law and History Review* 2 (1984): 44–78; Chused, "Late Nineteenth Century Married Women's Property Law: Reception of the Early Married Women's Property Acts by Courts and Legislatures," *The American Journal of Legal History* 29, no. 1 (January 1985): 3–35; Chused, "Married Women's Property Law: 1800–1850," *Georgetown Law Journal* 71 (1983): 1359–1425; Oregon Supreme Court, Frances E. Brooks *v.* Henry E. Ankeny, C. M. Cartwright, B. F. Harding, and J. M. Pritchard, 7 Ore. 461, 1879; Oregon Supreme Court, Mary J. Atteberry *v.* Thomas F. Atteberry, 8 Ore. 224, 1880; Paul Bourke and Donald DeBats, *Washington County: Politics and Community in Antebellum America* (Baltimore: Johns Hopkins University Press, 1995), 120–21; MCMWPR; CCWSPR; LCWSPR; PCMWSPR; WCWSRR; Boag, *Environment and Experience*; Dean L. May, *Three Frontiers: Family, Land, and Society in the American West, 1850–1900* (New York: Cambridge University Press, 1994).

24. John D. Unruh, *The Plains Across: Emigrants, Wagon Trains and the American West* (Urbana: University of Illinois Press, 1979); Faragher, *Sugar Creek*; Faragher,

Women and Men on the Overland Trail; Bowen, *The Willamette Valley*; Boag, *Environment and Experience*.

25. Richard Bunting, "Michael Luark and Settler Culture in the Western Pacific Northwest, 1853–1899," *Pacific Northwest Review* 96, no. 4 (Fall 2005): 198–205; David Blanke, *Sowing the American Dream: How Consumer Culture Took Root in the Rural Midwest* (Athens: Ohio University Press, 2000); Allan Kulikoff, "Households and Markets: Toward a New Synthesis of American Agrarian History," *William and Mary Quarterly*, 3d series, 50, no. 2 (1993): 342–55; Michael Merrill, "Cash is Good to Eat: Self-Sufficiency and Exchange in the Rural Economy of the United States," *Radical History Review* 3 (1997): 42–71; Kenneth Michael Sylvester, *The Limits of Rural Capitalism: Family, Culture, and Markets in Montcalm, Manitoba, 1780–1940* (Toronto: University of Toronto Press, 2001), chap. 2.

26. May, *Three Frontiers*, 201.

27. White, *"It's Your Misfortune*," 303.

28. Faragher, *Sugar Creek*, 56, 144, 249.

29. Bowen, *The Willamette Valley*; May, *Three Frontiers*; Bourke and DeBats, *Washington County*; David Peterson del Mar, *What Trouble I Have Seen*; Boag, *Environment and Experience*.

30. Karen J. Blair, *The Clubwoman as Feminist: True Womanhood Defined, 1868–1914* (New York: Holmes & Meier Publishers, 1980); Sandra Haarsager, *Organized Womanhood: Cultural Politics in the Pacific Northwest, 1840–1920* (Norman: University of Oklahoma Press, 1997); Karen J. Blair, ed., *Women in Pacific Northwest History: An Anthology* (Seattle: University of Washington Press, 2001); Ruth Barnes Moynihan, *Rebel for Rights: Abigail Scott Duniway* (New Haven: Yale University Press, 1983). On consumption, see Richard L. Bushman, *The Refinement of America: Persons, Houses, Cities* (New York: Vintage Books, 1993); Karen Dubinsky, *Second Greatest Disappointment: Honeymooning and Tourism at Niagara Falls* (Toronto: Between the Lines, 1999); William Leach, *Land of Desire: Merchants, Power, and the Rise of a New American Culture* (New York: Random House, Inc., 1993); Marina Moskowitz, "Public Exposure: Middle-Class Material Culture at the Turn of the Twentieth Century" in Bledstein and Johnston, *The Middling Sorts*, 170–84; Andrea Volpe, "Cartes de Visite Portrait Photographs and the Culture of Class Formation," in Bledstein and Johnston, *The Middling Sorts*, 157–69.

31. William Deverell, *Railroad Crossing: Californians and the Railroad, 1850–1910* (Berkeley: University of California Press, 1994); White, *"It's Your Misfortune*," 246–58; David Blanke, *Sowing the American Dream*; Alan Trachtenberg, *The Incorporation of America: Culture and Society in the Gilded Age* (New York: Hill and Wang, 1982).

Chapter 1. Fashioning Women and Men on the Frontier

1. Maria Locey married in Oregon City in 1860, then later moved east of the Cascades with her husband and young children. She made this record in 1909 while living in eastern Oregon. Although her husband shifted to cattle ranching in the

more arid eastern portion of the state, and altered his work responsibilities, Maria's daily routine varied little from that of her fellow settlers who remained in the Willamette Valley. Locey Family, OHS 2968.

2. I use "the early years" and "the first years of settlement" interchangeably to refer to the period of approximately five years that each family required to become economically established in the Willamette Valley. Because families arrived at different times, settling different areas of the vast Willamette Valley, for a given family this period might begin as early as 1843 or end as late as 1870. As with my use of the term "generation," my periodization is dependent on each individual's experience of the migration process rather than on a strict chronology across every family in my study.

3. Julie Roy Jeffrey, *Frontier Women: The Trans-Mississippi West 1840–1880* (New York: Hill and Wang, 1979); John Mack Faragher, *Women and Men on the Overland Trail* (New Haven: Yale University Press, 1979); Sandra Myers, *Westering Women and the Frontier Experience, 1800–1915* (Albuquerque: University of New Mexico Press, 1982); Lillian Schlissel, *Women's Diaries of the Westward Journey* (New York: Schocken Books, 1982); Robert L. Griswold, "Anglo Women and Domestic Ideology in the American West in the Nineteenth and Early Twentieth Centuries," in *Western Women: Their Land, Their Lives*, ed. Lillian Schlissel, Vicki L. Ruiz & Janice Monk (Albuquerque: University of New Mexico Press, 1988); Nancy F. Cott, *The Bonds of Womanhood: "Woman's Sphere" in New England, 1780–1835* (New Haven: Yale University Press, 1977); Mary P. Ryan, *Cradle of the Middle Class: The Family in Oneida County, New York, 1790–1865* (New York: Cambridge University Press, 1981); Jeanne Boydston, *Home & Work: Housework, Wages, and the Ideology of Labor in the Early Republic* (New York: Oxford University Press, 1990); Glenda Riley, ed., *Prairie Voices: Iowa's Pioneering Women* (Ames: Iowa State University Press, 1996); Welborn Beeson, *The Oregon & Applegate Trail Diary of Welborn Beeson in 1853: The Unabridged Diary* (Medford, Ore.: Webb Research Group, 1987); Eliza W. Farnham, *Life in Prairie Land* (New York: Harper & Bros., 1855); Christiana Holmes Tillson, *A Woman's Story of Pioneer Illinois* (Chicago: Lakeside Press, 1919); Adrietta Applegate Hixon, *On to Oregon! A True Story of a Young Girl's Journey into the West*, ed. Waldo Taylor (Weiser, Idaho: Signal-American, 1947); John Mack Faragher, *Sugar Creek: Life on the Illinois Prairie* (New Haven: Yale University Press, 1986); Wiliam Oliver, *Eight Months in Illinois; With Information for Emigrants* (Newcastle Upon Tyne: William Andrew Mitchell, 1843; Chicago: Walter M. Hill, 1924); Susan Sessions Rugh, *Our Common Country: Family Farming, Culture, and Community in the Nineteenth-Century Midwest* (Bloomington: Indiana University Press, 2001).

4. I adapt the concept of a "borderland" of interaction hardening into clearly defined "borders" from Jeremy Adelman and Stephen Aron, "From Borderlands to Borders: Empires, Nation-States, and the Peoples in Between in North American History," *American Historical Review* 104, no. 3 (June 1999): 814–41.

5. Riley, *Prairie Voices*, 8–19, 48–70; Faragher, *Women and Men on the Overland Trail*; Faragher, *Sugar Creek*.

6. Ezra Meeker and Howard R. Driggs, *Ox-Team Days on the Oregon Trail* (Yonkers-on-Hudson, N.Y.: World Book Company, 1925); Riley, *Prairie Voices*; John Kent Folmar, ed., *"This State of Wonders": The Letters of an Iowa Frontier Family, 1858–1861* (Iowa City: University of Iowa Press, 1986); Beeson, *The Oregon & Applegate Trail*, 16–22; Ruth Barnes Moynihan, *Rebel for Rights: Abigail Scott Duniway* (New Haven: Yale University Press, 1983); Faragher, *Sugar Creek*; Faragher, *Women and Men on the Overland Trail*; Jo B. Paoletti, "The Gendering of Infants' and Toddlers' Clothing in America," in *The Material Culture of Gender, The Gender of Material Culture*, Katharine Martinez and Kenneth L. Ames, eds. (Winterthur, Del.: Henry Francis du Pont Winterthur Museum, 1997), 27–36.

7. Riley, *Prairie Voices*, 13–19, 25; Tillson, *A Woman's Story*; Farnham, *Life in Prairie Land*; Faragher, *Women and Men on the Overland Trail*, 126–27; Faragher, *Sugar Creek*, 112.

8. Faragher, *Women and Men on the Overland Trail*; Schlissel, *Women's Diaries*; Jeffrey, *Frontier Women*.

9. Perhaps Jenny Scott's journal-writing responsibility helped prepare her for her later work writing and publishing the pro-women's suffrage newspaper the *New Northwest* under her married name, Abigail Scott Duniway.

10. Kenneth L. Holmes, ed., *Covered Wagon Women: Diaries and Letters from the Western Trails, 1841–1890*, vol. 5 (Glendale, Calif.: Arthur H. Clark Company, 1983); Moynihan, *Rebel for Rights*.

11. Holmes, *Covered Wagon Women* vols. 1, 3–6; J. Quinn Thornton, *Oregon and California in 1848* (New York: Harper & Brothers, 1849; Arno Press, 1973); George Belshaw, "Journal from Indiana to Oregon," Tms. (Southern Oregon State College Library, Ashland, Ore., 1943); Hixon, *On to Oregon!*; Eleanor Allen, *Canvas Caravans* (Portland, Ore.: Binfords & Mort, 1946); Basil N. Longworth, "Diary of Basil N. Longworth, Oregon Pioneer," Tms. (Historical Records Survey, Division of Women's and Professional Projects); Charlotte Pengra, *Diary of Mrs. Bynon J. Pengra, Maiden Name Charlotte Emily Stearns* (Eugene, Ore.: Lane County Pioneer-Historical Society, Inc., 1959?); Jasper N. Cranfill Papers, UO Ax 128; Riley, *Prairie Voices*; Rebecca Ketcham, "From Ithaca to Clatsop Plains: Miss Ketcham's Journal of Travel," ed. Leo M. Kaiser and Priscilla Knuth, *Oregon Historical Quarterly* 62 (1961): 237–87, 337–402; Edward Evans Parrish, *Diary of Rev. Edward Evans Parrish: Crossing the Plains in 1844* (Fairfield, Wash.: Ye Galleon Press, 1988); Thornton, *Oregon and California in 1848*; Agnes Ruth Sengstacken, *Destination West! A Pioneer Woman on the Oregon Trail*, 2d ed. (Portland, Ore.: Binfords & Mort, 1972); Helen Stewart, *Diary of Helen Stewart 1853* (Eugene, Ore.: Lane County Pioneer-Historical Society, 1961).

12. Edward E. Parrish Papers, OHS 648; Fred Lockley, *Oregon's Yesterdays* (New York: Knickerbocker Press, 1928), 196–202; Mary Jane Hayden, *Pioneer Days* (San Jose, Calif.: Murgotten's Press, 1915); Fabritus Smith Papers, UO A 191; Locey Family Papers, OHS 2968; Aitken Family Papers, OHS 1630.

13. Eliza Spalding Warren and Henry Harmon Spalding, *Memoirs of the West*

(Portland, Ore: Press of the Marsh Printing Company, 1916), 81; Edward Parrish, OHS 648; Abraham J. Wigle Papers, OHS 587.

14. Butler-Smith Family Papers, OHS 2623.

15. James Gibson Papers, OHS 141; Butler-Smith Family, OHS 2623; Martha Gay Masterson, *One Woman's West: Recollections of the Oregon Trail and Settling the Northwest Country*, ed. Lois Barton (Eugene, Ore.: Spencer Butte Press, 1986); Benjamin Franklin Fletcher Family Papers, OHS 1432.

16. Butler-Smith Family, OHS 2623; Eva (Emery) Dye Papers, OHS 1089; Calvin M. Reed, Account Book, 1850–1856, OHS 606; Clingman-Crewse Family Papers, OHS 2645; Sengstacken, *Destination West!*; John McCoy Papers, OHS 1166; Charles Stevens Letters, OHS 2624; (Nathaniel) Coe Family Papers, OHS 431; Seth Lewelling Papers, OHS 23 and 23–B; Fred Lockley, *Conversations with Pioneer Women*, ed. Mike Helm (Eugene, Ore.: Rainy Day Press, 1981), 148, 171–72, 292; Lockley, *Oregon's Yesterdays*, 200.

17. MCDR 329, Harriet Coulton *v.* W. W. Coulton, 1853. Nearly identical language appears in MCDR 489, Nancy Crane *v.* Wyatt Crane, 1857, and other 1850s cases.

18. MCDR 1670, Lucinda Coones *v.* Felix Coones, 1867. See also Elizabeth Geer Letters, OHS 1512; Native Daughters of Oregon, Biographical Sketches of Early Settlers, OHS 59.

19. Richard H. Chused, "The Oregon Donation Act of 1850 and Nineteenth Century Federal Married Women's Property Law," *Law and History Review* 2 (1984), 44–78; Chused, "Late Nineteenth Century Married Women's Property Law: Reception of the Early Married Women's Property Acts by Courts and Legislatures," *The American Journal of Legal History* 29, no. 1 (January 1985), 3–35; Chused, "Married Women's Property Law: 1800–1850," *Georgetown Law Journal* 71 (1983): 1359; Dean L. May, *Three Frontiers: Family, Land, and Society in the American West, 1850–1900* (New York: Cambridge University Press, 1994), 128, 149, 157; Paul Bourke and Donald DeBats, *Washington County: Politics and Community in Antebellum America* (Baltimore: Johns Hopkins University Press, 1995); William A. Bowen, *The Willamette Valley: Migration and Settlement on the Oregon Frontier* (Seattle: University of Washington Press, 1978); Peter G. Boag, *Environment and Experience: Settlement Culture in Nineteenth-Century Oregon* (Berkeley: University of California Press, 1992); Clingman-Crewse Family, OHS 2645; Locey Family, OHS 2968; Oregon Pioneer Association, *Transactions of the Twenty-second Annual Reunion of the Oregon Pioneer Association for 1894* (Portland, Ore: Geo. H. Himes and Company, 1895), 48.

20. Mrs. M. A. Minto, "Female Pioneering in Oregon," Bancroft Papers, OHS 176 microfilm.

21. David M. Guthrie Papers, OHS 1509; Locey Family, OHS 2968; Amanda (Humes) McDaniel Diaries, OHS 1509; Coe Family, OHS 431; Edward Parrish, OHS 648; Joseph Gragg Papers, UO Ax 139; Nellie May Young, *An Oregon Idyl; a Tale of a Transcontinental Journey, and Life in Oregon in 1883–1884, Based on the Diary of Janette Lewis Young* (Glendale, Calif.: A. H. Clark Co., 1961), 59–60; Catherine Julia

(Bartlett) Adams, "Transcription of the Diary of Catherine Julia (Bartlett) Adams, 1885–1898," WCHS 436.

22. Coe Family, OHS 431.

23. Mrs. E. Woodward Diary, Dorothy O. Johansen Papers, OHS 1652.

24. Locey Family, OHS 2968. Emphasis in the original.

25. Locey Family, OHS 2968; David Guthrie, OHS 1509; Templeton Family Papers, OHS 1232-B; Caroline Cock Dunlap Recollections, OHS 657; Edward Parrish, OHS 648; Adams, "Transcription of Diary," WCHS MSS 436; Lockley, *Conversations with Pioneer Women*, 134–45; Lucinda Smith Papers, OHS 1020; David Guthrie, OHS 1509; Edward Parrish, OHS 648; Locey Family, OHS 2968; Adams, "Transcription of Diary," WCHS MSS 436.

26. Locey Family, OHS 2968; Edward Parrish, OHS 648; Jasper Cranfill Papers, UO Ax 128; MCDR 1912, Catherine Wehnum *v.* Henry Wehnum, 1871.

27. Coe Family, OHS 431; Joseph Gragg, UO Ax 139; Adams, "Transcription of Diary," WCHS 436.

28. Fred Lockley, OHS 2168.

29. Locey Family, OHS 2968.

30. Coe Family, OHS 431; Julia A. Holt Papers, UO SFM 113; Myra Davenport Letter to Fred Lockley, UO CA 1949 February 7; James B. Riggs Family Papers, OHS 749; NDO, Biographical Sketches, OHS 59; Robertson Family Papers, OHS 1076; Locey Family, OHS 2968; Isom Cranfill Papers, UO Ax 127; Edward Parrish, OHS 648; George Merrill Diaries, OHS 1509; Willis Dunagan Papers, UO Ax 133; David Guthrie, OHS 1509.

31. William Tagg Papers, OHS 1500; Oliver Jory Correspondence, OHS 2928.

32. Oregon Supreme Court, Leah Linnville *v.* Green B. Smith, 14 Or. 284, 1876. See also MCDR; Oregon Supreme Court, Mary J. Atteberry *v.* Thomas F. Atteberry, 8 Ore. 224, 1880; Oregon Supreme Court, Frances E. Brooks *v.* Henry E. Ankeny, C. M. Cartwright, B. F. Harding, and J. M. Pritchard, 7 Ore. 461, 1879; David Peterson del Mar, *What Trouble I Have Seen: A History of Violence Against Wives* (Cambridge: Harvard University Press, 1996), 17–18.

33. LCWSPR. See also CCWSPR; MCDR; MCMWPR; PCMWSPR; WCWSRR; Lucy Eldersveld Murphy, "Her Own Boss: Businesswomen and Separate Spheres in the Midwest, 1850–1880," *Illinois Historical Journal* 80, no. 3 (1987): 155–76.

34. LCWSPR. See also CCWSPR; MCMWPR; PCMWSPR; WCWSRR.

35. *Polk County Pioneer Sketches*, vol. 1 (Dallas, Ore: Polk County Explorer, 1927).

36. Fred Lockley, OHS 2168; Henry Fancher Diary, CCHS; Margaret Caples Recollections, OHS 1508; Linda Young, *Middle-Class Culture in the Nineteenth Century: America, Australia and Britain* (New York: Palgrave Macmillan, 2003), 178–79; Diane M. Douglas, "The Machine in the Parlor: A Dialectical Analysis of the Sewing Machine," *Journal of American Culture* 5, no. 1 (Spring 1992): 20–29.

37. Sallie Applegate Long, "History of the Applegate Family Circa 1900 & Correspondence," OHS 233.

38. Margaret Caples, OHS 1508; Long, "History of the Applegate Family," OHS

233; Butler-Smith Family, OHS 2623; Welborn Beeson Papers, UO Ax 799; Lockley, *Conversations with Pioneer Women*, 280–81; William and Deborah Andrews, "Technology and the Housewife in Nineteenth Century America," *Women's Studies* 2 (1974): 309–28; David Blanke, *Sowing the American Dream: How Consumer Culture Took Root in the Rural Midwest* (Athens: Ohio University Press, 2000), 38–45; Jacqueline Williams, "Much Depends on Dinner: Pacific Northwest Foodways, 1843–1900" *Pacific Northwest Quarterly* 90, no. 2 (1999): 68–76.

39. Lockley, *Conversations with Pioneer Women*, 280–81.

40. Seth Lewelling, OHS 23.

41. Locey Family, OHS 2968.

42. CCWSPR; LCWSPR; MCMWPR; PCMWSPR; WCWSRR; MCDR 2825, Mary A. Creswell *v.* Donald Creswell, 1878; Marion County Probate Case Files, 1843–1908, OSA; Marion County Probate Will Records, 1853–1951, OSA.

43. The Grange (Order of the Patrons of Husbandry) Records, OHS 1511.

44. Joseph Gragg, UO Ax 139; Ansel Hemenway, UO A 49; Locey Family, OHS 2968; Jean Gordon and Jan McArthur, "American Women and Domestic Consumption, 1800–1920: Four Interpretive Themes," in *Making the American Home: Middle-Class Women & Domestic Material Culture 1840–1940*, ed. Marilyn Ferris Motz and Pat Browne (Bowling Green, Ohio: Bowling Green State University Popular Press, 1988), 27–47.

45. John Franklin Sutherlin Correspondence, OHS 1500.

46. Stanton Family Letters, OHS 475; Charles Stevens Letters, OHS 2624; Caroline Cock Dunlap, OHS 657; James Gibson, OHS 141; Jessie Benton Frémont, *Far West Sketches* (Boston: D. Lothrop Company, [c. 1890]), 12–14; Robert Glass Cleland, ed., *Apron Full of Gold: The Letters of Mary Jane Megquier from San Francisco, 1849–1856* (San Marino, Calif.: Huntington Library, 1949); Lilian A. Cross, *Appreciation of Loved Ones Who Made Life Rich for Many. My Father, John Francis Cross; My Mother, Sarah Jane Cross* (Oakland, Calif.: [The Tribune Press], 1933); Allison Varzally, "Reordering Western Womanhood: Anti-Chinese Boycotts and White Women at the Close of the Nineteenth Century" (presented at the Western Association of Women Historians conference, 10 June 2000).

47. Locey Family, OHS 2968.

48. Edward Parrish, OHS 648; Seth Lewelling, OHS 23; Lucinda Smith, OHS 1020; Clarence Elzy Talbott Papers, OHS 2454–B; Lucy Preston (Wilson) Peters Reminiscences, MSS OHS 2406–B; Stephen James Chadwick Recollections, OHS 2258; Gordon and McArthur, "American Women and Domestic Consumption"; Laurel Thatcher Ulrich, *A Midwife's Tale: The Life of Martha Ballard, Based on Her Diary, 1785–1812* (New York: Random House, Inc., 1990); Ulrich, *Good Wives: Image and Reality in the Lives of Women in Northern New England, 1650–1750* (New York: Random House, Inc., 1980); Christine Stansell, *City of Women: Sex and Class in New York, 1789–1860* (New York: Alfred A. Knopf, Inc., 1982); Young, *Middle-Class Culture in the Nineteenth Century*.

49. David Guthrie, OHS 1509; Edward Parrish, OHS 648.

50. Cott, *The Bonds of Womanhood*; Jeanne Boydston, *Home & Work: House-work, Wages, and the Ideology of Labor in the Early Republic* (New York: Oxford University Press, 1990); Glenna Matthews, *"Just a Housewife": The Rise and Fall of Domesticity in America* (New York: Oxford University Press, 1987); Mary P. Ryan, *Cradle of the Middle Class: The Family in Oneida County, New York, 1790–1865* (New York: Cambridge University Press, 1981); Faragher, *Women and Men on the Over-land Trail*; Jeffrey, *Frontier Women*; Jeanne H. Watson, "Traveling Traditions: Victorians on the Overland Trails," *Journal of the West* 33, no. 1 (1994): 74–83.

51. MCDR 1912; Jon Gjerde, *The Minds of the West: Ethnocultural Evolution in the Rural Middle West, 1830–1917* (Chapel Hill: University of North Carolina Press, 1997).

52. See, for example, "Home and Women" and "Who is the True Lady?" in *The Oregon [City] Statesman*, 19 August 1851.

53. Cott, *The Bonds of Womanhood*; Boydston, *Home & Work*; Jeffrey, *Frontier Women*; Faragher, *Women and Men on the Overland Trail*; Griswold, "Anglo Women and Domestic Ideology"; Richard L. Bushman, *The Refinement of America: Persons, Houses, Cities* (New York: Vintage Books, 1993).

54. Adams, "Transcription of Diary," WCHS MSS 436; "Nicholas and Sarah Hopper Lee," *Polk County Pioneer Sketches*, vol. 1; Locey Family, OHS 2968.

55. Justin Chenoweth, OHS 237.

56. Mother and grandmother letter to Ellenora, April 4, 1912, Clingman-Crewse Family, OHS 2645.

57. Emma Barker Galloway Book of Clippings, William Galloway Family Papers, OHS 730–1; Coe Family, OHS 431.

58. "A Sermon," Galloway Family, OHS 730–1; *Willamette Farmer*.

59. LCDR 410, Martha Ann Maupin *v.* Garret Maupin, 1860. See also Coe Family, OHS 431; Elvin John Crawford Papers, OHS 1509; Eva Dye, OHS 1089; Locey Family, OHS 2968.

60. LCDR 1175, John Harris *v.* Anna Harris, 1870. See also MCDR 2145, Eli H. Stege *v.* Elizabeth F. Stege, 1872; Andrew Smith, OHS 1834.

61. MCDR 2145.

62. Andrew Smith, OHS 305; MCDR 1834, Paul Oberheim *v.* Penelope Ober-heim, 1869.

63. Galloway Family, OHS 730–1.

64. To balance the largely anecdotal evidence available through traditional written sources, I built a collective biography of sixty-seven families that traveled overland to the Willamette Valley between 1843 and 1865. Relying on manuscript family papers, genealogical files, published histories of the Willamette Valley, and local court and probate records, I created a database of demographic, professional, property, and inheritance information for these families. Because all of this information was not available for every family, throughout this study I have excluded from statistical analyses those families for which I was unable to gather relevant information. For a full listing of the resources utilized in creating this database, see Cynthia D. Culver, "Gender and Generation on the Pacific Slope Frontier, 1845–1900"

(Ph.D. diss., University of California, Los Angeles, 2004), 173–74.

65. Locey Family, OHS 2968; Albert Kelly Family Papers, OHS 871–2; Joseph Gragg, UO Ax 139.

66. NDO, Biographical Sketches, OHS 59; Butler-Smith Family, OHS 2623; Galloway Family, OHS 730–1.

67. Locey Family, OHS 2968; Coe Family, OHS 431; Welborn Beeson, UO Ax 799; Edward Parrish, OHS 648; Mary Bywater Cross, *Treasures in the Trunk: Quilts of the Oregon Trail* (Nashville: Rutledge Hill Press, 1993).

68. Locey Family, OHS 2968. Emphasis added.

69. Edward Parrish, OHS 648; see also Welborn Beeson, UO Ax 799.

70. Edward Parrish, OHS 648.

71. George Merrill Papers, OHS 1184-B; Locey Family, OHS 2968; Edward Parrish, OHS 648; Willis Dunagan, UO Ax 133; Welborn Beeson, UO Ax 799.

Chapter 2. Masculine Providers and Manly Men

1. Oliver Jory Correspondence, OHS 2928.

2. I use the term "family" to refer to a nuclear family (husband, wife and their children) or in the broader sense of a group of people who share kinship ties. All the people residing in one home constitute a "household" and might include three generations of related kin, more than one nuclear family, or unrelated paid laborers.

3. On the Midwest, see John Mack Faragher, *Women and Men on the Overland Trail* (New Haven: Yale University Press, 1979); Faragher, *Sugar Creek: Life on the Illinois Prairie* (New Haven: Yale University Press, 1986). Fred Lockley, *Oregon's Yesterdays* (New York: Knickerbocker Press, 1928), 339–40; Myra Davenport, Letter to Fred Lockley, UO CA 1949 February 7; Seth Lewelling Papers, OHS 23 and 23–B; Locey Family Papers, OHS 2968; George Merrill Papers, OHS 1509; Isom Cranfill Papers, UO Ax 127; Fabritus Smith Papers, UO A 191; Willis Dunagan Papers, UO Ax 133; Locey Family, OHS 2968; Edward E. Parrish Papers, OHS 648; Julia A. Holt Papers, UO SFM 113; J. C. Yates, Account Books, UO A 138; Willis Dunagan, UO Ax 133; Edward Long Papers, OHS 1304; Fabritus Smith, UO A 191; Clingman-Crewse Family Papers, OHS 2645; Calvin M. Reed, Account Book, 1850–1856, OHS 606; David M. Guthrie Papers, OHS 1509; Maria Beard Sweek Diary, WCHS 183; Catherine Adams, "Transcription of the Diary of Catherine Julia (Bartlett) Adams, 1885–1898," WCHS 436.

4. Fred Lockley, *Conversations with Pioneer Women*, ed. Mike Helm (Eugene, Ore.: Rainy Day Press, 1981), 143. See also Virginia Dexter, "Meadowbrook as it was in the 1880's," OHS 1252–1.

5. I use the term "patriarchal" to describe gender relations in which men dominate every aspect of household and family life. Men's right and ability to control the labor, finances, social interaction, and all other elements of their wives' and children's lives declined over the course of the nineteenth century. David Peterson del Mar, *What Trouble I Have Seen: A History of Violence Against Wives* (Cambridge: Harvard University Press, 1996).

6. MCDR 744, Francis Waddle *v.* Margaret Waddle, 1858.

7. MCDR 1565, Mary Blanton *v*. Isaac Blanton, 1867.

8. Eva (Emery) Dye Papers, OHS 1089. See also MCDR 744; MCDR 1443, Louisa A. Taylor *v*. William Taylor, 1865; MCDR 1565; MCDR 1806, Isabella Rude *v*. Thompson Rude, 1869; (Nathaniel) Coe Family Papers, OHS 431; Elizabeth Geer Letters, OHS 1512.

9. MCDR 1443.

10. MCDR 1912, Catherine Wehnum *v*. Henry Wehnum, 1871. See also MCDR 1806.

11. MCDR.

12. LCDR.

13. *Census Reports. Compiled from the Original Returns of the Ninth Census (June 1, 1870)* (Washington, D.C.: Government Printing Office, 1872), 1:401; *Twelfth Census of the United States, Taken in the Year 1900* (Washington, D.C.: United States Census Office, 1902), 1:517–18.

14. Christopher Dean Carlson, "The Rural Family in the Nineteenth Century: A Case Study in Oregon's Willamette Valley" (Ph.D. diss., University of Oregon, 1980); Daniel Vickers, *Farmers and Fishermen: Two Centuries of Work in Essex County, Massachusetts, 1630–1850* (Chapel Hill: University of North Carolina Press, 1994).

15. Fred Lockley Papers, OHS 2168.

16. Isom Cranfill, UO Ax 127; Coe Family, OHS 431; Butler-Smith Family, OHS 2623; Locey Family, OHS 2968; Elliott West, *Growing Up With the Country* (Albuquerque: University of New Mexico Press, 1989).

17. Fabritus Smith, UO A 191; Amanda (Humes) McDaniel Diaries, OHS 1509; Cyrus Hamlin Walker Papers, OHS 264; Locey Family, OHS 2968; Clarence Elzy Talbott Papers, OHS 2454–B; Joseph Gragg Papers, UO Ax 139; Agnes Ruth Sengstacken, *Destination, West! A Pioneer Woman on the Oregon Trail*, 2d ed. (Portland, Ore: Binfords & Mort, 1972), 187; Ansel Hemenway Papers, UO A 49; G. W. Kennedy, *The Pioneer Campfire. In Four Parts* (Portland, Ore.: Clarke-Kundret Printing Co., 1914); Coe Family, OHS 431.

18. I use such modern terms as "adolescent," "pre-teen" and "teenager" to distinguish stages in boys' physical and psychological development and training. Joseph F. Kett, *Rites of Passage: Adolescence in America, 1790 to the Present* (New York: Basic Books, 1977).

19. Adams, "Transcription of the Diary," WCHS 436; McDaniel Diaries, OHS 1509; Edward Parrish, OHS 648; Isom Cranfill, UO Ax 127; Joseph Gragg, UO Ax 139; Fabritus Smith, UO A 191; David Guthrie, OHS 1509; Margaret Rice Brockway Correspondence, OHS 1500; Adams, "Transcription of the Diary," WCHS 436; Lois Barton, ed., *One Woman's West: Recollections of the Oregon Trail and Settling the Northwest Country by Martha Gay Masterson 1838–1916* (Eugene, Ore.: Spencer Butte Press, 1986); Fabritus Smith, UO A 191; Cyrus Walker, OHS 264; Lockley, *Oregon's Yesterdays*, 238; Lucien M. Davidson, *The Diaries of Lucien M. Davidson, Oswego, Oregon for the Years 1876–78, 1883–94, 1903–1909 and 1911*, ed. Glenn D. Harris (Mesa, Ariz.: privately printed, 1996); Carlson, "The Rural Family in the Nineteenth Century," chap. 7–8.

20. Carlson, "The Rural Family in the Nineteenth Century," 302–03.

21. Ansel Hemenway, UO A 49; Adams, "Transcription of the Diary," WCHS 436; Jasper N. Cranfill Papers, UO Ax 128; Isom Cranfill, UO Ax 127; Locey Family, OHS 2968; Cyrus Walker, OHS 264.

22. Cyrus Locey and his wife married in the Willamette Valley in 1860. They eventually settled in the more arid region of Oregon east of the Cascades (Malheur County), where Cyrus became primarily a cattle and horse rancher. Although the men's daily work differed from that of men in western Oregon due to their emphasis on animal husbandry rather than wheat farming, Cyrus and his sons reflect the tensions inherent in having sons grow up within a kinship network of mutual exchange. I use the Loceys as a case study due to the remarkably rich written records that Cyrus and his wife left behind. Locey Family, OHS 2968.

23. Locey Family, OHS 2968.

24. Davidson, *The Diaries of Lucien M. Davidson*; Seth Lewelling, OHS 23.

25. Locey Family, OHS 2968.

26. Locey Family, OHS 2968.

27. Locey Family, OHS 2968.

28. Locey Family, OHS 2968.

29. Abraham J. Wigle Recollections, OHS 587.

30. See chap. 1, note 64.

31. Shawn Johansen, *Family Men: Middle-Class Fatherhood in Early Industrializing America* (New York: Routledge, 2001).

32. Susan E. Gray, *The Yankee West: Community Life on the Michigan Frontier* (Chapel Hill: University of North Carolina Press, 1996), 91–118. On New England inheritance patterns, see Vickers, *Farmers and Fishermen*.

33. Oliver Jory, OHS 2928; Edward Parrish, OHS 648; Davidson, *The Diaries of Lucien M. Davidson*; Welborn Beeson Papers, UO Ax 799.

34. Edward Parrish, OHS 648.

35. MCDR 3790, Johan M. Fahey *v.* Michael Fahey, 1885; Isom Cranfill, UO Ax 127; Jasper Cranfill, UO Ax 128; Fabritus Smith, UO A 191; Edward Parrish, OHS 648; William Tagg to his sister, 29 August 1886, William Tagg, OHS 1500; David Guthrie, OHS 1509; Welborn Beeson, UO Ax 799.

36. William Chapman Papers, OHS 2460; Edward Parrish, OHS 648; Coe Family, OHS 431; Fabritus Smith, UO A 191; Locey Family, OHS 2968; Templeton Family Papers, OHS 1232-B; Welborn Beeson, UO Ax 799.

37. *Ninth Census*, 1:241–43.

38. *Twelfth Census*, 1:569, 637.

39. Coe Family, OHS 431; Seth Lewelling, OHS 23.

40. Hill Family Papers, UO Ax 47; Davidson, *The Diaries of Lucien M. Davidson*; Eliza Spalding Warren and Henry Harmon Spalding, *Memoirs of the West* (Portland, Ore: Press of the Marsh Printing Company, 1916), 81.

41. Lucy Preston (Wilson) Peters Reminiscences, OHS 2406–B. See also Stephen James Chadwick, Recollections, OHS 2258; Clarence Talbott, OHS 2454–B.

42. Coe Family, OHS 431; Seth Lewelling, OHS 23; Allion Varzally, "Reordering Western Womanhood: Anti-Chinese Boycotts and White Women at the Close of the Nineteenth Century" (Paper presented at the Western Association of Women Historians conference, 10 June 2000).

43. *Ninth Census*, 3:231; *Report on the Productions of Agriculture as Returned at the Tenth Census (June 1, 1880)* (Washington, D. C.: Government Printing Office, 1883), 202, 305–07. Willamette Valley figures calculated from aggregate census data for Benton, Clackamas, Lane, Linn, Marion, Multnomah, Polk, Washington, and Yamhill counties.

44. *Population of the United States in 1860; Compiled from the Original Returns of the Eighth Census* (Washington, D.C.: Government Printing Office, 1864), 405; *Agriculture at the Tenth Census*, 724; *Occupations at the Twelfth Census* (Washington, D.C.: Government Printing Office, 1904), 368–71. See also Welborn Beeson, UO Ax 799; William Chapman, OHS 2460; Jasper Cranfill, UO Ax 128; Ansel Hemenway, UO A 49; Fabritus Smith, UO A 191; Davidson, *The Diaries of Lucien M. Davidson*.

45. *Ninth Census*, 3:231; *Agriculture at the Tenth Census*, 305–07; *Twelfth Census of the United States, Taken in the Year 1900*, 6:586 (Washington, D.C.: United States Census Office, 1902). See also *American Beer: Glimpses of Its History and Description of Its Manufacture* (New York: United States Brewers' Association, 1909) http://brewery.org/library/ambeer/ (04 July 2006).

46. *Twelfth Census*, 1:471; *Agriculture of the United States in 1860; Compiled from the Original Returns of the Eighth Census* (Washington, D.C.: Government Printing Office, 1864), 120–21; *Ninth Census*, 3:230–31; *Agriculture at the Tenth Census*, 167, 202, 304–07; *Report on the Statistics of Agriculture in the United States at the Eleventh Census: 1890*, 381, 526 (Washington, D.C.: Government Printing Office, 1895); Davidson, *The Diaries of Lucien M. Davidson*; William Chapman, OHS 2460; Welborn Beeson, UO Ax 799; Jasper Cranfill, UO Ax 128.

47. Davidson, *The Diaries of Lucien M. Davidson*; William Chapman, UO Ax 799; Jasper Cranfill, UO Ax 128.

48. Davidson, *The Diaries of Lucien M. Davidson*; "Salem Pioneer Cemetery Data," http://www.open.org/pioneerc/ (26 June 2006); Charles Stevens Letters, OHS 2624; Linus Wilson Darling Papers, OHS 129; William Chapman, OHS 2460; Locey Family, OHS 2968; Welborn Beeson, UO Ax 799.

49. *Agriculture at the Eleventh Census*, 2:331.

50. Sweek Diary, WCHS 183; Oliver Jory, OHS 2928; Joseph Gragg Papers, UO Ax 139; "Jerry E. Hinkle," Leah Collins Menefee Collection, OHS 2519; Hendee Family Papers, OHS 1351.

51. Faragher, *Women and Men on the Overland Trail*, 88–143; Faragher, *Sugar Creek*, 151–55; Peterson del Mar, *What Trouble I Have Seen*, 21–46. On eastern standards of masculinity, see Mark Carnes and Clyde Griffen, *Meanings for Manhood: Constructions of Masculinity in Victorian America* (Chicago: University of Chicago Press, 1990); E. Anthony Rotundo, *American Manhood: Transformations in Masculinity from the Revolution to the Modern Era* (New York: Basic Books, 1993);

Rotundo, "Learning About Manhood: Gender Ideals and the Middle-Class Family in Nineteenth-Century America," in *Manliness and Morality: Middle-Class Masculinity in Britain and America 1800–1940,* J. A. Mangan and James Walvin, eds. (Manchester: Manchester University Press, 1987), 75–91.

52. MCDR 1808, Mary E. Dinsmore *v.* James C. Dinsmore, 1869.

53. MCDR; LCDR.

54. MCDR 1808; Elinor Meacham Redington Reminiscences, OHS 2562; MCDR 1899, Anna B. Gamble *v.* James W. Gamble, 1870; Oregon Pioneer Association, *Transactions of the Eleventh Annual Re-Union of the Oregon Pioneer Association for 1883* (Salem, Ore.: E. M. Waite, 1884); Locey Family, OHS 2968.

55. Edward Parrish, OHS 948; Galloway Family, OHS 730–1; MCDR 1724, Thomas B. Ward *v.* Sarah Ward, 1868; MCDR 2079, Sarah A. Sanderson *v.* Charles H. Sanderson, 1871; BCDR 642–A, Mary Frances Belfils *v.* Louis Belfils, 1865; Coe Family, OHS 431.

56. Oregon Pioneer Association, *Transactions of the Tenth Annual Re-Union of the Oregon Pioneer Association for 1882* (Salem, Ore.: E. M. Waite, 1883), 86.

57. For a discussion of manliness in *fin-de-siècle* America, see Gail Bederman, *Manliness and Civilization: A Cultural History of Gender and Race in the United States, 1880–1917* (Chicago: University of Chicago Press, 1995).

58. *Albany Evening Democrat,* 14 February 1876.

59. MCDR 2949, Harriet E. Strohm *v.* Christian Strohm, 1879.

60. MCDR 6634, Ida M. Loughmiller *v.* W. E. Loughmiller, 1897; MCDR 6634; MCDR 4477, W. H. Simmons *v.* Emma Simmons, 1887; Redington Reminiscences, OHS 2562.

61. MCDR; Peterson del Mar, *What Trouble I Have Seen,* 2, 9–46.

62. MCDR 1850, Susan Lindsey *v.* George W. Lindsey, 1870.

63. See, for example, MCDR 1496, Rebecca Scott *v.* John Scott, 1866; MCDR 1849, Rebecca Henry *v.* W. P. Henry, 1870; MCDR 1850; MCDR 2885, Hattie Kemp *v.* R. C. Kemp, 1879; MCDR 3978, Frances B. Johnson *v.* George B. Johnson, 1885.

Chapter 3. Love, Power, and Marital Choice

An earlier version of this chapter was published in the *Western Historical Quarterly* 38, no.1 (Spring 2007): 25–46.

1. William VitzJames Johnson to his parents, 29 April 1853, Aitken Family Papers, OHS 1630.

2. "Marrying Without Love," *Willamette Farmer,* 23 July 1875, 2.

3. Conceptions of romantic love have changed over time. I use "romantic love" to refer to the sharing of emotions and sexual passion. A marriage could be "companionate"—sharing common interests and concern for one another's well-being— while lacking the passion that characterized romance. Karen Lystra, *Searching the Heart: Women, Men, and Romantic Love in Nineteenth-Century America* (New York: Oxford University Press, 1989); Ellen K. Rothman, *Hands and Hearts: A History of Courtship in America* (New York: Basic Books, Inc., 1984); Ruth H. Bloch, "Chang-

ing Conceptions of Sexuality and Romance in Eighteenth-Century America," *William and Mary Quarterly*, 3d Series, 60, no. 1 (January 2003): 13–42.

4. Lystra, *Searching the Heart*; Rothman, *Hands and Hearts*; John Mack Faragher, *Women and Men on the Overland Trail* (New Haven: Yale University Press, 1979).

5. David Peterson del Mar, *What Trouble I Have Seen: A History of Violence against Wives* (Cambridge: Harvard University Press, 1996), 10–18.

6. LCDR 174, Rhoda McCord *v*. Thomas McCord, 1858.

7. Locey Family Papers, OHS 2968.

8. Aitken Family, OHS 1630. See also (Nathaniel) Coe Family Papers, OHS 431; Abigail Scott Duniway, *Path Breaking: An Autobiographical History of the Equal Suffrage Movement in Pacific Coast States*, 2d ed. (Portland, Ore: James, Kerns & Abbott Co., 1914); T. T. Geer, *Fifty Years in Oregon* (New York: Neale Publishing Company, 1916), 530–31.

9. Paul Bourke and Donald DeBats, *Washington County: Politics and Community in Antebellum America* (Baltimore: Johns Hopkins University Press, 1995), 121.

10. See chap. 1, note 64.

11. John Mack Faragher, *Sugar Creek: Life on the Illinois Prairie* (New Haven: Yale University Press, 1986), 87–88.

12. Lucy Henderson Deady, "Crossing the Plains to Oregon in 1846," *Transactions of the Fifty-Sixth Annual Oregon Pioneer Association* (Salem, Ore.: E. M. Waite, 1928), 57–64.

13. *New Northwest*, 2 June 1871, 1.

14. Fred Lockley, *Conversations with Pioneer Women*, ed. Mike Helm (Eugene, Ore.: Rainy Day Press, 1981), 250.

15. Lockley, *Conversations with Pioneer Women*; Julia A. Holt Letters, UO SFM 113; Agnes Ruth Sengstacken, *Destination, West! A Pioneer Woman on the Oregon Trail*, 2d ed. (Portland, Ore.: Binfords & Mort, 1972), 97–98; BCDR 369, James Coffey *v*. Mary J. Coffey, 1861; LCDR 2003, Eliza Francis Ramsey *v*. George C. Ramsey, 1867.

16. "Hog and Hominy," quoted in Faragher, *Women and Men on the Overland Trail*, 157–58.

17. LCDR 96, Jonathan Keeney *v*. Sarah Catharine Keeney, 1856.

18. Mrs. Robert A. Miller, "Women in Pioneer Times," *Transactions of the Twenty-Third Annual Reunion of the Oregon Pioneer Association for 1895* (Portland, Ore.: Press of Geo. H. Himes, 1895), 58.

19. Sandra L. Myres, *Westering Women and the Frontier Experience, 1800–1915* (Albuquerque: University of New Mexico Press, 1982), 102.

20. Faragher, *Women and Men on the Overland Trail*; Lillian Schlissel, *Women's Diaries of the Westward Journey* (New York: Schocken Books Inc., 1982); Myres, *Westering Women*.

21. MCDR 439, William Cassiday *v*. Mary Ann Cassiday, 1856.

22. MCDR 439; MCDR 248, Lucius Danforth *v*. Sophia A. Danforth, 1855.

23. Mary Jane Hayden, *Pioneer Days* (San Jose, Calif.: Murgotten's Press, 1915), 28; MCDR 2108, Matilda Penter *v.* Samuel Penter, 1872; MCDR 1546, L. B. Morgan *v.* W. W. Morgan, 1866; Clingman-Crewse Family Papers, OHS 2645; Locey Family, OHS 2968; Coe Family, OHS 431; Seth Lewelling Papers, OHS 23 and 23–B; Calvin M. Reed, Account Book, 1850–1856, OHS 606; Levi Scott Papers, OHS 2340.

24. Hayden, *Pioneer Days*, 28; MCDR 2108; MCDR 1546; Clingman-Crewse Family, OHS 2645; Locey Family, OHS 2968; Coe Family, OHS 431; Seth Lewelling, OHS 23; Reed Account Book, OHS 606; Levi Scott, OHS 2340; Laurel Thatcher Ulrich, *A Midwife's Tale: The Life of Martha Ballard, Based on Her Diary, 1785–1812* (New York: Random House, Inc., 1990).

25. Joan M. Jensen, *Loosening the Bonds: Mid-Atlantic Farm Women, 1750–1850* (New Haven: Yale University Press, 1986); Jensen, "Butter-Making and Economic Development in Mid-Atlantic America, 1750–1850," in *Promise to the Land: Essays on Rural Women* (Albuquerque: University of New Mexico Press, 1991), 170–85.

26. MCDR 4664, Eleanor Shrum *v.* Henry Shrum, 1889; Edward E. Parrish Papers, OHS 648; Clingman-Crewse Family, OHS 2645; Locey Family, OHS 2968; Coe Family, OHS 431; Seth Lewelling, OHS 23; Reed Account Book, OHS 606; Levi Scott, OHS 2340.

27. Locey Family, OHS 2968. Emphasis in the original.

28. Locey Family, OHS 2968. Most women did not achieve as much financial independence as Maria Locey did, but many did make significant gains in household authority over their lifetimes. See, for example, Coe Family, OHS 431; LC-WSPR; MCMWPR; PCMWSPR.

29. Richard H. Chused, "The Oregon Donation Act of 1850 and Nineteenth Century Federal Married Women's Property Law," *Law and History Review* 2 (1984), 44–78; Chused, "Late Nineteenth Century Married Women's Property Law: Reception of the Early Married Women's Property Acts by Courts and Legislatures," *The American Journal of Legal History* 29, no. 1 (January 1985), 3–35; Chused, "Married Women's Property Law: 1800–1850," *Georgetown Law Journal* 71 (1983): 1359.

30. MCDR 3654, Catherine Egan *v.* Patrick Egan, 1877.

31. Coe Family, OHS 431; Clingman-Crewse Family, OHS 2645; MCDR 2666, Leona Holt *v.* Thomas Holt, 1877; PCMWSPR; Edward Parrish, OHS 648.

32. MCDR: 3588, Anna P. Janz *v.* Carl Janz, 1883; 2783, Malvina Whitlock *v.* Mitchell Whitlock, 1878; 3076, James Whitney *v.* Elizabeth Whitney, 1880; 2906, D. M. Jones *v.* J. Ellen Jones, 1879; 3463, David Weaver *v.* Rebecca Weaver, 1882; 3461, Fisher Gaines *v.* L. N. Gaines, 1882; 2343, Evaline Smith *v.* David H. Smith, 1874; 2825, Mary A. Creswell *v.* Donald Creswell, 1878.

33. MCDR 1224, Maria Rhoades *v.* Alphonso Rhoades, 1862.

34. MCDR 1426, John Rudolph *v.* Pyra Rudolph, 1865.

35. MCDR 2878, D. C. Creswell *v.* Mary A. Creswell, 1878; MCDR 1224; MCDR 1426; Locey Family, OHS 2968. Contributing to the household income and responsibility for trading goods outside the family conferred prestige within the family unit. Faragher, *Women and Men on the Overland Trail*, 62.

36. "Matrimony," *Oregon [City] Statesman*, 21 October 1851.

37. *Oregon [City] Statesman*, 21 October 1851; Agnes Plummer Burns, "On to Oregon," Albert Kelly Family Papers, OHS 871–2; Elinor Meacham Redington, Reminiscences, OHS 2562; Coe Family, OHS 431; Homer Davenport, *The Country Boy: The Story of His Own Early Life* (Chicago: M. A. Donohue & Company, 1910).

38. Letter from Maria Locey to Mary and Addie Locey, 6 October 1904, Locey Family, OHS 2968.

39. Locey Family, OHS 2968.

40. Edward Parrish, OHS 648.

41. Locey Family, OHS 2968; Albert Kelly Family, OHS 871–2; *Oregon [City] Statesman*, 21 October 1851.

42. MCDR 329, Harriet Coulton *v.* W. W. Coulton, 1853.

43. MCDR 996, William Larkins *v.* Caroline Larkins, 1860; MCDR 1834, Paul Oberheim *v.* Penelope Oberheim, 1869.

44. *Statistics of the Population of the United States at the Tenth Census (June 1, 1880)* (Washington, D.C.: Government Printing Office, 1882), 620, 741–42, 800–06, 842.

45. Faragher, *Sugar Creek*, 88.

46. "Nelly Hill to Mamma," 1 April 1894, Hill Family Papers, UO Ax 47.

47. Linus Wilson Darling Papers, OHS 129.

48. "Who are Rich?" *Willamette Farmer*, 19 February 1875, 2.

49. Libbie Hendershott to Billy [Willard Hall Rees], 22 July 1872, Hendershott Family Correspondence, OHS 109.

50. Lockley, *Conversations with Pioneer Women*, 227.

51. "Advice to Young Ladies," *Willamette Farmer*, 10 September 1875, 2, reprinted 6 April 1877, 7.

52. "A Happy Couple," in Coe Family Papers, OHS 431.

53. Advertisement for Parker's Hair Balsam, *Oregon [City] Statesman*, 2 January 1885, 5. See also Hendershott Family Correspondence, OHS 109; Mollie Hill Scrapbooks, OHS 1352B; Locey Family, OHS 2968; *Eugene City Guard*, 29 June 1889; "Who are Rich?" *Willamette Farmer*, 19 February 1875; *Willamette Farmer*, 6 April 1877, 2; *Willamette Farmer*, 20 April 1877; "A Chapter on Marriage," *New Northwest*, 2 April 1875; "A Loveless Marriage," *New Northwest*, 25 June 1885; "What Men Need Wives For," *New Northwest*, 10 September 1875; *New Northwest*, 2 March 1882; *Oregon Cultivator*, 16 December 1875, 1; "What Men Need Wives For," *Oregon Cultivator*, 30 December 1875, 2.

54. *Willamette Farmer*, 6 April 1877.

55. LCDR 1175, John Harris *v.* Anna Harris, 1870.

56. LCDR 2025, Mary E. Howard *v.* Lyttle Howard, 1877; LCDR 2049, B. P. Goodman *v.* Susan Goodman, 1886; LCDR 2050, Rosina B. Whitney *v.* William M. Whitney, 1886.

57. Hill Scrapbooks, OHS 1352B.

58. Lockley, *Conversations with Pioneer Women*, 146, 250.

59. Hill Family, UO Ax 47; Locey Family, OHS 2968; Welborn Beeson Papers, UO Ax 799; Oliver Jory Correspondence, OHS 2928.

60. Hill Family, UO Ax 47.

61. Lockley, *Conversations with Pioneer Women*, 134–45, 250; Linus Darling Papers, OHS 129; Locey Family, OHS 2968; Welborn Beeson, UO Ax 799.

62. Lockley, *Conversations with Pioneer Women*, 181.

63. "Why Girls Don't Marry," *Willamette Farmer*, 11 February 1887, 3.

64. Julia A. Holt Letters, UO SFM 113; Lockley, *Conversations with Pioneer Women*, 181, 227; *Oregon [City] Statesman*, 17 April 1885, 1; Locey Family, OHS 2968; Hill Family Papers, UO Ax 47; Cyrus Hamlin Walker Papers, OHS 264; "For What is a Wife Wanted?" *Willamette Farmer*, 6 June 1874; MCDR 4548, D. H. Close *v*. Hattie J. Close, 1889; MCDR 3259, Martha E. Wilson *v*. Albert Wilson, 1881.

65. Harry Denlinger to Nellie Hill, 9 March 1896, Hill Family, UO Ax 47.

66. Oliver Jory to Ella Hodean, 16 December 1892, Jory Correspondence, OHS 2928. Emphasis added.

67. Hill Scrapbooks, OHS 1352B; BCDR 642–A, Mary Frances Belfils *v*. Louis Belfils, 1865; Julia A. Holt, UO SFM 113; Locey Family, OHS 2968; MCDR 4548, D. H. Close *v*. Hattie J. Close, 1889; MCDR 3259; "Marriage Maxims," *Willamette Farmer*, 9 April 1870, 55.

68. "Tell Your Wife," *Willamette Farmer*, 6 November 1874, 2.

69. "A Wife's Rights," *Willamette Farmer*, 22 November, 1874.

70. Jory Correspondence, OHS 2928.

71. Welborn Beeson, UO Ax 799.

72. "How to Manage Him," *Willamette Farmer*, 18 June 1885.

73. "She Cured Him," *Willamette Farmer*, 18 September 1884; "How to Manage Him," Hill Scrapbooks, OHS 1352B.

74. LCWSPR.

75. "How to Manage Him," *Willamette Farmer*, 18 June 1885; "She Cured Him," *Willamette Farmer*, 18 September 1884; "How to Manage Him," Hill Scrapbooks, OHS 1352B; MCDR 4275, Selena Potter *v*. George Potter, 1887; LCWSPR; Peterson del Mar, *What Trouble I Have Seen*.

76. MCDR 3400, Laura J. Woodworth *v*. George W. Woodworth, 1882.

77. MCDR 4275.

78. MCDR 4275; "How to Manage Him," *Willamette Farmer*, 18 June 1885; "She Cured Him," *Willamette Farmer*, 18 September 1884; "How to Manage Him," Hill Scrapbooks, OHS 1352B; LCWSPR; Peterson del Mar, *What Trouble I Have Seen*.

79. MCDR 2783.

80. MCDR 4659, John A. McCarl *v*. Diana McCarl, 1889.

81. MCDR 4659.

82. "Flirtation," *Willamette Farmer*, 6 August 1875.

83. MCDR 4500, Mary A. Bushey *v*. William M. Bushey, 1888; MCDR 2490, S. T. Garrison *v*. Florence Garrison, 1876; MCDR 2825; CCWSPR; LCWSPR; MCMWPR; PCMWSPR; WCWSRR; Sallie Applegate Long, History of the Applegate Family

Circa 1900 & Correspondence, OHS 233; Margaret Caples Recollections, OHS 1508; Seth Lewelling, OHS 23; Locey Family, OHS 2968; Joseph Gragg, UO Ax 139; Ansel Hemenway, UO A 49.

84. MCDR 2490.

85. MCDR 1724, Thomas B. Ward *v.* Sarah Ward, 1868.

86. MCDR: 1724; 1372, Frances Ann Godfrey *v.* Robert Godfrey, 1865; 3865, Rachel Wait *v.* T. B. Wait, 1886; 3161, W. R. Parker *v.* Nancy E. Parker, 1880; 1724; 981, Theresa Coil *v.* Michael Coil, 1858; 1848, Arnold Myers *v.* Mary Myers, 1870; 2363, Josette Berneir *v.* Louis Bernier, 1874; 2634, Fannie B. Dixon *v.* J. H. Dixon, 1877; 4665, J. H. Lunn *v.* Victoria A. Lunn, 1889; 6521, Cora Ramsden *v.* W. T. Ramsden, 1896.

87. LCDR.

88. Edward Parrish, OHS 648.

89. MCDR 1848.

90. MCDR: 1724; 1372; 3865; 3161; 981; 1848; 2363; 2634; 4665, J. H. Lunn *v.* Victoria A. Lunn, 1889; LCDR 1480, Eleanor Huff *v.* James W. Huff, 1877; LCDR 2343, Margaret A. Taylor *v.* I. J. Taylor, 1889; LCDR 2622, Mary E. Pyle *v.* John F. Pyle, 1887; Hill Scrapbooks, OHS 1352B; "Origin of the Word 'Husband,'" *Willamette Farmer*, 9 April 1870, 55; Peterson del Mar, *What Trouble I Have Seen*; E. Anthony Rotundo, "Learning About Manhood: Gender Ideals and the Middle-Class Family in Nineteenth-Century America," in *Manliness and Morality: Middle-Class Masculinity in Britain and America 1800–1940*, J. A. Mangan and James Walvin, eds. (Manchester: Manchester University Press, 1987), 75–91; Jesse F. Battan, "The 'Rights' of Husbands and the 'Duties' of Wives: Power and Desire in the American Bedroom, 1850–1910," *Journal of Family History* 24 (April 1999): 165–86.

91. MCDR 3161.

92. MCDR 3161; MCDR 4471, Rebecca H. Minto *v.* John W. Minto, 1888; Locey Family, OHS 2968; Mary P. Ryan, *Cradle of the Middle Class: The Family in Oneida County, New York, 1790–1865* (New York: Cambridge University Press, 1981).

93. "The Divorce Evil," Hill Scrapbooks, OHS 1352B.

Chapter 4. Refining the Domestic Sphere

1. Zeralda Carpenter Bones Stone, Churn dash quilt, circa 1860, OHSM 67–368.

2. Minnie Biles Brazee Knapp, Crazy quilt, circa 1890, OHSM 86–97.

3. Fred Lockley, *Conversations with Pioneer Women*, ed. Mike Helm (Eugene, Ore.: Rainy Day Press, 1981), 169.

4. Lockley, *Conversations with Pioneer Women*, 164–69, 207; Julia A. Holt Papers, UO SFM 113; Nellie May Young, *An Oregon Idyl; a Tale of a Transcontinental Journey, and Life in Oregon in 1883–1884, Based on the Diary of Janette Lewis Young* (Glendale, Calif., A. H. Clark Co., 1961); Joseph Hardin Cornwall Recollections, OHS 1509.

5. "Conveniences on the Farm," *Willamette Farmer*, 6 August 1886, 3.

6. Joan M. Jensen, "Butter-Making and Economic Development in Mid-Atlantic America, 1750–1850," *Promise to the Land: Essays on Rural Women* (Albuquerque:

University of New Mexico Press, 1991): 170–85; Joan M. Jensen, *Loosening the Bonds: Mid-Atlantic Farm Women, 1750–1850* (New Haven, Conn.: Yale University Press, 1986).

7. *Report on the Productions of Agriculture as Returned at the Tenth Census (June 1, 1880)* (Washington, D. C.: Government Printing Office, 1883), 167; *Twelfth Census of the United States, Taken in the Year 1900*, 5:616–17 (Washington, D.C.: United States Census Office, 1902).

8. *Report on Population of the United States at the Eleventh Census: 1890* (Washington, D.C.: Government Printing Office, 1897), 2:331.

9. Clingman-Crewse Family Papers, OHS 2645; Fred Lockley Papers, OHS 2168; MCDR 3400, Laura J. Woodworth *v.* George W. Woodworth, 1882; Virginia Dexter, "Meadowbrook as it was in the 1880's," OHS 1252–1; Victoria Case, ed., *This I Remember: Personal Pioneer Experiences* (Portland, Ore.: Rose Villa, Inc., 1972); Oliver Jory Correspondence, OHS 2928; Locey Family Papers, OHS 2968; short course dairy class, 1900–1909, Harriet's Photographic Collection (no. 413), OSU; sewing class, 1890, College of Home Economics Photographic Collection (no. 044), OSU; food preparation class, 1890–1899, College of Home Economics Photographic Collection (no. P44:43), OSU.

10. "Women as Poultry Raisers," *Oregon Cultivator*, 30 March 1876, 2.

11. Lucien M. Davidson, *The Diaries of Lucien M. Davidson, Oswego, Oregon for the Years 1876–78, 1883–94, 1903–1909 and 1911*, ed. Glenn D. Harris (Mesa, Ariz.: privately printed, 1996); Welborn Beeson Papers, UO Ax 799; Templeton Family Papers, OHS 1232–B; Locey Family, OHS 2968; "Money Crops for Daughters," *Willamette Farmer*, 15 July 1887, 3; "Women as Poultry Raisers, *Oregon Cultivator*, 30 March 1876, 2; "Poultry Raising as Profitable Employment for Women," *Willamette Farmer*, 19 January 1883, 3.

12. *Statistics of the Population of the United States at the Tenth Population at the Tenth Census (June 1, 1880)* (Washington, D.C.: Government Printing Office, 1882), 305–06; *Report on the Statistics of Agriculture in the United States at the Eleventh Census: 1890*, 344 (Washington, D.C.: Government Printing Office, 1895); *Twelfth Census*, 5:660.

13. Davidson, *The Diaries of Lucien M. Davidson*; Welborn Beeson, UO Ax 799; Templeton Family, OHS 1232–B; Locey Family, OHS 2968; Madeline Buckendorf, "The Poultry Frontier: Family Farm Roles and Turkey Raising in Southwest Idaho, 1910–1940," *Idaho Yesterdays* 37, no. 2 (Summer 1993): 2–8.

14. MCDR 4477, W. H. Simmons *v.* Emma Simmons, 1887.

15. MCDR 7040, Jessie R. Parkes *v.* Arthur D. Parkes, 1898.

16. Pamphlet for the Stoddard churn, circa 1885, ISAW 90.91.39; hand-powered tabletop butter churn, Coquille River Museum Collection, Bandon Historical Society, Bandon, Ore.; hand-powered tabletop butter churn, MAW 87.171.2; L. Lockwood, "Improved Washing Machine, United States Patent Office patent no. 69,567," http://www.tmm.utexas.edu/exhibits/past'exh/laundry/index.html (6 August 2003); washing machine, circa 1890s, MAW 90.143.19; *1897 Sears, Roebuck and Co. Cata-*

logue, ed. Fred L. Israel (New York: Chelsea House Publishers, 1968); *Sears, Roebuck & Co. 1908 Catalogue No. 117, The Great Price Maker*, ed. Joseph J. Schroeder Jr. (Chicago: Gun Digest Company, 1969); International Publishing Company, *Supply Department Catalog no. 47* (n.p., 1900); *Montgomery Ward & Co. Catalogue & Buyers Guide No. 56, Fall & Winter 1894–95*, ed. Joseph J. Schroeder Jr. (Northfield, Ill.: DBI Books, Inc., 1977); Locey Family, OHS 2968; "Lighten the Work," *Willamette Farmer*, 19 August 1887; "Advantages and Disadvantages of the Sewing Machine," *New Northwest*, 23 November 1877.

17. Jacqueline Williams, "Much Depends on Dinner: Pacific Northwest Foodways, 1843–1900," *Pacific Northwest Quarterly* 90, no. 2 (1999): 68–76; Rob Schorman, *Selling Style: Clothing and Social Change at the Turn of the Century* (Philadelphia: University of Pennsylvania Press, 2003); Priscilla J. Brewer, "Home Fires: Cookstoves in American Culture, 1815–1900," *Dublin Seminar for New England Folklife. Annual Proceedings* 13 (1988): 68–88; Linda Young, *Middle-Class Culture in the Nineteenth Century: America, Australia and Britain* (New York: Palgrave Macmillan, 2003), 106–08.

18. Ricky Clark, George W. Knepper, and Ellice Ronsheim, *Quilts in Community: Ohio's Traditions* (Nashville, Tenn.: Rutledge Press, 1991), 58.

19. Rebecca Mapel Parrish, linen blouse, OHSM 1743; Calvin M. Reed, Account Book, 1850–1856, OHS 606; Clingman-Crewse Family, OHS 2645; Welborn Beeson, UO Ax 799; J. C. Yates, Account Books, UO A 138; (Nathaniel) Coe Family Papers, OHS 431; Elaine Hedges, Pat Ferrero, and Julie Silber, *Hearts and Hands: Women, Quilts, and American Society* (Nashville, Tenn.: Rutledge Hill Press, 1987), 32–38; Jane Ashelford and Andreas Einsiedel, *The Art of Dress: Clothes and Society, 1500–1914* (New York: Abrams, 1996), 211–72.

20. Beverly Gordon, "Meanings in Mid-Nineteenth Century Dress: Images from New England Women's Writings," *Clothing and Textiles Research Journal* 10, no. 3 (1992): 44–53; Kathryn Clippinger Kosto, " 'some work . . . to be kept': Textiles and Memories of Victorian Domesticity," *Dublin Seminar for New England Folklife Annual Proceedings* 24 (1999): 173–94; Young, *Middle-Class Culture*.

21. Black and white cotton print dress, circa 1860, OHSM 68–500.3. See also challis and wool dress, circa 1850, MAW 91.67.1; lavender and purple print cotton dress, circa 1845, MAW 88.147.1; printed ombre wool dress, circa 1840s, MAW 92.204.1; red and brown leaf print cotton dress, circa 1845, MAW 90.55.1.

22. Agnes Ruth Sengstacken, *Destination West! A Pioneer Woman on the Oregon Trail*, 2d ed. (Portland, Ore.: Binfords & Mort, 1972), 94.

23. Sarah and W. A. Finley as bride and groom, Harriet's Photographic Collection (no. 224), OSU; chocolate-brown silk taffeta dress, circa 1850–1865, OHSM 68–441.1; Lockley, *Conversations with Pioneer Women*, 100; Elaine Pedersen and Jan Loverin, "Historic Costume Dating: Further Exploration of Schlick's Algorithm," *Dress* 15 (1989): 38–49; Elaine L. Pedersen, "Deciphering the Ormsby Gown: What Does it Tell?" *Nevada Historical Society Quarterly* 38, no. 2 (1995): 75–88; Sally Helvenston, "Fashion on the Frontier," *Dress* 17 (1990), 141–55.

24. MCDR 3400.

25. The Farmers' & Mechanics' Store advertisements, *New Northwest*, 9 June 1881 and 15 October 1885; The White House advertisements, *New Northwest*, 3 December 1875 and 10 August 1877; Olds & King advertisement, *New Northwest*, 15 July 1880.

26. "Belles of the 1870's, Portland, Oregon," UO PH035_08000; graduating class, St. Helen's Hall, Portland, 1877, UO PH035_06312; Louisa Gay, circa 1875, OHS CN 017711; Ida Humphries, 1888, OHS OrHi 0195G073.

27. "What to Wear and How, No. II," *New Northwest*, 22 September 1881.

28. "Fashion Notes," *New Northwest*, 10 July 1884.

29. "What to Wear and How, No. I," *New Northwest*, 15 September 1881. See also "What to Wear and How, No. III" *New Northwest*, 13 October 1881.

30. "Fashion Notes," *New Northwest*, 27 March 1884; "What to Wear and How, No. I," *New Northwest*, 15 September 1881; "What to Wear and How, No. II," *New Northwest*, 22 September 1881; "What to Wear and How, No. III" *New Northwest* 13 October 1881; "For Women Only," *New Northwest*, 21 February 1884; "Fashion Notes," *New Northwest*, 15 November 1883; "Fashion Chit-Chat," *New Northwest*, 29 April 1880; "Fashion Notes," *New Northwest*, 5 November 1885; "Fashion Notes," *New Northwest*, 14 January 1886; "What to Wear," *New Northwest*, 30 September 1880; "Fashion Notes," *New Northwest*, 1 May 1884.

31. Andrew Orus Brown (grandson of Tabitha Brown) and his wife Asenaath Carey Brown, wedding portrait, OHS OrHi 9999Y523; Sarah and W. A. Finley as bride and groom, HC no. 224; ivory brocade and satin wedding gown, OHSM 71–136.1; Uncle Arthur and Aunt Lucy, UO PH200_0010; wedding portrait of Mrs. W. A. Carter of Gold Hill, Oregon, OHS OrHi 0172G028; wedding portrait by Hayes & Hayes, circa 1900–1905, OU PH200.

32. "What to Wear and How, No. II," *New Northwest*, 22 September 1881; "Brief Fashion Hints," *New Northwest*, 3 July 1884; ivory wool wedding gown, OHSM 73–40.1, .2.

33. Mr. and Mrs. A. J. Burdett and child, 1890, OHS OrHi 0199G067; Addie Burdett, 1890, OHS OrHi 0205G019.

34. Ida Burley, OHS OrHi 0207G018; Ella Burley, OHS OrHi 0203G071; the Burley sisters—Ida and Ella, holding cherry blossoms, 1894, OHS OrHi 0178G017. See also Blanche Albert and Ada Stapleton, OHS OrHi 0202G029; Cami Anderson, OHS OrHi 1215G055; Mr. and Mrs. G. W. Ashby, OHS OrHi 0203G032; Mrs. Mattie Baker, OHS OrHi 0199G001; Addie Burdett, OHS OrHi 0206G019; Mr. and Mrs. A. J. Burdett and child, OHS OrHi 0199G067; Lulu Bernhart and friends, OHS OrHi 0217G015; Mrs. C. A. Brown, OHS OrHi 0196G039; Effie Chamness and Miss Cox, OHS OrHi 0215G028; Mrs. Mary B. Churchill, OHS OrHi 0215G068; Ethel Cusick and Miss Breyman with large flowered hats, OHS OrHi 0214G002; Nettie Driveler and friend, OHS OrHi 0209G001; Alice Estes in front of painted backdrop in dark dress, with umbrella, OHS OrHi 0192G032; Mrs. Richard Hensley, OHS OrHi 0207G028; Narcissa Gloves, OHS OrHi 0207G015.

35. "What to Wear and How, No. III," *New Northwest*, 13 October 1881.

36. "My Striped Dress," *New Northwest*, 22 August 1876.

37. Mr. and Mrs. John Baker, OHS OrHi 0182G006; "What to Wear and How, No. I," *New Northwest*, 15 September 1881; "What to Wear and How, No. II," *New Northwest*, 22 September 1881; "What to Wear and How, No. III," *New Northwest*, 13 October 1881; "A Severe Lesson," *Willamette Farmer*, 2 April 1886.

38. White organdy shirtwaist, OHSM 3778; printed cotton day dress, circa 1896, MAW 91.132.5; advertisement for Butterick patterns sold by Mrs. E. S. Wass, *New Northwest*, 26 October 1882; *1897 Sears, Roebuck and Co. Catalogue*; *Sears, Roebuck & Co. 1908 Catalogue No. 117*; *Montgomery Ward & Co. Catalogue & Buyers Guide No. 56, Fall & Winter 1894–95*; *Supply Department Catalog no. 47*.

39. Herbert E. Cooper Papers, OHS 931; Fishel & Roberts advertisements, *New Northwest*, 10 August 1877 and 15 July 1880; A. Roberts advertisement, *New Northwest*, 3 April 1884; Benjamin R. Holtgrieve Papers, OHS 2; Ansel Hemenway Papers, UO A 49; Davidson, *The Diaries of Lucien M. Davidson*; J. C. Yates, UO A 138; Linus Wilson Darling Papers, OHS 129; *Samuel's Directory of Portland and East Portland, for 1873* (Portland, Ore.: L. Samuel, Newspaper Advertising Agent, 1873); *Portland City Directory. 1885*, vol. 23 (Portland, Ore.: R. L. Polk & Co., Publishers, 1885); *Portland City Directory 1895: Embracing a Complete Alphabetical and Classified Directory, Miscellaneous Information and Street Guide*, vol. 33 (Portland, Ore.: R.L. Polk & Co., Publishers, 1895); *1897 Sears, Roebuck and Co. Catalogue*; *Sears, Roebuck & Co. 1908 Catalogue No. 117*; *Montgomery Ward & Co. Catalogue & Buyers Guide No. 56, Fall & Winter 1894–95*; *Supply Department Catalog no. 47*.

40. "Girls and the Needle," *Willamette Farmer*, 18 June 1880, p. 3.

41. "As Viewed By a Woman," *Willamette Farmer*, 29 November 1895; "Advantages and Disadvantages of the Sewing Machine," *New Northwest*, 23 November 1877; gold silk day dress with brocade trim, circa 1883, MAW 91.132.2; black faille evening dress, 1883–87, MAW 90.245.3; white voile and cotton day dress, circa 1885, MAW 93.89.1; royal blue silk day dress, circa 1886, MAW 91.132.1; red floral print cotton day dress, circa 1895, MAW 91.35.1; printed cotton day dress, circa 1896, MAW 91.132.5.

42. William Leach, *Land of Desire: Merchants, Power, and the Rise of a New American Culture* (New York: Random House, Inc., 1993); Jane H. Hunter, *How Young Ladies Became Girls: The Victorian Origins of American Girlhood* (New Haven: Yale University Press, 2002); Diane M. Douglas, "The Machine in the Parlor: A Dialectical Analysis of the Sewing Machine," *Journal of American Culture* 5, no. 1 (Spring 1992): 20–29; Diana Di Zerega Wall, "Sacred Dinners and Secular Teas: Constructing Domesticity in Mid-19th-Century New York," *Historical Archaeology* 25, no. 4 (1991): 69–81; David Blanke, *Sowing the American Dream: How Consumer Culture Took Root in the Rural Midwest* (Athens: Ohio University Press, 2000).

43. Jacob Hunsaker Family Reminiscences, CCHS.

44. "Our Letter Box," *Willamette Farmer*, 9 February 1883, p. 3; *Willamette Farmer*, 3 June 1887, p. 3; *Willamette Farmer*, 27 March 1884; MCDR 3400; quilting bee, Mehama, Ore., circa 1900, OHS OrHi 21876; Julia Holt, UO SFM 113; Davidson,

The Diaries of Lucien M. Davidson; Lucinda Smith Papers, OHS 1020; Willard Hall Rees Papers, OHS 109; Robertson Family Papers, OHS 1076; "For the Children" column, *Willamette Farmer*, 1880s; Sarah Hathaway Bixby Smith, *Adobe Days* (Cedar Rapids, Iowa: Torch Press, 1925); "Our Letter Box," *Willamette Farmer*, 9 February 1883, p. 3; *Willamette Farmer*, 3 June 1887, p. 3; *Willamette Farmer*, 27 March 1884; Patricia Mainardi, "Quilts: The Great American Art," *The Feminist Art Journal* 2, no. 1 (Winter 1973): 1, 18–23; Patricia Cooper and Norma Bradley Allen, *The Quilters: Women and Domestic Art: An Oral History* (New York: Doubleday, 1989); Ferrero et al. *Hearts and Hands*, 60–64; John Mack Faragher, *Women and Men on the Overland Trail* (New Haven: Yale University Press, 1979), 55–56, 126–27.

45. Whig rose quilt, circa 1860–1870, MAW 88.18.2; Stone churn dash quilt, circa 1860, OHSM 67–368; Ferrero et al. *Hearts and Hands*, 50–64; Jonathan Holstein, "The American Block Quilt," in *In the Heart of Pennsylvania*, ed. Jeanette Lasansky (Lewisburg, Penn.: Oral Traditions Project, 1986), 16–27.

46. Robertson Family, OHS 1076.

47. *Willamette Farmer*, regular feature on knitting and lace patterns, 1884; "Fashion Notes," *New Northwest*, 17 July 1884; "The Fancy-Work Department," *New Northwest*, 21 October 1886; Eliza Archard article on fancy work, reprinted from *New York World* in *New Northwest* 26 June 1884; Beverly Gordon, "Victorian Fancywork in the American Home: Fantasy and Accommodation," in *Making the American Home: Middle-Class Women & Domestic Material Culture 1840–1940*, ed. Marilyn Ferris Motz and Pat Browne (Bowling Green, Ohio: Bowling Green State University Popular Press, 1988), 48–68.

48. Knapp crazy quilt, circa 1890, OHSM 86–97; Ellen Wright and Annie Wright Reynolds, crazy quilt, circa 1900, OHSM 89–240.1; "The Fancy-Work Department," *New Northwest*, 21 October 1886; "Something New," *Willamette Farmer*, 22 April 1887; "Items for Ladies," *New Northwest*, 3 April 1884; Jane Przybysz, "Quilts, Old Kitchens, and the Social Geography of Gender at Nineteenth-Century Sanitary Fairs," *The Material Culture of Gender, The Gender of Material Culture*, ed. Katharine Martinez and Kenneth L. Ames (Winterthur, Del.: Henry Francis du Pont Winterthur Museum, 1997), 411–41.

49. Ellen Fickling Eanes, Erma Hughes Kirkpatrick, Sue Barker McCarter, Joyce Joines Newman, Ruth Haislip Roberson, and Kathlyn Fender Sullivan, *North Carolina Quilts*, ed. Ruth Haislip Roberson (Chapel Hill: University of North Carolina Press, 1988), 162.

50. Knapp crazy quilt, OHSM 86–97; Bonnett crazy quilt, pictured in Mary Bywater Cross, *Treasures in the Trunk: Quilts of the Oregon Trail* (Nashville, Tenn.: Rutledge Hill Press, 1993), 88–89.

51. "Something New," *Willamette Farmer*, 22 April 1887, 3; Penny McMorris, *Crazy Quilts* (New York: E. P. Dutton, 1984); Barbara Brackman, *Clues in the Calico: A Guide to Identifying and Dating Antique Quilts* ([McLean, Va.]: EPM Publications, 1989).

52. Wright and Reynolds, crazy quilt, circa 1900, OHSM 89–240.1.

53. Maria Anne Peas Warner, Harriet Griffith Wise, and Laura Etta Warner, grandmother's fan quilt, circa 1890, OHSM 71–186.84; Amelia Peck, *American Quilts and Coverlets in The Metropolitan Museum of Art* (New York: Dutton Studio Books, 1990), 101.

54. LCWSPR.

55. MCMWPR.

56. "Home Adornment," *New Northwest*, 4 February 1996; Richard L. Bushman, *The Refinement of America: Persons, Houses, Cities* (New York: Vintage Books, 1992), 273–79; Beverly Gordon, "Woman's Domestic Body: the Conceptual Conflation of Women and Interiors in the Industrial Age," *Winterthur Portfolio* 31, no. 4 (1996): 281–301.

57. MCMWPR.

58. MCMWPR; PCMWSPR.

Chapter 5. New Roles for "New Women"

1. Mary Murdoch Mason, *Mae Madden* (Chicago: Jansen, McClurg & Co., 1876), 19.

2. *Albany Evening Democrat*, 20 January 1876.

3. "The Duty of a Woman Is to be a Lady," *Willamette Farmer*, 20 November 1874.

4. Hill Family Papers, UO Ax 47; John McCoy Family Papers, OHS 1166; BCDR 642-A, Mary Frances Belfils *v.* Louis Belfils, 1865; MCDR 3865, Rachel Wait *v.* T. B. Wait, 1886; (Nathaniel) Coe Family Papers, OHS 431; Martha Gay Masterson, *One Woman's West: Recollections of the Oregon Trail and Settling the Northwest Country*, ed. Lois Barton (Eugene, Ore: Spencer Butte Press, 1986); *Albany Evening Democrat*, 31 December 1875; Caroline Couch (Burns) Hoffman Papers, OHS 2546; Elinor Meacham Redington Reminiscences, OHS 2562; Clingman-Crewse Family Papers, OHS 2645; Thomas Van Buren Embree Papers, OHS 164; "The Duty of a Woman is to be a Lady," *Willamette Farmer*, 4 May 1877, 7; "Womanly Modesty," *Willamette Farmer*, 13 December 1873, 6; "Should Women Smoke?" *Eugene City Guard*, 29 June 1889; "A Wife's Power," *Willamette Farmer*, 23 February 1877.

5. *Report on Population of the United States at the Eleventh Census: 1890* (Washington, D.C.: Government Printing Office, 1897), 2:76, 127.

6. Albert Kelly Family Papers, OHS 871–2; Locey Family Papers, OHS 2968; Joseph Hardin Cornwall Recollections, OHS 1509; Edward E. Parrish Papers, OHS 648; Robertson Family Papers, OHS 1076; Joseph Gragg Papers, UO Ax 139; Clingman-Crewse Family Papers, OHS 2645; Lucien M. Davidson, *The Diaries of Lucien M. Davidson, Oswego, Oregon for the Years 1876–78, 1883–94, 1903–1909 and 1911*, ed. Glenn D. Harris (Mesa, Ariz.: privately printed, 1996); Charles Stevens Papers, OHS 2624; Lucy Preston (Wilson) Peters Reminiscences, OHS 2406-B; Welborn Beeson Papers, UO Ax 799; Jasper N. Cranfill Papers, UO Ax 128; "The prairie flower," 18 December 1874, Mary E. Lacey Papers, OHS 2536; Supreme Court, Harris *v.* Burr, 32 Ore. 348, 1898; "Don't," *Willamette Farmer*, 28 March 1884, 3; Locey Family, OHS

2968; Jane H. Hunter, *How Young Ladies Became Girls: The Victorian Origins of American Girlhood* (New Haven: Yale University Press, 2002).

7. *Oregon [City] Statesman*, 23 September 1851.

8. "Educate the Women," *Willamette Farmer*, 21 January 1871, 380; "Motherhood," *The Oregon Cultivator*, 13 April 1876, 2; "A Word Fitly Spoken," *Willamette Farmer*, 18 July 1874, 2; *Oregon [City] Statesman*, 23 September 1851; Mary Lacey, OHS 2536; Cyrus Hamlin Walker Papers, OHS 264; Margaret Kuhn Caples Recollections, OHS 1508; Peters Reminiscences, OHS 2406-B; Hunter, *How Young Ladies Became Girls*.

9. Dean L. May, *Three Frontiers: Family, Land, and Society in the American West, 1850–1900* (Cambridge: Cambridge University Press, 1994), 135; *Report on Population of the United States at the Eleventh Census: 1890* (Washington, D.C.: Government Printing Office, 1897), 2:xxxiv.

10. "Our Future Housekeepers," *Willamette Farmer*, 14 May 1870, 95.

11. *Willamette Farmer*, 26 May 1876.

12. "Equal Rights," *Willamette Farmer*, 8 June 1877, 7.

13. Hill Family, UO Ax 47.

14. Oliver Jory Correspondence, OHS 2928.

15. *Willamette Farmer*, 27 November 1874, 2.

16. "Educating Boys For Husbands," *Oregon Cultivator*, 5 October 1876; "Make Home Beautiful," *Willamette Farmer*, 22 November 1873, 6; *Willamette Farmer*, 20 December 1873; "A Pleasant Home," *Willamette Farmer*, 10 June 1887, 3; "Imperceptible Presence," reprinted from *Rural Home* in *Willamette Farmer*, 11 July 1874, 2; "A Hint to Housekeepers," *Willamette Farmer*, 18 August 1872, 7.

17. "Aunt Hetty's Visit, Its Results," *Willamette Farmer*, 10 September 1886, 3; "The Home Circle" column, *Willamette Farmer*, 1873–87; Cornwall Recollections, OHS 1509; Clingman-Crewse Family, OHS 2645; Lockley, *Conversations with Pioneer Women*; Holt Papers, UO SFM 113; Nellie May Young, *An Oregon Idyl; A Tale of a Transcontinental Journey, and Life in Oregon in 1883–1884, Based on the Diary of Janette Lewis Young* (Glendale, Calif.: A. H. Clark Co., 1961); Eunice Waters Robbins Luckey Letters, OHS 1167; Stewart B. Eakin Diary, WCHS 360; Hill Family, UO Ax 47; "Home Duties; Or, Woman's Influence," *Willamette Farmer*, 4 July 1879, 3; "A Hint to Housekeepers," *Willamette Farmer*, 18 August 1872; "Visitors," *Willamette Farmer*, 20 May 1887; "Woman's Purity," *Willamette Farmer*, 20 December 1895, 1; Hunter, *How Young Ladies Became Girls*.

18. "Photo of 'High Five' Club of 40 Years Ago Stirs Memories," Scrapbook, Fletcher Family, OHS 1432.

19. Larkin Ball Family History, WCHS; Wilbur P. Ball, *Descendants of Rebecca, Perry, and Albert Ball; A Genealogical Study from 1839 to 1969* (Providence, Utah: K. W. Watkins, 1969); "Douglas Jones Genealogy," CCHS; Davidson, *The Diaries of Lucien M. Davidson*; William Galloway Family Papers, OHS 730–1; Masterson, *One Woman's West*; Isaiah Kelsey Family Genealogy, MCHS; George Merrill Diaries, OHS 1509; Edward Parrish, OHS 648; Lorna Borman, *History and Genealogy of the*

Pomeroy and Allied Families (Yakima, Wash.: L. Borman, 1983); *The Webfoot* (Eugene, Ore.: University of Oregon, 1902); Sandra Haarsager, *Organized Womanhood: Cultural Politics in the Pacific Northwest, 1840–1920* (Norman: University of Oklahoma Press, 1997).

20. "Street Suits," reprinted from *Philadelphia Times* in *Willamette Farmer*, 4 July 1879, 3; Coe Family, OHS 431; "Woman's Virtues," *Willamette Farmer*, 14 January 1887, 3; "A Word to Girls," *Willamette Farmer*, 9 June 1882, 3; Hunter, *How Young Ladies Became Girls*.

21. "Fashion," *Willamette Farmer*, 9 February 1877, 7.

22. "A Woman's Defense of Dress," Emma Barker Galloway Book of Clippings, Galloway Family, OHS 730–1.

23. Coe Family, OHS 431; "Woman's Virtues," *Willamette Farmer*, 14 January 1887, 3; "Girls," *Willamette Farmer*, 18 July 1874, 2; "Young Housekeepers of the Home Circle," *Willamette Farmer*, 14 November 1879, [7]; *The Oregon Cultivator*, 1874–76; "Women-Planners," *Willamette Farmer*, 3 June 1887, 3.

24. *Population at the Eleventh Census*, 2:76–77, 138–39, 149; Rebecca Force, "Gambling on Higher Education: A History of the Founding of the University of Oregon," *Oregon Historical Quarterly* 102, no. 4 (Winter 2001), 500–09.

25. Melinda Tims, "Discovering the Forty-Three Percent Minority: Pioneer Women in Pleasant Hill, Oregon, 1848–1900" (M.A. thesis, Université de Poitiers, 1982), 100.

26. Caples Recollections, OHS 1508, 43; Kelly Family, OHS 871–2; Locey Family, OHS 2968; Hill Family, UO Ax 47; "Girl Graduates," *New Northwest*, 1 February 1883; Fletcher Family, OHS 1432; Hillsboro Coffee Club Papers, WCHS 390; Young, *An Oregon Idyl*; Ida Everitt Papers, WCHS 116; Hill Family, UO Ax 47; Davidson, *The Diaries of Lucien M. Davidson*.

27. Rebecca J. Mead, *How the Vote Was Won: Woman Suffrage in the Western United States, 1868–1914* (New York: New York University, 2004); Ruth Barnes Moynihan, *Rebel for Rights: Abigail Scott Duniway* (New Haven: Yale University Press, 1983), 171–88 and 214–16; Ellen Carol DuBois, *Woman Suffrage and Women's Rights* (New York: New York University Press, 1998), 1–29.

28. *The Organic and Other General Laws of Oregon, Together with the National Constitution and Other Public Acts and Statutes of the United States, 1845–1864*, ed. M. P. Deady (Portland, Ore.: Henry L. Pittock, State Printer, 1866).

29. Oregon Supreme Court, Harris v. Burr, 1898; May, *Three Frontiers*, 135.

30. Oregon Supreme Court, Stevens v. Carter, 27 Ore. 553, 1895.

31. Oregon Supreme Court, State Ex Rel. v. Stevens, 29 Ore. 464, 1896.

32. Oregon Supreme Court, Harris v. Burr, 1898.

33. "Woman's Rights," *Willamette Farmer*, 13 April 1877, [7].

34. Susan Coolidge, "My Rights," *Willamette Farmer*, 3 October 1884.

35. "Why Should She Want to Vote?" Galloway Family, OHS 730–1; Locey Family, OHS 2968; Susan Coolidge, "My Rights," *Willamette Farmer*, 3 October 1884; Susan Coolidge, "My Rights," *New Northwest*, 29 September 1881.

36. "Woman," *Willamette Farmer*, 5 October 1872, 2.

37. "Woman's Sphere," *Willamette Farmer*, 9 February 1877.

38. "Equal Rights," *Willamette Farmer*, 8 June 1877, 7. Emphasis appears in the original.

39. "What Woman's Rights Are," *Oregon Cultivator*, 31 August 1876, 2.

40. "Why Should She Want to Vote?" Galloway Family, OHS 730–1; "Woman," *Willamette Farmer*, 5 October 1872, 2; "Woman's Sphere," *Willamette Farmer*, 9 February 1877; "What Girls Shall Read," *Willamette Farmer*, 13 April 1877, [7]; "Woman," *Willamette Farmer*, 5 November 1872, 2; "Home Duties; Or, Woman's Influence," *Willamette Farmer*, 4 July 1879, 3; "Women and Politics," *Willamette Farmer*, 11 November 1871, 3; "The Old Types," *Willamette Farmer* 27 December 1873, 6; "Women and Politics," *Willamette Farmer*, 11 November 1871; "Women's Rights," *New Northwest*, 28 April 1876.

41. "Woman's Rights," *Willamette Farmer*, 13 April 1877, [7].

42. "The Woman Question," *Willamette Farmer*, 11 May 1877, 7.

43. "Woman's Rights," *Willamette Farmer*, 4 May 1877, 7.

44. "What Girls Should Read, and Woman's Rights," *Willamette Farmer*, 4 May 1877, 7.

45. "Shall Women Vote on the License Question?" *Willamette Farmer*, 14 August 1876, 6.

46. *Oregon City Argus*, 23 April 1859, quoted in Moynihan, *Rebel for Rights*, 66.

47. Abigail Scott Duniway, *Path Breaking: An Autobiographical History of the Equal Suffrage Movement in Pacific Coast States*, 2d ed. (Portland, Ore.: James, Kerns & Abbott Co., 1914); Moynihan, *Rebel for Rights*, 1–70.

48. "The Coming Housewife," *Golden Age*, reprinted in *New Northwest*, 12 July 1872.

49. "Your Dress-Coat, Your Money, and Your Vote," *New Northwest*, 21 January 1876.

50. "A True Lady," *New Northwest*, 29 September 1881; "What Woman Should Do," *New Northwest*, 9 October 1884; "A Word to Those Who Have All the Rights They Want," *New Northwest*, 18 December 1874; Oregon Pioneer Association, *Transactions of the Tenth Annual Re-Union of the Oregon Pioneer Association for 1882* (Salem, Ore: E. M. Waite, 1883), 36–39; "Your Dress-Coat, Your Money, and Your Vote," *New Northwest*, 21 January 1876; "Masculine Women," *New Northwest*, 7 August 1874; " 'No Lady Wants to Vote,' " *New Northwest*, 10 November 1881; Susan Coolidge, "My Rights," *New Northwest*, 29 September 1881; "What Woman Should Do," *New Northwest*, 9 October 1884; "The Coming Housewife," *Golden Age*, reprinted in *New Northwest*, 12 July 1872; "Feminine Men and Masculine Women," *New Northwest*, 5 May 1871; "Women at Work in Oregon City," *New Northwest*, 9 March 1882; "Girl Graduates," *New Northwest*, 1 February 1883; Duniway, *Path Breaking*.

51. "Your Dress-Coat, Your Money, and Your Vote," *New Northwest*, 21 January 1876.

52. "Woman Suffrage and the Farm," *New Northwest*, 8 May 1884. See also "Equality of Difference," *New Northwest*, 18 January 1881; "Objections to Woman Suffrage Reviewed," *New Northwest*, 22 September 1876; "Woman Suffrage and the Farm," *New Northwest*, 8 May 1884; "Your Dress-Coat, Your Money, and Your Vote," *New Northwest*, 21 January 1876.

53. Locey Family, OHS 2968. Emphasis in the original.

54. Locey Family, OHS 2968; Duniway, *Path Breaking*; "Objections to Woman Suffrage Reviewed," *New Northwest*, 22 September 1876.

55. Abigail Scott Duniway to Nellie Hill, 15 February 1890, Hill Family, UO Ax 47.

56. Hill Family, UO Ax 47.

57. Hill Family, UO Ax 47.

58. Hill Family, UO Ax 47. Emphasis in the original.

59. Hill Family, UO Ax 47; Haarsager, *Organized Womanhood*, 262–66; OPA, *Transactions of the Tenth Annual Re-Union*, 37–38.

60. Hill Family, UO Ax 47; OPA, *Transactions of the Tenth Annual Re-Union*, 37–38; Locey Family, OHS 2968; Emma Barker Galloway Book of Clippings, Galloway Family, OHS 730–1.

Chapter 6. Remembering and Reinventing Oregon Pioneers

1. Oregon Native Daughters, Odell Cabin No. 8. Papers, OHS MSS 772.

2. Gail Bederman, *Manliness & Civilization: A Cultural History of Gender and Race in the United States, 1880–1917* (Chicago: University of Chicago Press, 1995); Frederick Jackson Turner, "The Significance of the Frontier in American History," *Annual Report of the American Historical Association for the Year 1893* (Washington, D.C., 1894), reprinted in John Mack Faragher, *Rereading Frederick Jackson Turner: "The Significance of the Frontier in American History" and Other Essays* (New York: Henry Holt and Company, 1994), 31–60.

3. I have avoided using the term "pioneer" to refer to early settlers because of the word's complex cultural associations. The early Willamette Valley settler was indeed "one who went before, preparing the way for others," as "pioneer" is defined in *Webster's New World Dictionary* (New York: Warner Books, 1984), 454. However, this term also suggests a degree of cultural superiority, of one leading "civilization" to a land that was either empty or dominated by savagery. In contrast to previous chapters, I use the term "pioneer" in this chapter because that was the word the members of the pioneer associations used to describe themselves. I continue to use "settler" when referring to their actual experiences during the early years on the frontier, but use "pioneer" when referring to the settlers' conceptions of themselves. See also Clyde A. Milner II, "The View from Wisdom: Four Layers of History and Regional Identity" in *Under an Open Sky: Rethinking America's Western Past*, ed. William Cronon, George Miles and Jay Gatlin (New York: W. W. Norton & Company, 1992), 203–22.

4. On "historical memory," see Joan Didion, *Where I Was From* (New York: Alfred A. Knopf, Inc., 2003); Richard W. Etulain, *Re-Imagining the American West: A*

Century of Fiction, History and Art (Tucson: University of Arizona Press, 1996); Milner, "The View from Wisdom"; Malcolm J. Rohrbough, *Days of Gold: The California Gold Rush and the American Nation* (Berkeley: University of California Press, 1997); Richard White, *Remembering Ahanagran: Storytelling in a Family's Past* (New York: Hill and Wang, 1998).

5. On intergenerational conflict throughout the United States in the early twentieth century, see Paula S. Fass, *The Damned and the Beautiful: American Youth in the 1920s* (New York: Oxford University Press, 1977).

6. *Thirteenth Census of the United States Taken in the Year 1910* (Washington, D. C.: Government Printing Office, 1914), 3:509, 4:73.

7. Eva (Emery) Dye Papers, OHS 1089; Fred Lockley Papers, OHS MSS 2168; John McCoy (Family) Papers, OHS 1166; Albert Kelly Family Papers, OHS 871–2.

8. Fred Lockley, *Conversations with Pioneer Women*, ed. Mike Helm (Eugene, Ore.: Rainy Day Press, 1981), 24–25.

9. Fred Lockley, OHS 2168; Lockley, *Conversations with Pioneer Women*, 24–25.

10. Lockley, *Conversations with Pioneer Women*, 134.

11. Clingman-Crewse Family Papers, OHS 2645; Lockley, *Conversations with Pioneer Women*, 24–25, 134; Fred Lockley, OHS 2168; Fass, *The Damned and the Beautiful*, 23; Kelly Schrum, *Some Wore Bobby Sox: The Emergence of Teenage Girls' Culture, 1920–1945* (New York: Palgrave Macmillan, 2004).

12. For more on the women's club movement in Oregon, see Sandra Haarsager, *Organized Womanhood: Cultural Politics in the Pacific Northwest, 1840–1920* (Norman: University of Oklahoma Press, 1997).

13. Oregon Pioneer Association, *Transactions of the Third Annual Re-Union of the Oregon Pioneer Association* (Salem, Ore.: E. M. Waite, 1876), 12.

14. OPA, *Transactions of the Third Annual Re-Union*, 12. Emphasis added.

15. OPA, *Transactions of the Third Annual Re-Union*, 12; Oregon Pioneer Association, *Transactions of the Fourth Annual Re-Union; for 1876* (Salem, Ore.: E. M. Waite, 1877), 14, 21; Oregon Pioneer Association, *Transactions of the Sixteenth Annual Reunion of the Oregon Pioneer Association for 1888* (Portland, Ore.: Press of Himes the Printer, 1889), 156; Abner Sylvester Baker III, "The Oregon Pioneer Tradition in the Nineteenth Century: A Study of Recollection and Self-Definition" (Ph.D. diss., University of Oregon, Eugene, 1968).

16. Oregon Pioneer Association, *Transactions of the Nineteenth Annual Reunion of the Oregon Pioneer Association for 1891* (Portland, Ore.: A. Anderson & Co., 1893), 7.

17. OPA, *Transactions of the Nineteenth Annual Reunion*, 7, 12; Oregon Pioneer Association, *Transactions of the Twenty-Third Annual Reunion of the Oregon Pioneer Association for 1895* (Portland, Ore.: Press of Geo. H. Himes, 1895), 9.

18. OPA, *Transactions of the Twenty-Third Annual Reunion*, 9.

19. OPA, *Transactions of the Nineteenth Annual Reunion*, 7, 12; OPA, *Transactions of the Twenty-Third Annual Reunion*, 9.

20. Polk County Pioneers Papers, OHS 1511.

21. Polk County Pioneers, OHS 1511. On sports and masculinity, see Bederman, *Manliness & Civilization*; J. A. Mangan and James Walvin, eds., *Manliness and Morality: Middle-Class Masculinity in Britain and America, 1800–1940* (Manchester: Manchester University Press, 1987).

22. "Women in Pioneer Times," in OPA, *Transactions of the Twenty-Third Annual Reunion*, 58. Miller used the term "wonderful" in the sense of something that causes wonder; she likely did not anticipate the modern colloquial use of the term to mean something that was excellent or altogether positive. *Webster's New World Dictionary*, 688.

23. Oregon Pioneer Association, *Transactions of the Tenth Annual Re-Union of the Oregon Pioneer Association for 1882* (Salem, Ore.: E. M. Waite, 1883), 36.

24. OPA, *Transactions of the Tenth Annual Re-Union*, 37–38.

25. Oregon Pioneer Association, *Transactions of the Twenty-Fourth Annual Reunion of the Oregon Pioneer Association for 1896* (Portland, Ore.: Press of Geo. H. Himes, 1897), 16.

26. The only other issue that was not adopted unanimously was to award an honorarium to association Secretary George H. Himes. Resolutions to change the membership guidelines, and votes of thanks to various parties who contributed to the reunion, were adopted unanimously. OPA, *Transactions of the Twenty-Fourth Annual Reunion*, 14–16.

27. Oregon Pioneer Association, OHS 1511.

28. OPA, OHS 1511.

29. Sons and Daughters of Oregon Papers, OHS 1511.

30. Native Daughters of Oregon Papers, OHS 1511.

31. NDO, OHS 1511; SDO, OHS 1511.

32. George Henry Himes Papers, OHS 1462; Native Daughters of Oregon, Tabitha Brown Cabin No. 24, OHS 107-B; Oregon Native Daughters, Odell Cabin No. 8. Papers, OHS 772; Sons and Daughters of Oregon Pioneers, OHS 1511.

33. NDO, OHS 1511.

34. NDO, OHS 1511; Laurel Thatcher Ulrich, *The Age of Homespun: Objects and Stories in the Creation of an American Myth* (New York: Alfred A. Knopf, Inc., 2001).

35. NDO, OHS 1511; OND, OHS 772.

36. NDO, Tabitha Brown Cabin No. 24, OHS 107B; Native Sons and Daughters of Oregon, WCHS 310.

37. Medorum Crawford, "Opening Address" in OPA, *Transactions of the Tenth Annual Re-Union*, 5.

38. John Minto, "The Occasional Address," OPA, *Transactions of the Fourth Annual Re-Union*, 38.

39. Milner, "The View from Wisdom." On republican motherhood, see Nancy F. Cott, *The Bonds of Womanhood: "Woman's Sphere" in New England, 1780–1835* (New Haven: Yale University Press, 1977), 101–25; Linda K. Kerber, *Women of the Republic: Intellect & Ideology in Revolutionary America* (Chapel Hill: University of North Carolina Press, 1980), 189–288; Mary Beth Norton, *Liberty's Daughters: The Revolu-*

tionary Experience of American Women, 1750–1800 (Boston: Little, Brown, 1980), 228–99.

40. "On This Day in Oregon," http://www.onthisdayinoregon.com/05'20.html (18 August 2006).

41. Mrs. Minto, "Female Pioneering in Oregon," Bancroft Papers, OHS 176 microfilm; OPA, *Transactions of the Fourth Annual Re-Union*, 24, 38, 42; OPA, *Transactions of the Twenty-Second Re-Union of the Oregon Pioneer Association for 1894* (Portland, Ore.: Geo. H. Himes and Company, 1895), 5; Native Sons & Daughters of Oregon, Miscellaneous Papers, WCHS 310; Lockley, *Conversations with Pioneer Women*, 79.

42. Hon. W. Lair Hill, "Annual Address," *Transactions of the Eleventh Annual Reunion of the Oregon Pioneer Association for 1883* (Salem, Ore.: E. M. Waite, 1884), 21.

43. Charles Grafly, *The Pioneer Mother*, bronze, 1915, Palace of Fine Arts, San Francisco, Calif.; "The Pioneer Mother," http://www.books-about-california.com/Pages/The_City_of_Domes/Illustration_Pages/The_Pioneer_Mother.html (18 August 2006).

44. Quoted in Annabelle Amick, "Madonna of the Trail," http://www.baxtercountyonline.com/arkdar/madonna.htm (18 August 2006).

45. August Leimbach, *Pioneer Mother/Madonna of the Trail*, crushed granite, stone, marble, cement and lead, 1928, Bethesda, Md.; Beallsville, Penn.; Wheeling, W.Va.; Springfield, Ohio; Richmond, Ind.; Vandalia, Ill.; Lexington, Mo.; Council Grove, Kan.; Lamar, Colo.; Albuquerque, N.M.; Springerville, Ariz.; and Upland, Calif.; Bryant Baker, *Pioneer Woman*, bronze, 1930, Pioneer Woman Museum, Ponca, Okla.; "Pioneer Woman Museum," http://www.poncacity.com/attractions/pioneer_woman.htm (18 August 2006).

46. Paul Donald, "Oregon's New State Library," *[Portland] Oregon Sunday Journal*, 2 April 1939, http://www.osl.state.or.us/home/lib/oslart39.html (18 August 2006).

47. Gabriel Lavare, *Pioneer Mother*, marble, circa 1939, Oregon State Library, Salem.

48. Leo Friedlander, *The Covered Wagon*, marble, circa 1937, Oregon Statehouse, Salem. Emphasis added.

49. Friedlander, *The Covered Wagon*; Avard Fairbanks, *The Old Oregon Trail*, bronze, 1924, Baker City and Seaside, Ore.

50. The 1926 *Pioneer Mother* statue erected in Kansas City was copied from the bronze mother and baby that were part of Proctor's earlier life-size bronze grouping that included a mountain man carrying his rifle, a mother with a baby, a frontiersman, and two horses. A. Phimister Proctor, *Mountain Man, Pioneer Mother, Frontiersman and Two Horses*, bronze, circa 1924, Santa Barbara Museum of Art, Santa Barbara, Calif.; Proctor, *Pioneer Mother*, bronze, circa 1926, Kansas City, Mo.

51. Proctor, *Mountain Man, Pioneer Mother, Frontiersman and Two Horses*; Proctor, *Pioneer Mother*, Kansas City, Mo.; Peter H. Hassrick, "The Oregon Art of Alexander Phimister Proctor," *Oregon Historical Quarterly* 104, no. 3 (Fall 2003), 394–413.

52. Frederick V. Holman, "Qualities of the Oregon Pioneers," *The Quarterly of the Oregon Historical Society* XX, no. 3 (September 1919), "A Place Called Oregon," http://gesswhoto.com/ohs-pioneers.html (18 August 2006).

53. A. Phimister Proctor, *Pioneer*, bronze, 1918, University of Oregon Museum of Art, Eugene; Ulric Ellerhusen, *Oregon Pioneer*, circa 1937, Oregon Statehouse, Salem.

54. Burt Brown Barker to A. P. Proctor, 3 November 1927, quoted in Hassrick, "Proctor in Oregon," 412.

55. A. Phimister Proctor, *Pioneer Mother*, bronze, 1932, University of Oregon Museum of Art, Eugene.

56. Lockley, *Conversations with Pioneer Women*, 143.

Conclusion

1. "Symbols, Mother of Oregon: Tabitha Moffatt Brown," http://www.statehousegirls.net/or/symbols/motheroforegon/ (18 August 2006).

2. "Symbols, Mother of Oregon"; Jerry Easterling, "Oregon's Pioneer Mother," *Statesman Journal* (Salem, Ore.), 7 May 1987, quoted in "Salem Pioneer Cemetery Data," http://www.open.org/pioneerc/pg06.html (18 August 2006).

3. Fred Lockley, *Conversations with Pioneer Women*, ed. Mike Helm (Eugene, Ore.: Rainy Day Press, 1981), 143.

4. "Sons and Daughters of Oregon Pioneers," http://www.oregonpioneers.com/sdop.htm (18 August 2006).

5. Tom Brokaw, *The Greatest Generation* (New York: Random House, 1998).

SELECTED BIBLIOGRAPHY

Manuscript Sources

Adams, Catherine. "Transcription of the Diary of Catherine Julia (Bartlett) Adams, 1885–1898." WCHS 436.

Adams, Charles. Letters. OHS 1500.

Aitken Family. Papers. OHS 1630.

Ball, Larkin. Family History. WCHS.

Beeson, Welborn. Papers. UO Ax 799.

Belknap, Wilda (Ketchum). Autobiography. OHS 304.

Brockway, Margaret Rice. Correspondence. OHS 1500.

Bullard, Philip Alva. Letters. OHS 1500.

Butler-Smith Family. Papers. OHS 2623.

Caples, Margaret. Recollections. OHS 1508.

Chadwick, Stephen James. Recollections. OHS 2258.

Chapman, William. Papers. OHS 2460.

Chenoweth, Justin. Papers. OHS 237.

Clingman-Crewse Family. Papers. OHS 2645.

Coe (Nathaniel) Family. Papers. OHS 431.

Cooper, Herbert E. Papers. OHS 931.

Cornwall, Joseph Hardin. Recollections. OHS 1509.

Cranfill, Isom. Papers. UO Ax 127.

Cranfill, Jasper N. Papers. UO Ax 128.

Crawford, Elvin John. Papers. OHS 1509.

Cummins/Fischbuch Family. Family History. WCHS.

Darling, Linus Wilson. Papers. OHS 129.

Davenport, Myra. Letter to Fred Lockley. UO CA 1949 February 7.

Deady, Lucy Ann. Papers. OHS 48.

Dexter, Virginia. "Meadowbrook as it was in the 1880's." OHS 1252-1.

"Douglas Jones Genealogy." CCHS.

Dunagan, Willis. Papers. UO Ax 133.

Dunlap, Caroline. Reminiscences. OHS 657.

Dye, Eva (Emery). Papers. OHS 1089.

Eakin, Stewart B. Diary. WCHS 360.

Embree, Thomas Van Buren. Papers. OHS 164.

Everitt, Ida. Papers. WCHS 116.

Fancher, Henry. Diary. CCHS.

Flanary, Thomas. Family History. WCHS.

Fletcher (Benjamin Franklin) Family. Papers. OHS 1432.

Galloway, Mildred C. Papers. OHS 2574.

Galloway (William) Family. Papers. OHS 730-1.

Garrison, Abraham Henry. Recollections. OHS 874.

Geer, Elizabeth. Letters. OHS 1512.

Geer Family. Genealogy. MCHS.

Gibson, James. Recollections. OHS 141.

Gould Family. Papers. OHS 2680.

Gragg, Joseph. Papers. UO Ax 139.

The Grange (Order of the Patrons of Husbandry). Records. OHS 1511.

Guthrie, David M. Papers. OHS 1509.

Hayden, Mary. "Pioneer Days." OHS 1508.

Hemenway, Ansel. Papers. UO A 49.

Hendee Family. Papers. OHS 1351.

Hendershott Family. Correspondence. OHS 109.

Hill Family. Papers. UO Ax 47.

Hill, Mollie. Scrapbooks. OHS 1352B.

Hillsboro Coffee Club. Papers. WCHS 390.

Himes, George Henry. Papers. OHS 1462.

Hoffman, Caroline Couch (Burns). Papers. OHS 2546.

Holt, Julia A. Papers. UO SFM 113.

Holtgrieve, Benjamin R. Papers. OHS 2.

Hunsaker, Jacob, Family. Reminiscences. CCHS.

Johansen, Dorothy O. Papers. OHS 1652.

Jones, Victor W. "Some Antecedents and Descendants of Mr. and Mrs. Earl Douglas Jones." CCHS.

Jory, Oliver. Correspondence. OHS 2928.

Kelly, Albert, Family. Papers. OHS 871-2.

Kelsey, Isaiah. Family Genealogy. MCHS.

Lacey, Mary E. Papers. OHS 2536.

Lewelling, Seth. Papers. OHS 23 and 23-B.

Locey Family. Papers. OHS 2968.

Lockley, Fred. Papers. OHS 2168.

Long, Edward. Papers. OHS 1304.

Long, Sallie Applegate. "History of the Applegate Family Circa 1900 & Correspondence." OHS 233.

Luckey, Eunice Waters Robbins. Letters. OHS 1167.

McCoy, John, Family. Papers. OHS 1166.

McDaniel, Amanda (Humes). Diaries. OHS 1509.

McKinney Family. Family History. WCHS.

Menefee, Leah Collins. Collection. OHS 2519.

Merrill, George. Papers. OHS 1184-B.

Merrill, George. Diaries. OHS 1509.

Minto, Mrs. M. A. "Female Pioneering in Oregon," Bancroft Papers. OHS 176 microfilm.

"Miriam Wright Long Eagon 1819–1908." Tms. CCHS.

Native Daughters of Oregon. Biographical Sketches of Early Settlers. OHS 59.

Native Daughters of Oregon. Papers. OHS 1511.

Native Daughters of Oregon, Tabitha Brown Cabin No. 24. Papers. OHS 107B.

Native Sons and Daughters of Oregon. Miscellaneous Papers. WCHS 310.

Oregon Native Daughters, Odell Cabin No. 8. Papers. OHS 772.

Oregon Pioneer Association. OHS 1511.

"Oregon Pioneers of 1847, with Collateral Ancestors & Descendants of Allied Families." Tss. CCHS.

Pamphlet for the Stoddard churn. Circa 1885. Institute for the Study of the American West at the Autry National Center, Los Angeles, Calif., 90.91.39.

Parrish, Edward E. Papers. OHS 648.

Peters, Lucy Preston (Wilson). Reminiscences. OHS 2406-B.

Polk County Pioneers. Papers. OHS 1511.

Redington, Elinor Meacham. Reminiscences. OHS 2562.

Reed, Calvin M. Account Book, 1850–1856. OHS 606.

Rees, Willard Hall. Papers. OHS 109.

Richey Family. Papers. OHS 1508.

Riggs, James B., Family. Papers. OHS 749.

Robertson Family. Papers. OHS 1076.

Scott, Levi. Papers. OHS 2340.

Skinner, Eugene Franklin. Correspondence. OHS 594.

Smith, Andrew. Papers. OHS 305.

Smith, Fabritus. Papers. UO A 191.

Smith, Lucinda. Papers. OHS 1020.

Sons and Daughters of Oregon. Papers. OHS 1511.

Stanton Family. Letters. OHS 475.

Stevens, Charles. Letters. OHS 2624.

Sutherlin, John Franklin. Correspondence. OHS 1500.

Sweek, Maria Beard. Diary. WCHS 183.

Tagg, William. Papers. OHS 1500.

Talbott, Clarence Elzy. Papers. OHS 2454-B.

Templeton Family. Papers. OHS 1232-B.

Walker, Cyrus Hamlin. Papers. OHS 264.

Walker, Elkanah and Mary. Papers. OHS 1204.

Wigle, Abraham J. Recollections. OHS 587.

Wood, Elizabeth Lambert. Papers. OHS 1509.

Yates, J. C. Account Books. UO A 138.

Government Documents in the Oregon State Archives, Salem

Benton County Circuit Court Divorce Records, 1852–1937.

Benton County Probate Case Files, 1850–1900.

Clackamas County Probate Case Files, 1844–1928.

Clackamas County Women's Separate Property Register, 1859–1909.

Lane County Probate Case Files, 1853–1937.

Linn County Probate Will Records, 1860–1889.

Linn County Women's Separate Property Register, 1862–1912.

Marion County Circuit Court Divorce Records, 1848–1900.

Marion County Married Women's Property Register, 1859–1897.

Marion County Probate Case Files, 1843–1908.

Marion County Probate Will Records, 1853–1951.

Multnomah County Probate Case Files, 1856–1900.

Polk County Married Women's Separate Property Register, 1859–1897.

Polk County Probate Case Files, 1853–1921.

Polk County Probate Will Records, 1853–1926.

Washington County Probate Case Files, 1848–1921.

Washington County Women's Separate Rights Records, 1881–1882.

Yamhill County Probate Case Files, 1854–1946.

Yamhill County Probate Will Records, 1854–1958.

Newspapers

Albany Evening Democrat, 1875–1876

Eugene City Guard, 1870–1890

New Northwest, 1871–1886

Oregon Cultivator, 1874–1876

Oregon Granger, 1873–1877

The Oregon [City] Statesman, 1851–1885

Willamette Farmer, 1869–1887

Material Culture

Baker, Bryant. *Pioneer Woman*. Bronze, 1930. Pioneer Woman Museum, Ponca, Okla.

Black and white cotton housedress. MAW 91.207.1.

Black and white cotton housedress. MAW 91.207.2.

Black and white cotton print dress. OHSM 68–500.3.

Black faille evening dress. 1883–1887. MAW 90.245.3.

Bronze taffeta silk dress. Circa 1864–1866. MAW 90.245.6.

Brown striped dress. Circa late 1850s. MAW 90.143.25.

Castro, Mary Mardocco. Crazy quilt top. MAW 98.13.7.

Challis and wool dress. Circa 1850. MAW 91.67.1.

Chocolate-brown silk taffeta dress. Circa 1850–1865. OHSM 68–441.1.

Elgin, Mrs. George. Blazing sun quilt. Circa 1860. OHSM 81–98.f.

Ellerhusen, Ulric. *Oregon Pioneer*. Circa 1937. Oregon Statehouse, Salem.

Fairbanks, Avard. *The Old Oregon Trail*. Bronze, 1924. Baker City and Seaside, Ore.

Friedlander, Leo. *The Covered Wagon*. Marble, circa 1937. Oregon Statehouse, Salem.

Giesy, John, Family. Crown and square quilt. Circa 1870. Old Aurora Colony Museum, Aurora, Ore.

Gold silk day dress with brocade trim. Circa 1883. MAW 91.132.2.

Grafly, Charles. *The Pioneer Mother*. Bronze, 1915. Palace of Fine Arts, San Francisco, Calif.

Hand-powered tabletop butter churn. Coquille River Museum Collection, Bandon Historical Society, Bandon, Ore.

Hand-powered tabletop butter churn. MAW 87.171.2.

Ivory brocade and satin wedding gown. OHSM 71–136.1.

Ivory wool wedding gown. OHSM 73–40.1, .2.

Knapp, Minnie Biles Brazee. Crazy quilt. Circa 1890. OHSM 86–97.

Lavare, Gabriel. *Pioneer Mother*. Marble, circa 1939. Oregon State Library, Salem.

Lavender and purple print cotton dress. Circa 1845. MAW 88.147.1.

Leimbach, August. *Pioneer Mother/Madonna of the Trail*. Crushed granite, stone, marble, cement and lead, 1928. Bethesda, Md.; Beallsville, Penn.; Wheeling, W.Va.; Springfield, Ohio; Richmond, Ind.; Vandalia, Ill.; Lexington, Mo.; Council Grove, Kan.; Lamar, Colo.; Albuquerque, N.M.; Springerville, Ariz.; and Upland, Calif.

Lockwood, L. "Improved Washing Machine, United States Patent Office patent no. 69,567." http://www.tmm.utexas.edu/exhibits/past_exh/laundry/index .html (6 August 2003).

Parrish, Rebecca Mapel. Linen blouse. OHSM 1743.

Plum-colored taffeta dress with black lace detail. Circa 1875. MAW 2002.58.2.

Printed cotton day dress. Circa 1896. MAW 91.132.5.

Printed ombre wool dress. Circa 1840s. MAW 92.204.1.

Proctor, A. Phimister. *Mountain Man, Pioneer Mother, Frontiersman and Two Horses*. Bronze, circa 1924. Santa Barbara Museum of Art, Santa Barbara, Calif.

——. *Pioneer*. Bronze, 1918. University of Oregon Museum of Art, Eugene, Ore.

——. *Pioneer Mother*. Bronze, circa 1926. Kansas City, Mo.

——. *Pioneer Mother*. Bronze, 1932. University of Oregon Museum of Art, Eugene, Ore.

Red and brown leaf print cotton dress. Circa 1845. MAW 90.55.1.

Red floral print cotton day dress. Circa 1895. MAW 91.35.1.

Royal blue silk day dress. Circa 1886. MAW 91.132.1.

Rust-colored satin dress. Circa 1875. MAW 2002.58.1.

Stone, Zeralda Carpenter Bones. Churn dash quilt. Circa 1860. OHSM 67–368.

Warner, Maria Anne Pease, Harriet Griffith Wise, and Laura Etta Warner. Grandmother's fan quilt. Circa 1890. OHSM 71–186.84.

Washing machine. Circa 1890s. MAW 90.143.19

Whig rose quilt. Circa 1860–1870. MAW 88.18.2.

White organdy shirtwaist. OHSM 3778.

White voile and cotton day dress. Circa 1885. MAW 93.89.1.

Wright, Ellen, and Annie Wright Reynolds. Crazy quilt. Circa 1900. OHSM 89–240.1.

Photographs

Addie Burdett, 1890. OHS OrHi 0205G019.

Alice Estes in front of painted backdrop in dark dress, with umbrella. OHS OrHi 0192G032.

Andrew Orus Brown (grandson of Tabitha Brown) and his wife Asenaath Carey Brown, wedding portrait. OHS OrHi 9999Y523.

Belles of the 1870s, Portland, Oregon. UO PH035_08000.

Blanche Albert and Ada Stapleton. OHS OrHi 0202G029.

The Burley sisters—Ida and Ella, holding cherry blossoms, 1894. OHS OrHi 0178G017.

Cami Anderson. OHS OrHi 1215G055.

Effie Chamness and Miss Cox. OHS OrHi 0215G028.

Ella Burley. OHS OrHi 0203G071.

Ethel Cusick and Miss Breyman with large flowered hats. OHS OrHi 0214G002.

Food preparation class, 1890–1899. College of Home Economics Photographic Collection (no. P44:43), OSU.

Graduating class, St. Helen's Hall, Portland, 1877. UO PH035_06312.

Ida Burley. OHS OrHi 0207G018.

Ida Humphries, 1888. OHS OrHi 0195G073.

Louisa Gay, circa 1875. OHS OrHi CN 017711.

Lulu Bernhart and friends. OHS OrHi 0217G015.

Mrs. C. A. Brown. OHS OrHi 0196G039.

Mrs. Mary B. Churchill. OHS OrHi 0215G068.

Mrs. Mattie Baker. OHS OrHi 0199G001.

Mrs. Richard Hensley. OHS OrHi 0207G028.

Mr. and Mrs. A. J. Burdett and child, 1890. OHS OrHi 0199G067.

Mr. and Mrs. G. W. Ashby. OHS OrHi 0203G032.

Mr. and Mrs. John Baker. OHS OrHi 0182G006.

Narcissa Gloves. OHS OrHi 0207G015.

Nettie Driveler and friend. OHS OrHi 0209G0ol.

Quilting bee, Mehama, Ore., circa 1900. Ray C. Stout Collection. OHS OrHi 21876.

Sarah and W.A. Finley as bride and groom. Harriet's Photographic Collection (no. 224), OSU.

Sewing class, 1890. College of Home Economics Photographic Collection (no. 044), OSU.

Short course dairy class, 1900–1909. Harriet's Photographic Collection (no. 413), OSU.

Uncle Arthur and Aunt Lucy. UO PH200_0010.

Wedding portrait by Hayes & Hayes, circa 1900–1905. OU PH200.

Wedding portrait of Mrs. W. A. Carter of Gold Hill, Oregon. OHS OrHi 0172G028.

Published Primary Sources

Agriculture of the United States in 1860; Compiled from the Original Returns of the Eighth Census. Washington, D.C.: Government Printing Office, 1864.

Allen, Eleanor. *Canvas Caravans*. Portland, Ore.: Binfords & Mort, 1946.

Ball, Wilbur P. *Descendants of Rebecca, Perry, and Albert Ball; A Genealogical Study from 1839 to 1969*. Providence, Utah: K. W. Watkins, 1969.

Barton, Lois, ed. *One Woman's West: Recollections of the Oregon Trail and Settling the Northwest Country by Martha Gay Masterson 1838–1916*. Eugene, Ore.: Spencer Butte Press, 1986.

Beeson, Welborn. *The Oregon & Applegate Trail Diary of Welborn Beeson in 1853: The Unabridged Diary*. Medford, Ore.: Webb Research Group, 1987.

Belshaw, George. "Journal from Indiana to Oregon." Tms. Southern Oregon State College Library, Ashland, Ore., 1943.

"Bits for Breakfast." *Salem Statesman*. 21 February 1930.

"Bits for Breakfast." *Salem Statesman*. 11 June 1930.

Case, Victoria, ed. *This I Remember: Personal Pioneer Experiences*. Portland, Ore.: Rose Villa, Inc., 1972.

Census Reports. Compiled from the Original Returns of the Ninth Census. (June 1, 1870). 3 vols. Washington: Government Printing Office, 1872.

Chambers, Edith Lois Kerns. *Genealogical Narrative: A History of Three Pioneer Families: The Kerns, Popes, and Gibsons*. Portland, Ore.: Binfords & Mort, 1943.

Cleland, Robert Glass, ed. *Apron Full of Gold: The Letters of Mary Jane Megquier from San Francisco, 1849–1856*. San Marino, Calif.: Huntington Library, 1949.

Compendium of the Tenth Census (June 1, 1880). Washington, D.C.: Government Printing Office, 1883.

Cooke, Lucy Rutledge. *Crossing the Plains in 1852*. Fairfield, Wash: Ye Galleon Press, 1988.

Cross, Lilian A. *Appreciation of Loved Ones Who Made Life Rich for Many. My Father, John Francis Cross; My Mother, Sarah Jane Cross.* Oakland, Calif.: [The Tribune Press], 1933.

Davenport, Homer. *The Country Boy: The Story of His Own Early Life.* Chicago: M. A. Donohue & Company, 1910.

Davidson, Lucien M. *The Diaries of Lucien M. Davidson, Oswego, Oregon for the Years 1876–78, 1883–94, 1903–1909 and 1911.* Edited by Glenn D. Harris. Mesa, Ariz.: privately printed, 1996.

Davis, Charles George. *David D. Davis, Hannah Donahoe Davis, Their Family, Their Friends in Two Generations of Oregon Pioneers.* Aloha, Ore: C. G. Davis, 1993.

Deady, Lucy Henderson. "Crossing the Plains to Oregon in 1846." *Transactions of the Fifty-Sixth Annual Reunion of the Oregon Pioneer Association.* Salem, Ore.: E. M. Waite, 1928: 57–64.

Donald, Paul. "Oregon's New State Library." *[Portland] Oregon Sunday Journal,* 2 April 1939. http://www.osl.state.or.us/home/lib/oslart39.html (18 August 2006).

Duniway, Abigail Scott. *Path Breaking: An Autobiographical History of the Equal Suffrage Movement in Pacific Coast States.* 2d ed. Portland, Ore: James, Kerns & Abbott Co., 1914.

1897 Sears, Roebuck and Co. Catalogue. Edited by Fred L. Israel. New York: Chelsea House Publishers, 1968.

Farnham, Eliza W. *Life in Prairie Land.* New York: Harper & Bros., 1855.

Folmar, John Kent, ed. *"This State of Wonders": The Letters of an Iowa Frontier Family, 1858–1861.* Iowa City: University of Iowa Press, 1986.

Frémont, Jessie Benton. *Far West Sketches.* Boston: D. Lothrop Company, [1890].

Geer, T. T. *Fifty Years in Oregon.* New York: Neale Publishing Company, 1916.

Handsaker, Samuel. "Autobiography, Diary, and Reminiscences of Oregon, 1853." Tms. Yale University, New Haven.

Hayden, Mary Jane. *Pioneer Days.* San Jose, Calif.: Murgotten's Press, 1915.

Hixon, Adrietta Applegate. *On to Oregon! A True Story of a Young Girl's Journey into the West.* Edited by Waldo Taylor. Weiser, Idaho: Signal-American, 1947.

Hewitt, James, ed. *Eye-Witnesses to Wagon Trains West.* New York: Charles Scribner's Sons, 1973.

Holman, Frederick V. "Qualities of the Oregon Pioneers." *The Quarterly of the Oregon Historical Society* XX, no. 3 (September 1919), reproduced in "A Place Called Oregon." http://gesswhoto.com/ohs-pioneers.html (18 August 2006).

Holmes, Kenneth L., ed. *Covered Wagon Women: Diaries and Letters from the*

Western Trails, 1841–1890. 11 vols. Glendale, Calif.: Arthur H. Clark Company, 1983.

International Publishing Company. *Supply Department Catalog no. 47.* N.p.: 1900.

Kennedy, G. W. *The Pioneer Campfire. In Four Parts.* Portland, Ore.: Clarke-Kundret Printing Co., 1914.

Ketcham, Rebecca. "From Ithaca to Clatsop Plains: Miss Ketcham's Journal of Travel." Edited by Leo M. Kaiser and Priscilla Knuth. *Oregon Historical Quarterly* 62 (1961): 237–87 and 337–402.

Lockley, Fred. *Conversations with Pioneer Women.* Edited by Mike Helm. Eugene, Ore.: Rainy Day Press, 1981.

Lockley, Fred. *Oregon's Yesterdays.* New York: Knickerbocker Press, 1928.

Longworth, Basil N. "Diary of Basil N. Longworth, Oregon Pioneer." Tms. Historical Records Survey, Division of Women's and Professional Projects.

Mason, Mary Murdoch. *Mae Madden.* Chicago: Jansen, McClurg & Co., 1876.

Masterson, Martha Gay. *One Woman's West: Recollections of the Oregon Trail and Settling the Northwest Country.* Edited by Lois Barton. Eugene, Ore.: Spencer Butte Press, 1986.

Meeker, Ezra, and Howard R. Driggs. *Ox-Team Days on the Oregon Trail.* Yonkers-on-Hudson, N.Y.: World Book Company, 1925.

Montgomery Ward & Co. Catalogue & Buyers Guide No. 56, Fall & Winter 1894–95. Edited by Joseph J. Schroeder Jr. Northfield, Ill.: DBI Books, Inc., 1977.

Myres, Sandra L., ed. *Ho for California! Women's Diaries from the Huntington Library.* San Marino, Calif.: Huntington Library, 1988.

Newsom, David. *David Newsom: The Western Observer, 1805–1882.* Portland, Ore.: Oregon Historical Society, Glass Dahlstrom Printers, 1972.

Occupations at the Twelfth Census. Washington, D.C.: Government Printing Office, 1904.

Oliver, Wiliam. *Eight Months in Illinois; With Information for Emigrants.* Newcastle Upon Tyne: William Andrew Mitchell, 1843; Chicago: Walter M. Hill, 1924.

Oregon Pioneer Association. *Transactions of the Eighteenth Annual Reunion of the Oregon Pioneer Association for 1890.* Portland, Ore.: A. Anderson & Co., 1892.

——. *Transactions of the Eleventh Annual Re-Union of the Oregon Pioneer Association for 1883.* Salem, Ore.: E. M. Waite, 1884.

——. *Transactions of the Fourth Annual Re-Union; for 1876.* Salem, Ore.: E. M. Waite, 1877.

——. *Transactions of the Nineteenth Annual Reunion of the Oregon Pioneer Association for 1891.* Portland, Ore.: A. Anderson & Co., 1893.

——. *Transactions of the Sixteenth Annual Reunion of the Oregon Pioneer Association for 1888.* Portland, Ore.: Press of Himes the Printer, 1889.

——. *Transactions of the Tenth Annual Re-Union of the Oregon Pioneer Association for 1882*. Salem, Ore.: E. M. Waite, 1883.

——. *Transactions of the Third Annual Re-Union of the Oregon Pioneer Association*. Salem, Ore.: E. M. Waite, 1876.

——. *Transactions of the Twenty-second Annual Reunion of the Oregon Pioneer Association for 1894*. Portland, Ore: Geo. H. Himes and Company, 1895.

——. *Transactions of the Twenty-Third Annual Reunion of the Oregon Pioneer Association for 1895*. Portland, Ore.: Press of Geo. H. Himes, 1895.

Oregon Supreme Court. Atteberry, Mary J. *v*. Thomas F. Atteberry. 8 Ore. 224, 1880.

——. Brooks, Frances E. *v*. Henry E. Ankeny, C. M. Cartwright, B. F. Harding, and J. M. Pritchard. 7 Ore. 461, 1879.

——. Harris *v*. Burr. 32 Ore. 348, 1898.

——. Linnville, Leah *v*. Green B. Smith. 14 Or. 284, 1876.

——. State Ex Rel. *v*. Stevens, 29 Ore. 464, 1896.

——. Stevens *v*. Carter, 27 Ore. 553, 1895.

The Organic and Other General Laws of Oregon, Together with the National Constitution and Other Public Acts and Statutes of the United States, 1845–1864. Edited by M. P. Deady. Portland, Ore.: Henry L. Pittock, State Printer, 1866.

Parrish, Edward Evans. *Diary of Rev. Edward Evans Parrish: Crossing the Plains in 1844*. Fairfield, Wash.: Ye Galleon Press, 1988.

Pengra, Charlotte. *Diary of Mrs. Bynon J. Pengra, Maiden Name Charlotte Emily Stearns*. Eugene, Ore.: Lane County Pioneer-Historical Society, Inc., 1959?.

Polk County Pioneer Sketches. 2 vols. Dallas, Ore: Polk County Explorer, 1927–1929.

Population of the United States in 1860; Compiled from the Original Returns of the Eighth Census. Washington, D.C.: Government Printing Office, 1864.

Portland City Directory. 1885, vol. 23. Portland, Ore.: R. L. Polk & Co., Publishers, 1885.

Portland City Directory, 1895: Embracing a Complete Alphabetical and Classified Directory, Miscellaneous Information and Street Guide, vol. 33. Portland, Ore.: R.L. Polk & Co., Publishers, 1895.

Report on Population of the United States at the Eleventh Census: 1890. 2 vols. Washington, D.C.: Government Printing Office, 1897.

Report on the Productions of Agriculture as Returned at the Tenth Census (June 1, 1880). Washington, D.C.: Government Printing Office, 1883.

Report on the Statistics of Agriculture in the United States at the Eleventh Census: 1890. Washington, D.C.: Government Printing Office, 1895.

Riley, Glenda, ed. *Prairie Voices: Iowa's Pioneering Women*. Ames: Iowa State University Press, 1996.

Samuel's Directory of Portland and East Portland, for 1873; Containing Every Thing Found in a Complete Directory. Portland, Ore.: L. Samuel, Newspaper Advertising Agent, 1873.

Sears, Roebuck & Co. 1908 Catalogue No. 117, The Great Price Maker. Edited by Joseph J. Schroeder Jr. Chicago: Gun Digest Company, 1969.

Sengstacken, Agnes Ruth. *Destination West! A Pioneer Woman on the Oregon Trail.* 2d ed. Portland, Ore.: Binfords & Mort, 1972.

Smith, Sarah Hathaway Bixby. *Adobe Days.* Cedar Rapids, Iowa: Torch Press, 1925.

Statistics of the Population of the United States at the Tenth Census (June 1, 1880). Washington, D.C.: Government Printing Office, 1882.

Stewart, Helen. *Diary of Helen Stewart 1853.* Eugene, Ore.: Lane County Pioneer-Historical Society, 1961.

Thirteenth Census of the United States Taken in the Year 1910. 11 vols. Washington, D. C.: Government Printing Office, 1914.

Thornton, J. Quinn. *Oregon and California in 1848.* New York: Harper & Brothers, 1849; Arno Press, 1973.

Tillson, Christiana Holmes. *A Woman's Story of Pioneer Illinois.* Chicago: Lakeside Press, 1919.

Twelfth Census of the United States, Taken in the Year 1900. 10 vols. Washington, D.C.: United States Census Office, 1902.

Warren, Eliza Spalding, and Henry Harmon Spalding. *Memoirs of the West.* Portland, Ore: Press of the Marsh Printing Company, 1916.

The Webfoot. Eugene, Ore.: University of Oregon, 1902.

Young, Nellie May. *An Oregon Idyl; a Tale of a Transcontinental Journey, and Life in Oregon in 1883–1884, Based on the Diary of Janette Lewis Young.* Glendale, Calif.: A. H. Clark Co., 1961.

Secondary Sources

Adelman, Jeremy, and Stephen Aron. "From Borderlands to Borders: Empires, Nation-States, and the Peoples in Between in North American History." *American Historical Review* 104, no. 3 (June 1999): 814–841.

Allen, Judy. "Children on the Overland Trails." *Overland Journal: The Official Journal of the Oregon-California Trails Association* 12, no. 1 (Spring 1994): 2–11.

Allerfeldt, Kristofer. *Race, Radicalism, Religion, and Restriction: Immigration in the Pacific Northwest, 1890–1924.* Westport, Conn.: Praeger Publishers, 2003.

Amick, Annabelle. "Madonna of the Trail." http://www.baxtercountyonline.com/arkdar/madonna.htm (18 August 2006).

Andrews, William and Deborah. "Technology and the Housewife in Nineteenth Century America." *Women's Studies* 2 (1974): 309–28.

Ashelford, Jane, and Andreas Einsiedel. *The Art of Dress: Clothes and Society, 1500–1914*. New York: Abrams, 1996: 211–72.

Baker, Abner Sylvester, III, "The Oregon Pioneer Tradition in the Nineteenth Century: A Study of Recollection and Self-Definition." Ph.D. diss., University of Oregon, Eugene, 1968.

Battan, Jesse F. "The 'Rights' of Husbands and the 'Duties' of Wives: Power and Desire in the American Bedroom, 1850–1910." *Journal of Family History* 24, no. 2 (April 1999): 165–86.

Bederman, Gail. *Manliness and Civilization: A Cultural History of Gender and Race in the United States, 1880–1917*. Chicago: University of Chicago Press, 1995.

Blair, Karen J. *The Clubwoman as Feminist: True Womanhood Defined, 1868–1914*. New York: Holmes & Meier Publishers, 1980.

——. (ed.) *Women in Pacific Northwest History: An Anthology*. Seattle: University of Washington Press, 2001.

Blanke, David. *Sowing the American Dream: How Consumer Culture Took Root in the Rural Midwest*. Athens: Ohio University Press, 2000.

Bledstein, Burton J. and Robert D. Johnston. *The Middling Sorts: Explorations in the History of the American Middle Class*. New York: Routledge, 2001.

Bloch, Ruth H. "Changing Conceptions of Sexuality and Romance in Eighteenth-Century America." *William and Mary Quarterly*, 3d Series, 60, no. 1 (January 2003): 13–42.

Boag, Peter G. *Environment and Experience: Settlement Culture in Nineteenth-Century Oregon*. Berkeley: University of California Press, 1992.

Borman, Lorna. *History and Genealogy of the Pomeroy and Allied Families*. Yakima, Wash.: L. Borman, 1983.

Bourke, Paul, and Donald DeBats. *Washington County: Politics and Community in Antebellum America*. Baltimore: Johns Hopkins University Press, 1995.

Bowen, William A. *The Willamette Valley: Migration and Settlement on the Oregon Frontier*. Seattle: University of Washington Press, 1978.

Boyer, Paul. *Urban Masses and Moral Order in America, 1820–1920*. Cambridge: Harvard University Press, 1978.

Brackman, Barbara. *Clues in the Calico: A Guide to Identifying and Dating Antique Quilts*. [McLean, Va.]: EPM Publications, 1989.

Brewer, Priscilla J. "Home Fires: Cookstoves in American Culture, 1815–1900." *Dublin Seminar for New England Folklife. Annual Proceedings* 13 (1988): 68–88.

Brokaw, Tom. *The Greatest Generation*. New York: Random House, Inc., 1998.

Buckendorf, Madeline. "The Poultry Frontier: Family Farm Roles and Turkey Raising in Southwest Idaho, 1910–1940." *Idaho Yesterdays* 37, no. 2 (Summer 1993): 2–8.

Bunting, Richard. "Michael Luark and Settler Culture in the Western Pacific Northwest, 1853–1899." *Pacific Northwest Review* 96, no. 4 (Fall 2005): 198–205.

Burgess, Barbara MacPherson. "Journals, Diaries, and Letters Written by Women on the Oregon Trail, 1836–1865." M.S. thesis, Kansas State University, 1984.

Bushman, Richard L. *The Refinement of America: Persons, Houses, Cities.* New York: Vintage Books, 1993.

Carlson, Christopher Dean. "The Rural Family in the Nineteenth Century: A Case Study in Oregon's Willamette Valley." Ph.D. diss., University of Oregon, 1980.

Carnes, Mark, and Clyde Griffen. *Meanings for Manhood: Constructions of Masculinity in Victorian America.* Chicago: University of Chicago Press, 1990.

Chudacoff, Howard. *How Old Are You? Age Consciousness in American Culture.* Princeton: Princeton University Press, 1989.

Chused, Richard H. "Late Nineteenth Century Married Women's Property Law: Reception of the Early Married Women's Property Acts by Courts and Legislatures." *The American Journal of Legal History* 29, no. 1 (January 1985), 3–35.

——. "Married Women's Property Law: 1800–1850." *Georgetown Law Journal* 71 (1983): 1359.

——. "The Oregon Donation Act of 1850 and Nineteenth Century Federal Married Women's Property Law." *Law and History Review* 2 (1984), 44–78.

Clark, Ricky, George W. Knepper, and Ellice Ronsheim. *Quilts in Community: Ohio's Traditions.* Nashville, Tenn.: Rutledge Press, 1991.

Cooper, Patricia and Norma Bradley Allen. *The Quilters: Women and Domestic Art: An Oral History.* New York: Doubleday, 1989.

Cott, Nancy F. *The Bonds of Womanhood: "Woman's Sphere" in New England, 1780–1835.* New Haven: Yale University Press, 1977.

Craig, Lee A. *To Sow One Acre More: Childbearing and Farm Productivity in the Antebellum North.* Baltimore: Johns Hopkins University Press, 1993.

Cross, Mary Bywater. *Treasures in the Trunk: Quilts of the Oregon Trail.* Nashville: Rutledge Hill Press, 1993.

Culver, Cynthia D. "Changing Lives, Consistent Roles: Family Life on the Overland Trail." A.B. thesis, Duke University, 1998.

——. "Gender and Generation on the Pacific Slope Frontier, 1845–1900." Ph.D. diss., University of California, Los Angeles, 2004.

Deutsch, Sarah. *No Separate Refuge: Culture, Class, and Gender on an Anglo-Hispanic Frontier in the American Southwest, 1880–1940.* New York: Oxford University Press, 1987.

Deverell, William. *Railroad Crossing: Californians and the Railroad, 1850–1910*. Berkeley: University of California Press, 1994.

Didion, Joan. *Where I Was From*. New York: Alfred A. Knopf, Inc., 2003.

Douglas, Diane M. "The Machine in the Parlor: A Dialectical Analysis of the Sewing Machine." *Journal of American Culture* 5, no. 1 (Spring 1992): 20–29.

Dubinsky, Karen. *Second Greatest Disappointment: Honeymooning and Tourism at Niagara Falls*. Toronto: Between the Lines, 1999.

DuBois, Ellen Carol. *Woman Suffrage and Women's Rights*. New York: New York University Press, 1998.

Eanes, Ellen Fickling, Erma Hughes Kirkpatrick, Sue Barker McCarter, Joyce Joines Newman, Ruth Haislip Roberson, and Kathlyn Fender Sullivan. *North Carolina Quilts*. Edited by Ruth Haislip Roberson. Chapel Hill: University of North Carolina Press, 1988.

Etulain, Richard W. *Re-Imagining the American West: A Century of Fiction, History and Art*. Tucson: University of Arizona Press, 1996.

Faragher, John Mack. *Rereading Frederick Jackson Turner: "The Significance of the Frontier in American History" and Other Essays*. New York: Henry Holt and Company, 1994.

———. *Sugar Creek: Life on the Illinois Prairie*. New Haven: Yale University Press, 1986.

———. *Women and Men on the Overland Trail*. New Haven: Yale University Press, 1979.

Fass, Paula S. *The Damned and the Beautiful: American Youth in the 1920s*. New York: Oxford University Press, 1977.

Force, Rebecca. "Gambling on Higher Education: A History of the Founding of the University of Oregon," *Oregon Historical Quarterly* 102, no. 4 (Winter 2001), 500–09.

Gjerde, Jon. *The Minds of the West: Ethnocultural Evolution in the Rural Middle West, 1830–1917*. Chapel Hill: University of North Carolina Press, 1997.

Gordon, Beverly. "Meanings in Mid-Nineteenth Century Dress: Images from New England Women's Writings." *Clothing and Textiles Research Journal* 10, no. 3 (1992): 44–53.

———. "Victorian Fancywork in the American Home: Fantasy and Accommodation." *Making the American Home: Middle-Class Women & Domestic Material Culture 1840–1940*. Edited by Marilyn Ferris Motz and Pat Browne. Bowling Green, Ohio: Bowling Green State University Popular Press, 1988: 48–68.

———. "Woman's Domestic Body: The Conceptual Conflation of Women and Interiors in the Industrial Age." *Winterthur Portfolio* 31, no. 4 (1996): 281–301.

Gordon, Jean, and Jan McArthur. "American Women and Domestic Consumption, 1800–1920: Four Interpretive Themes." *Making the American Home: Middle-Class Women & Domestic Material Culture 1840–1940*. Edited by Marilyn Ferris Motz and Pat Browne. Bowling Green, Ohio: Bowling Green State University Popular Press, 1988: 27–47.

Gray, Susan E. *The Yankee West: Community Life on the Michigan Frontier*. Chapel Hill: University of North Carolina Press, 1996.

Griswold, Robert L. "Anglo Women and Domestic Ideology in the American West in the Nineteenth and Early Twentieth Centuries." *Western Women: Their Land, Their Lives*. Edited by Lillian Schlissel, Vicki L. Ruiz & Janice Monk, Albuquerque: University of New Mexico Press, 1988.

——. *Family and Divorce in California, 1850–1890: Victorian Illusions and Everyday Realities*. Albany: State University of New York Press, 1982.

Gutiérrez, David G. *Walls and Mirrors: Mexican Americans, Mexican Immigrants, and the Politics of Ethnicity*. Berkeley: University of California Press, 1995.

Haarsager, Sandra. *Organized Womanhood: Cultural Politics in the Pacific Northwest, 1840–1920*. Norman: University of Oklahoma Press, 1997.

Halttunen, Karen. *Confidence Men and Painted Women: A Study of Middle-Class Culture in America, 1830–1870*. New Haven: Yale University Press, 1982.

Hassrick, Peter H. "The Oregon Art of Alexander Phimister Proctor." *Oregon Historical Quarterly* 104, no. 3 (Fall 2003): 394–413.

Hedges, Elaine, Pat Ferrero, and Julie Silber. *Hearts and Hands: Women, Quilts, and American Society*. Nashville, Tenn.: Rutledge Hill Press, 1987.

Helvenston, Sally. "Fashion on the Frontier." *Dress* 17 (1990): 141–55.

Holstein, Jonathan. "The American Block Quilt." *In the Heart of Pennsylvania*. Edited by Jeanette Lasansky. Lewisburg, Penn.: Oral Traditions Project, 1986. 16–27.

Hunter, Jane H. *How Young Ladies Became Girls: The Victorian Origins of American Girlhood*. New Haven: Yale University Press, 2002.

Hurtado, Albert L. *Intimate Frontiers: Sex, Gender, and Culture in Old California*. Albuquerque: University of New Mexico Press, 1999.

Jameson, Elizabeth, and Susan Armitage, eds. *Writing the Range: Race, Class, and Culture in the Women's West*. Norman: University of Oklahoma Press, 1997.

Jeffrey, Julie Roy. *Frontier Women: The Trans-Mississippi West 1840–1880*. New York: Hill and Wang, 1979.

Jensen, Joan M. "Butter-Making and Economic Development in Mid-Atlantic America, 1750–1850." *Promise to the Land: Essays on Rural Women*. Albuquerque: University of New Mexico Press, 1991: 170–85.

——. *Loosening the Bonds: Mid-Atlantic Farm Women, 1750–1850*. New Haven: Yale University Press, 1986.

Johansen, Shawn. *Family Men: Middle-Class Fatherhood in Early Industrializing America*. New York: Routledge, 2001.

Johnson, Susan Lee. *Roaring Camp: The Social World of the California Gold Rush.* New York: W. W. Norton & Company, 2000.

Johnston, Robert D. *The Radical Middle Class: Populist Democracy and the Question of Capitalism in Progressive Era Portland, Oregon.* Princeton: Princeton University Press, 2003.

Kasson, John F. *Rudeness & Civility: Manners in Nineteenth-Century Urban America.* New York: Hill and Wang, 1990.

Kerber, Linda K. *Women of the Republic: Intellect & Ideology in Revolutionary America.* Chapel Hill: University of North Carolina Press, 1980.

Kett, Joseph F. *Rites of Passage: Adolescence in America, 1790 to the Present.* New York: Basic Books, Inc., 1977.

Kosto, Kathryn Clippinger. " 'some work . . . to be kept': Textiles and Memories of Victorian Domesticity." *Dublin Seminar for New England Folklife Annual Proceedings* 24 (1999): 173–94.

Kulikoff, Allan. "Households and Markets: Toward a New Synthesis of American Agrarian History." *William and Mary Quarterly*, 3d series, 50, no. 2 (1993): 342–55.

Laipson, Peter. " 'Kiss Without Shame, for She Desires it': Sexual Foreplay in American Marital Advice Literature, 1900–1925." *Journal of Social History* 29, no. 3 (Spring 1996): 507–26.

Leach, William. *Land of Desire: Merchants, Power, and the Rise of a New American Culture.* New York: Random House, Inc., 1993.

Levine, Lawrence W. *Highbrow/Lowbrow: The Emergence of Cultural Hierarchy in America.* Cambridge: Harvard University Press, 1988.

Limerick, Patricia Nelson. *The Legacy of Conquest: The Unbroken Past of the American West.* New York: W. W. Norton & Company, 1987.

Lystra, Karen. *Searching the Heart: Women, Men, and Romantic Love in Nineteenth-Century America.* New York: Oxford University Press, 1989.

Mainardi, Patricia. "Quilts: The Great American Art." *The Feminist Art Journal* 2, no. 1 (Winter 1973): 1, 18–23.

Mangan, J. A., and James Walvin, eds. *Manliness and Morality: Middle-Class Masculinity in Britain and America, 1800–1940.* Manchester: Manchester University Press, 1987.

Marsh, Margaret. "Suburban Men and Masculine Domesticity, 1870–1915." *American Quarterly* 40, no. 2 (1988): 165–86.

Martinez, Katharine, and Kenneth L. Ames, eds. *The Material Culture of Gender, The Gender of Material Culture.* Winterthur, Del.: Henry Francis du Pont Winterthur Museum, 1997.

Matthews, Glenna. *"Just a Housewife": The Rise and Fall of Domesticity in America.* New York: Oxford University Press, 1987.

May, Dean L. *Three Frontiers: Family, Land, and Society in the American West, 1850–1900.* New York: Cambridge University Press, 1994.

McMorris, Penny. *Crazy Quilts*. New York: E. P. Dutton, 1984.

McWilliams, Carey. *California: The Great Exception*. New York: Current Books, 1949.

Mead, Rebecca J. *How the Vote Was Won: Woman Suffrage in the Western United States, 1868–1914*. New York: New York University Press, 2004.

Merrill, Michael. "Cash is Good to Eat: Self-Sufficiency and Exchange in the Rural Economy of the United States." *Radical History Review* 3 (1997): 42–71.

Milner, Clyde A., II. "The View from Wisdom: Four Layers of History and Regional Identity." *Under an Open Sky: Rethinking America's Western Past*. Edited by William Cronon, George Miles, and Jay Gatlin. New York: W. W. Norton & Company, 1992: 203–222.

Moynihan, Ruth Barnes. *Rebel for Rights: Abigail Scott Duniway*. New Haven: Yale University Press, 1983.

Murphy, Lucy Eldersveld. "Her Own Boss: Businesswomen and Separate Spheres in the Midwest, 1850–1880." *Illinois Historical Journal* 80, no. 3 (1987): 155–76.

Myres, Sandra L. *Westering Women and the Frontier Experience, 1800–1915*. Albuquerque: University of New Mexico Press, 1982.

Norton, Mary Beth. *Liberty's Daughters: The Revolutionary Experience of American Women, 1750–1800*. Boston: Little, Brown, 1980.

Oliver, Celia Y. *Enduring Grace: Quilts from the Shelburne Museum Collection*. Lafayette, Calif.: C & T Publishing, 1997.

"On This Day in Oregon." http://www.onthisdayinoregon.com/05_20.html (18 August 2006).

Pascoe, Peggy. *Relations of Rescue: The Search for Female Moral Authority in the American West, 1874–1939*. New York: Oxford University Press, 1990.

Peck, Amelia. *American Quilts and Coverlets in The Metropolitan Museum of Art*. New York: Dutton Studio Books, 1990.

Pedersen, Elaine, and Jan Loverin. "Historic Costume Dating: Further Exploration of Schlick's Algorithm." *Dress* 15 (1989): 38–49.

Pedersen, Elaine L. "Deciphering the Ormsby Gown: What Does it Tell?" *Nevada Historical Society Quarterly* 38, no. 2 (1995): 75–88.

Peterson del Mar, David. *What Trouble I Have Seen: A History of Violence Against Wives*. Cambridge: Harvard University Press, 1996.

Petrik, Paula. *No Step Backward: Women and Family on the Rocky Mountain Mining Frontier, Helena, Montana, 1865–1900*. Helena: Montana Historical Society Press, 1987.

"The Pioneer Mother." http://www.books-about-california.com/Pages/The_City_of_Domes/Illustration_Pages/The_Pioneer_Mother.html (18 August 2006).

"Pioneer Woman Museum." http://www.poncacity.com/attractions/pioneer_ woman.htm (18 August 2006).

Rohrbough, Malcolm J. *Days of Gold: The California Gold Rush and the American Nation*. Berkeley: University of California Press, 1997.

Rothman, Ellen K. *Hands and Hearts: A History of Courtship in America*. New York: Basic Books, Inc., 1984.

Rotundo, E. Anthony. *American Manhood: Transformations in Masculinity from the Revolution to the Modern Era*. New York: Basic Books, Inc., 1993.

——. "Learning About Manhood: Gender Ideals and the Middle-Class Family in Nineteenth-Century America." *Manliness and Morality: Middle-Class Masculinity in Britain and America 1800–1940*. Edited by J. A. Mangan and James Walvin. Manchester: Manchester University Press, 1987: 75–91.

Rugh, Susan Sessions. *Our Common Country: Family Farming, Culture, and Community in the Nineteenth-Century Midwest*. Bloomington: Indiana University Press, 2001.

Ryan, Mary P. *Cradle of the Middle Class: The Family in Oneida County, New York, 1790–1865*. New York: Cambridge University Press, 1981.

"Salem Pioneer Cemetery Data." http://www.open.org/pioneerc/ (18 August 2006).

Sánchez, George J. *Becoming Mexican-American: Ethnicity, Culture and Identity in Chicano Los Angeles, 1900–1945*. New York: Oxford University, 1993.

Schlissel, Lillian. *Women's Diaries of the Westward Journey*. New York: Schocken Books, 1982.

Schorman, Rob. *Selling Style: Clothing and Social Change at the Turn of the Century*. Philadelphia: University of Pennsylvania Press, 2003.

Schrum, Kelly. *Some Wore Bobby Sox: The Emergence of Teenage Girls' Culture, 1920–1945*. New York: Palgrave Macmillan, 2004.

Smith-Rosenberg, Carroll. "The Female World of Love and Ritual: Relations between Women in Nineteenth-Century America," *Signs* 1 (1975): 1–29.

"Sons and Daughters of Oregon Pioneers," http://www.oregonpioneers.com/ sdop.htm (18 August 2006).

Sylvester, Kenneth Michael. *The Limits of Rural Capitalism: Family, Culture, and Markets in Montcalm, Manitoba, 1780–1940*. Toronto: University of Toronto Press, 2001.

"Symbols, Mother of Oregon: Tabitha Moffatt Brown." http://www.statehouse girls.net/or/symbols/motheroforegon/ (18 August 2006).

Tims, Melinda. "Discovering the Forty-Three Percent Minority: Pioneer Women in Pleasant Hill, Oregon, 1848–1900." M.A. thesis, Université de Poitiers, 1982.

Trachtenberg, Alan. *The Incorporation of America: Culture and Society in the Gilded Age*. New York: Hill and Wang, 1982.

Ulrich, Laurel Thatcher. *The Age of Homespun: Objects and Stories in the Creation of an American Myth*. New York: Alfred A. Knopf, Inc., 2001.

———. *Good Wives: Image and Reality in the Lives of Women in Northern New England, 1650–1750*. New York: Random House, Inc., 1980.

———. *A Midwife's Tale: The Life of Martha Ballard, Based on Her Diary, 1785–1812*. New York: Random House, Inc., 1990.

Unruh, John D. *The Plains Across: Emigrants, Wagon Trains and the American West*. Urbana: University of Illinois Press, 1979.

Varzally, Allison. "Reordering Western Womanhood: Anti-Chinese Boycotts and White Women at the Close of the Nineteenth Century." Paper presented at the Western Association of Women Historians conference, 10 June 2000.

Vickers, Daniel. *Farmers and Fishermen: Two Centuries of Work in Essex County, Massachusetts, 1630–1850*. Chapel Hill: University of North Carolina Press, 1994.

Wall, Diana Di Zerega. "Sacred Dinners and Secular Teas: Constructing Domesticity in Mid-19th-Century New York." *Historical Archaeology* 25, no. 4 (1991): 69–81.

Watson, Jeanne H. "Traveling Traditions: Victorians on the Overland Trails." *Journal of the West* 33, no. 1 (1994): 74–83.

Webster's New World Dictionary. New York: Warner Books, 1984.

Welter, Barbara. "The Cult of True Womanhood, 1820–1860." *American Quarterly* 18 (1966): 151–74.

West, Elliott. *Growing Up With the Country*. Albuquerque: University of New Mexico Press, 1989.

White, Richard. *"It's Your Misfortune and None of My Own": A History of the American West*. Norman: University of Oklahoma Press, 1991.

———. *The Middle Ground: Indians, Empires, and Republics in the Great Lakes Region, 1650–1815*. Cambridge: Cambridge University Press, 1991.

———. *Remembering Ahanagran: Storytelling in a Family's Past*. New York: Hill and Wang, 1998.

Williams, Jacqueline. "Much Depends on Dinner: Pacific Northwest Foodways, 1843–1900." *Pacific Northwest Quarterly* 90, no. 2 (1999): 68–76.

Yoo, David K. *Growing Up Nisei: Race, Generation, and Culture among Japanese Americans of California, 1924–49*. Urbana: University of Illinois Press, 2000.

Young, Linda. *Middle-Class Culture in the Nineteenth Century: America, Australia and Britain*. New York: Palgrave Macmillan, 2003.

Yung, Judy. *Unbound Feet: A Social History of Chinese Women in San Francisco*. Berkeley: University of California Press, 1995.

INDEX

Dinsmore, Mary, 56
division of labor, 1, 13, 14, 15, 18–19, 37
divorce, 29–30, 33, 41, 56, 66, 69–70, 75, 83–84,
    85; acceptability of, 86, 87; property and, 80–
    81
DLC. *See* donation land claims
DLCA. *See* Donation Land Claim Act
domestic abuse, 72, 83–84
domestic servants, 28, 36, 37; Chinese as, 50–51
domestic sphere, 2, 5, 154; hired help in, 28–29;
    men's investment in, 26–27; morality and,
    121–22; quilt making and, 110–14; romanti-
    cism of, 31–32; women in, 30–31, 40, 89–91;
    women's investment in, 24, 25, 82–83; and
    woman's rights movement, 126–33
domestic tasks, 14; butter production as, 23–
    24; labor-saving devices for, 26–27; older
    men and, 35–36; women and, 19–22, 120–21
domestic workers, 28, 76
Donation Land Claim Act (Donation Land
    Law) (DLCA), 9–10, 20, 161n22; access to
    land, 24, 68; marriage ages and, 62–63, 64–65
donation land claims (DLC), 1, 46; sales of, 68–
    69; women and, 24–25, 28
dresses: fashionable, 98–104, 105–7; wedding,
    104–5
Duniway, Abigail Scott, 63–64, 124, 129–30, 131,
    132, 154, 164n9; and Oregon Pioneer Associa-
    tion, 140–41
Dunn, Mary, 145

economy: household, 19, 67–68, 93–94; mar-
    riage and, 38, 60
Eddy, Marietta, 25
education: gender roles and, 119–20; second-
    ary, 123–24; on women's votes, 124–25
egg production. *See* poultry production
elections: women and, 125–26
Ellerhusen, Ulric: *Oregon Pioneer,* 149
employment: off-farm, 54–55; women's, 73, 136
epidemics, 7
equality, 13; in marriage, 61, 68, 77–78
estates: distribution of, 47–48
ethnicity, 28, 50
etiquette: middle-class, 31, 97–98
exchange: labor, 42–43; merchant-farmer, 39
exchange networks: informal, 67

Fairbanks, Avard T.: *The Old Oregon Trail,* 147,
    149
families, 15, 24, 34, 163n2, 169n2, 175n35; farm
    ownership by, 46–48; Locey, 43–46; men as
    heads of, 40–41, 57; on Oregon Trail, 17–18;
    settler, 18–19; shared labor, 1, 22
fashion: women's attention to, 98–104
fathers: and sons, 43–46, 48; teaching roles of,
    41–42, 43
femininity, 129–30
fields: as gendered spaces, 18
finances: household, 65, 66–68, 77–78, 79–82
financial success: indicators of, 26
Finley, Sarah, 98–99, 100(fig.)
Finley, W. A., 100(fig.)
Folsom, Freeman, 76
Folsom, Margaret LaFore, 76
food production, 22, 23–24
fraud as cause for divorce, 83, 85
French Prairie, 7
Friedlander, Leo: *The Covered Wagon,* 147,
    148(fig.)
Frink, Margaret B., 116–17
frontier, 22, 134, 159n3; gender roles on, 15–16,
    135; marriage on, 60, 61–72
fruit production, 22, 38, 52, 53–54

Gann, A. J., 33
gardens, 18, 20, 36, 94
Garrison, Florence, 82–83
Garrison, S. T., 82–83
Gay, Louisa, 101, 102(fig.)
gender ideals, 5, 118
gender identity, 12, 28–29, 57, 98, 153
gender ratios, 55–56
gender roles, 1, 2, 12, 13, 25, 119, 135, 136, 153–54,
    159–60n6; in barnyard, 23–24, 67; changes
    in, 36–37, 159n5; in fruit production, 53–54;
    masculine vs. feminine, 28–29, 169n5; men's,
    38–39; middle-class, 5–6, 159n5; on mid-
    western frontier, 15–16; of minorities, 49–51;
    in pioneer organizations, 138–43; in settler
    family, 18–19; shared labor and, 39–40; valu-
    ation of, 32–33
gifts: wedding, 25
Gilkey, Mary Robinson, 77
girls: education, 119–20

ABOUT THE AUTHOR

Cynthia Culver Prescott is an assistant professor of history at the University of North Dakota. She received her doctorate in history from the University of California, Los Angeles. Her current research interests include gender and consumer culture in rural America during the nineteenth and early twentieth centuries.